Praise for

TOUCH OF REDEMPTION

"To rightfully observe that *Touch of Redemption*, the second novel in Waights Taylor's *Joe McGrath and Sam Rucker Detective* series, is a page-turner—from first to last—fails to fully describe its considerable merits. Firmly grounded in the atmosphere of racially-charged late 1940's Southern *noir*, Taylor has created a universe of vivid characters, no doubt modeled on the many colorful individuals whom he clearly was familiar with growing up in Alabama. Following Joe McGrath's cracking of a sensational murder case in *Kiss of Salvation*, the series' first novel, he has left the Birmingham police department to start a private detective agency in secret partnership with 'the only colored private investigator in Birmingham,' Sam Rucker. Throughout the plot's initial misdirection, Taylor firmly establishes the relationship between Joe and Sam—a solid bond that will protect them in returning to Joe's roots attempting to solve the mystery of his father's murder years before. As if straight out of an episode of HBO's rural-gothic *True Detective* series, Joe and Sam encounter an intricate maze of small town graft, lakeside racist rituals, shape-shifting politicians and businessmen, and the occasional eccentric hero. Taylor spins a yarn that is simultaneously fantastic and yet entirely plausible. But after all, isn't that contradiction—among so many others—what the rest of us find eternally fascinating about the American South?"

—KEVIN KONICEK. Attorney and former Hollywood story editor

"Waights Taylor Jr. delivers a mystery that advances his detective series so that we better understand the time prior to the Civil Rights era. *Touch of Redemption* teaches us that black lives mattered long before the present day, and Taylor uses this mystery to inform us that sensitivity to race and racism was present in the harshest of times and circumstances. With an acute eye for detail, an ear for dialog in the streets, and a true sense of the Deep South, Taylor touches us with a mystery that defines the human condition."

—JOHN KOETZNER. Poet and author and Library
Director at Mendocino College

"Waights Taylor Jr. has done it again as he reconnects readers with Joe McGrath and Sam Rucker in *Touch of Redemption*. Taylor formed the unlikely friendship between the two in his first award-winning novel, *Kiss of Salvation*. Joe is white, Sam is black, and they now work together as private investigators in 1948 racist Alabama. Taylor masterfully weaves his story against the backdrop of the Deep South where there is as much to fear from the police and judiciary as from the murderers. No easy task, but Taylor's roots are deeply embedded in Alabama and prove to be his most valuable asset in understanding the sticky and perilous nuances. As in *Kiss of Salvation*, Taylor beautifully weaves the threads of racism and each characters' personal strengths, weaknesses, and challenges into a sturdy rope. I'm looking forward to the third novel that Taylor has promised to write to conclude the trilogy."

—ARMANDO GARCIA-DÁVILA. Award-winning poet and author of
Perfil: Poemas y Cuentos (Profile: Poems and Stories)

Touch of Redemption

A Joe McGrath and Sam Rucker Detective Novel

ALSO BY WAIGHTS TAYLOR JR.

NON-FICTION

Our Southern Home
Scottsboro to Montgomery to Birmingham
The Transformation of the South in the Twentieth Century (2011)

Alfons Mucha's Slav Epic
An Artist's History of the Slavic People (2008)

FICTION

Kiss of Salvation
A Joe McGrath and Sam Rucker Detective Novel (2014)

POETRY

Literary Ramblings
Poems and Short Stories (2010)

WORKS IN OTHER PUBLICATIONS

This Is What a Feminist Looks Like
The Sitting Room: A Community Library (2014)

Beyond Boundaries
Redwood Writers Anthology (2013)

Healdsburg Alive!
Eight Sonoma County Writers Pay Homage to a Great Northern
California Town—Healdsburg Literary Guild (2012)

Love—Poetry Valentines
Healdsburg Literary Guild (2011)

Healdsburg Area Poets from the Hearts
Healdsburg Literary Guild (2010)

To Kenneth Kelder
Hope you enjoy this. A big departure from
our Southern Home.

Waights

March 30, 2016

TOUCH OF REDEMPTION

A JOE MCGRATH AND SAM RUCKER DETECTIVE NOVEL

Waights Taylor Jr.

Waights Taylor Jr.

MCCAA BOOKS • SANTA ROSA

McCaa Books
1604 Deer Run
Santa Rosa, CA 95405-7535

First published in 2016 by McCaa Books, an imprint of McCaa Publications.

LIBRARY OF CONGRESS CONTROL NUMBER: 2016902796
ISBN 978-0-9960695-6-4

Printed in the United States of America
Set in Minion Pro
Cover design by Suzan Reed
Author's photograph by Star Dewar

www.mccaabooks.com

To
JUDGE, PETER, AND PAIGE

STANDARD OIL ROAD MAP OF CENTRAL ALABAMA
(*circa* 1948)

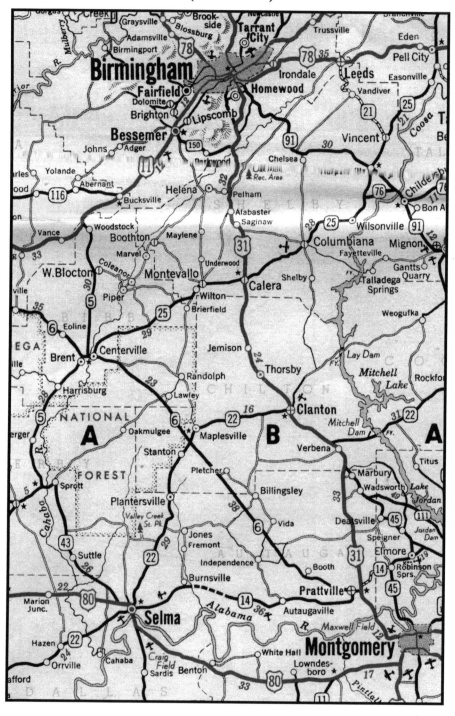

CHAPTER 1

THE LEAK

THURSDAY—DECEMBER 18, 1947

"Well, Big Dick, guess you thought you could hide from me. I was out back sorting new produce. How's my big-eared handsome detective doing?" Helen asked as she reached down and lightly touched his earlobe.

Joe McGrath looked up from his plate of scrambled eggs. He hadn't seen Helen when he entered the cops' diner, the favorite eating joint of Birmingham cops. He mustered a droll smile at her use of his nickname, knowing she tagged all her cop customers with one. He found Helen attractive, but her teasing entreaties didn't interest him. She had a habit of wearing provocatively short skirts and was about his age. Pushing forty, nice figure, red hair tied in a braid on top of her head with two pencils stuck in it for orders.

"I'm doing okay, Helen."

"Where's my young Puppy Dog? Haven't seen him in a long time."

"Brendan, your Puppy Dog, is probably still in bed. He worked the graveyard shift last night. The department moved him back to street patrol. He's no longer my sidekick. Things going okay for you?"

"Can't complain, but if I can't have you, it sure would be nice to be in bed with Puppy Dog and jus' cuddle up with him. Tell him I said so when you see him."

Joe shrugged his shoulders. "He'll probably come in here soon. Tell him yourself."

"At least, you could ask me out. If it ain't too much trouble."

"I'm working on it, Helen. Lots going on right now."

"So I hear. Sounds like a date may be a long time comin'."

Surprised, Joe asked, "Whaddaya mean?"

"Didn't you read Jack Ritter's column in yesterday's *Birmingham News*?"

"No. What's my favorite muckraking reporter said now?"

From a nearby table, Helen grabbed a copy of the paper that had been left behind. "Here, read this," she said, tossing it to him. "Hell, you're the talk of the town."

On the front page, Joe read Jack's popular column, *Birmingham Beat*.

Ace Homicide Detective Joe McGrath To Open Private Investigation Business

Reliable sources tell the "Beat" that Police Department Homicide Detective Joe McGrath has resigned the department effective the end of the year. He will open a private investigation firm.

On November 12, McGrath identified Warren Abernathy as the killer of three colored prostitutes over a two-month period. When McGrath and his sidekick, Officer Brendan O'Connor, tried to arrest Abernathy, he killed himself with a single gunshot to the head.

McGrath will prove a huge loss to the department's homicide unit. Homicide Captain Dick Oliver said, "Joe is the finest detective we've ever had on this force. He will be sorely missed."

Citizens can feel some solace knowing that McGrath will still be available to assist them as a private investigator.

Good luck, Joe.

Joe set the paper down. *How the hell did Ritter find out about this? I told the department not to announce it until year-end.*

He pushed his breakfast aside and paid the check. As he jaywalked across the street toward police headquarters, he looked up at the cold, gray sky, hoping like hell the forecast for a rare snowstorm didn't come to pass. It took only a few flakes to bring the city to its knees.

"Morning, Sally," Joe said to his secretary, a thirty-year employee with the Birmingham Police Department. Sixtyish and small in stature, she had never married and disliked being called a spinster. She dressed in plain, dark clothes and wore her gray hair in a tight bun.

"Good morning, Joe. Did you read Jack Ritter's article?"

"Just read it. I'm going to see the boss. Fill you in when I get back."

Homicide Captain Dick Oliver, dressed impeccably as usual, sat at his desk reading police reports from last night's activities. Joe couldn't help admiring the charcoal gray wool suit Oliver was wearing with a light blue shirt, tasteful red striped silk tie, and matching handkerchief in the jacket pocket.

Joe sat and didn't waste a moment on pleasantries. "Who leaked the story to Ritter?"

Dick looked up with a smug expression. "Why, Joe, you're the one always telling me Ritter's got sources in every nook and cranny in the city. I can tell you it wasn't me. But I can think of a number of people who might have. You know them all." Dick laughed and added, "Hell, consider it great free advertising."

Joe sighed and leaned back, not surprised Dick had responded this way. Although he had helped Joe get the search warrant that led to the attempt to arrest Abernathy, Dick played both sides of the fence, especially between Joe and the department's racist police chief, Big Bob Watson.

"Always the chameleon, Dick," Joe said. "But you bet, I'll take the free advertising."

CHAPTER 2

THE CONTRACT

THURSDAY—DECEMBER 18, 1947

"SALLY, LET'S TALK IN MY OFFICE," Joe said.

She sat down with her hands demurely crossed.

Joe struggled to get started. "I'm sorry you had to hear the news that way. I wanted to tell you in person. Ritter's article is accurate. The department and others are putting demands on me I can't accept. I've resigned effective the end of the year. I'm opening a private investigation office in the city."

"Joe, I'm not surprised. I don't know how you've put up with things around here for so long. As you know, I'm thinking about retiring next year."

Joe smiled. "Thanks for the great opening. Would you consider working for me as the office administrator? It'll be rough sledding for some time until we get our feet on the ground. There're two things you need to know. Sam Rucker will be working with us. And while I haven't talked to Brendan yet, I'm going to ask him to join us."

Sally looked pleased. "Joe, I would love to. But I have to explore my retirement possibilities with the department. I need the retirement check. Can I give you an answer in a few days?"

"I'll wait 'with bated breath and whisp'ring humbleness.'"

Sally grinned. "Shylock, in *The Merchant of Venice*."

Joe laughed. "I should know by now I can't slip a Shakespearean quote past you."

AFTER SALLY LEFT, Joe considered his next steps long and hard. He had found suitable office space, but he needed to talk with his partner, Sam Rucker—the only colored private investigator in Birmingham—about the office and a business contract. Sam had helped Joe solve the prostitute murders but had received none of the accolades and credit that came Joe's way in this segregated city, something that had grated on Joe ever since.

Joe dialed the phone.

"Sam Rucker."

"Hey Sam, it's Joe. We need to meet today. The cat's outta the bag. Did you read Ritter's article in the *News*?"

"Yeah. You should have bet money that would happen. Where do you want to meet?"

"How about your house at noon? I'll bring sandwiches."

"Good. See you then."

JOE PARKED IN SAM'S GARAGE in the alley behind his house to avoid arousing suspicion in the colored neighborhood. The two men had agreed on this approach when they started working together.

As always, Sam was waiting at his back door. "C'mon in, soon-to-be ex-Homicide Detective McGrath. How you doing, Joe?"

Joe smiled as he looked at this man who filled the doorframe. Sam, at six-four, had a handsome face seemingly chiseled from dark stone accented by a strong chin, and his broad shoulders and chest tapered to a slim waist. Clearly a man not to be trifled with.

"I was pissed when I read Ritter's article," Joe said. "Now I think it was for the best. People trust him, and he had his facts right. Makes it easier for us to go ahead. I've got sandwiches, potato salad, and Cokes."

"Well, bless you, white boy. Let's break bread. I'll grab a couple of plates and napkins. Take a seat in the dining room."

Joe unwrapped his sandwich and looked around. "Your house looks great. You'd never know those Klan clowns bombed it a few months ago."

"Yeah, everything's back to normal. Waiting for their next visit, which might come if they learn about our new arrangement."

"Ritter didn't mention anything about you, and that's good. We gotta write a business agreement. We'll need a lawyer who'll keep his mouth shut."

"I agree. Any suggestions?" Sam asked.

Perplexed, Joe said, "Not really. I know several white lawyers, but not well enough to trust them. What about Alfred Banks? Do you think he'd work with us? Can he be trusted?"

"Yeah. I'll call him right now. When should we meet with him?"

"Sooner the better."

"I'll call him from my study. Be right back."

Joe overheard parts of the conversation but not enough to put its context together.

When Sam returned, Joe had just taken a bite of his sandwich and mumbled, "Well?"

"He laughed."

"What?"

Sam chuckled. "Alfred loved the idea. He said the city needs more of this sort of thing. A business contract between two individuals is simple. Just has to be notarized. The colored accountant who works next door to Alfred is a notary public. That's all we need. He'll keep his mouth shut. We've got an appointment with him at nine o'clock tomorrow morning."

"Good," Joe replied. "I found some space on the fourth floor of a building on the corner of Third Avenue North and Twenty-First Street North. It's old and a little shabby, but it'll work. We can't afford top dollar. It has a reception area, a small supply room, and two rooms for offices. We can get three desks in the larger room, and one desk and a medium size conference table in the other one. A college buddy of mine who works commercial rentals got us a great deal on it, as long as we don't ask for any cleaning or remodeling before we move in. Wanna look at it in the morning after we see Banks?"

Sam nodded. "Sure. I'm glad it has space for a conference room. It'll make us look more professional with clients. But I'm gonna keep my current office open in Scratch Ankle. Two advantages. First, in this city with two faces, we need colored clients to make ends meet. It's the bread-and-butter stuff—divorce disputes, cheating spouses, runaway kids, petty business fights over money —it'll keep our heads above water financially. Colored folks will come to my office rather than one in the white business district. Of course, we'll work together on everything. Second, it'll give us some cover. A lot of folks won't take too kindly to our arrangement. With my office still open, it'll be easier for me to act like an employee, maybe even part-time, in the new office."

"Goddammit, you're right. I wish you weren't. It's like the dance of the seven veils. Only reveal what you have to, to get what you want."

Sam laughed. "A hell of a metaphor. So whose head will be on the platter?"

Joe grinned. "Probably mine if things blow up. Look, we need a contract with clauses that split the business fifty-fifty, including both locations. The new office will be called McGrath Detective Agency, and your old office will remain Sam Rucker—Private Investigator. You'll be considered an employee in order to deal with our enlightened Birmingham friends. Okay so far?"

"Sounds good," Sam said.

"Operating expenses will include equal, modest salaries for you and me, and reasonable salaries for any others with us. Any annual net after all expenses will be shared equally between us, and we'll consider year-end bonuses dependent upon our results. All decisions concerning the operation—financial, personnel, office space, etc.— must be agreed to by both of us or it doesn't happen. We also need a clause that allows either of us to terminate the agreement within a reasonable period of time, say three months, with an option for the remaining partner to buy the business. If a buy-out agreement can't be reached, the business will be liquidated, each of us bearing one-half the costs to do so."

Sam raised his eyebrows. "Goddamn, Joe, you sound like a fuckin' lawyer. You've been thinking a lot about this. Maybe you should draft the agreement."

"Yeah, I given it some thought," Joe said sheepishly, "along with the things you just suggested. Throw any of your ideas into the pot, and we'll let Banks clean it up."

"A good starting point. Anything else?"

The phone rang. "Excuse me, Joe." Sam went into his study. "Hello, Sam Rucker."

"You black son bitch, we knows where you live. Next bomb'll take your sorry ass out."

Sam snarled, "Why don't you kiss—." Sam heard a click.

"Is there a problem?" Joe asked when Sam returned.

"Probably a Klan hate call. I get 'em occasionally. So does Alfred."

"Have they done anything?"

"No. I think it's mostly bluster. So where were we?"

Joe knew Sam was trying to put a good face on a threatening situation. "Personnel matters. I asked my secretary, Sally Bowers, to work for us as our office administrator. She's about sixty years old and has worked for the police department for years. She knows our business well. You'll like this. After the Scottsboro Boys case started years ago, she's been donating money to the NAACP and ACLU. I haven't asked Brendan yet, but I want to ask him to join us."

"You're thinking big, Joe. I like it. I'm okay with Brendan, but I want to meet Sally before making a final decision. There's a Miles College student who works for me on occasion. After he graduates, I might want to bring him on board."

"Fair enough. Sally said she needed a couple of days to mull things over. I'll arrange a meeting with her. I think that's it."

"Yeah, good start." Sam wrote something on a piece of paper. "Here's Alfred's office address."

"See you there at nine. Hope those assholes don't call you again," Joe said.

"They're loose nuts, Joe, trying to act like big, tough guys."

CHAPTER 3

THE NEW OFFICE

MONDAY—JANUARY 12, 1948

"WHOA, NOT SO FAST. IT'S A TIGHT FIT," Joe said, as he and Sam lifted the last desk through the door into the office.

As they put the desk in place, sweat dripping from their brows, Sam said, "I don't care how tight we are with cash, I'll hire some guys to move us next time."

"Well, let's hope next time we move, we'll be flush and can afford it," Joe said.

They had spent the weekend cleaning up the place left a mess by the previous tenant—filthy windows, dust and dirt everywhere, and papers strewn about. Cobwebs the size of fishing nets had drooped from the corners of the ceilings.

Alfred Banks had done an excellent job of crafting a business contract satisfactory to both men. Sally would join them on February second, once her retirement was in place. Brendan would come on board March first. Things were falling into place.

While they arranged furniture, Joe asked, "Have you gotten any more hate calls?"

"No, but I will. I can handle it, Joe."

Joe nodded, looking unsure. "Hey, know what yesterday was?"

"Sunday."

"Good guess, smart-ass. It was also a new moon. Hell, you're the one who noticed the first two prostitute murders occurred on dates of new moons last September and October. And you predicted the third would happen on November's new moon, and it did. Since then no one in the city has been murdered during a new moon."

Sam put his fingers on his forehead and closed his eyes. "Ah, the Great Swami Rucker has triumphed again."

Both men laughed, and Sam continued. "Always good news to have quiet nights in the Magic City. And this adds more credence to Warren Abernathy as the murderer, even though he committed suicide the night you tried to arrest him."

Joe said nothing. It still bothered him that he and Brendan hadn't successfully arrested Abernathy before he killed himself.

When they finished, Joe opened the small refrigerator in the supply room, got two Cokes, and they sat on the small sofa in the reception room to admire their handiwork.

"Not bad for two guys," Sam said. "I'll bet our lady friends could dress it up a bit."

"And Sally too," Joe said, adding, "I guess this means we're open for business."

Both men looked at the front door where the glass panel had been painted—McGRATH DETECTIVE AGENCY.

"I wish to hell it said 'McGrath and Rucker Detective Agency,' " Joe said.

"Maybe someday it will. What I wanna know is where are all the customers?"

"They'll come." Joe took a final swig of his Coke and set it down on a small table next to the sofa. "Sam, after Abernathy's suicide, I told you about my Dad's murder years ago in Montevallo. You immediately agreed to help me find the murderers. It meant a lot to me and still does. I need to tell you more about it."

"Good. I've been wondering about his murder since you first mentioned it."

Joe's head drooped a little. "I was thirteen in 1923 when he was killed. His body was found tied to a tree in the woods west of town. He had been brutally beaten and shot once between the eyes as if the killer wanted him to see it coming." Joe paused, his heart pounding and his mouth dry. He took a deep breath.

Sam said, "God, it must have been hard for you at that young age."

"Yeah," Joe mumbled. Regaining his composure, he went on. "Dad was the only criminal defense attorney in Shelby County who handled both white and colored clients with equal vigor and fairness. As you might guess, many in the county were not too pleased with him. We had dinner at home the night before he disappeared. My Uncle Andrew, Dad's brother and the town's police chief, was with us. Dad mentioned a case he was handling in court the next day, and said he was concerned about hotheads in the community causing trouble. Uncle Andrew said not to worry. He'd take care of them. Dad left for the courthouse the next morning. I never saw him again."

"What was the case about?" Sam asked.

"Dad was defending a poor colored man who had been charged with the murder of a white man. I never quite understood why the colored man had supposedly killed the white man, but you know how that goes down here."

"Only too well," Sam replied.

"Uncle Andrew worked tirelessly on Dad's murder for years. He even let me help until I started college. He was never able to come up with a credible suspect. The community was completely uncooperative. Some thought it was the Klan, others said it was a member of the white man's family or maybe an ex-client with a grudge. That's about it. Will you still help me work on it?"

Sam looked concerned. "Of course I will, but this happened almost twenty-five years ago. Got our work cut out for us. When do you want to start?"

"The office should be in good shape by January twenty-sixth. I'd like to go to Montevallo alone part of that week. I need to do some spadework to figure out how to get started. Can you hold down the fort? Sally will start on February second."

"Sure. I'll play the office darkie to any white person who comes in. No problem with my office. When I'm out, I put an 'Out of Office' sign on the door, along with a notepad for visitors to write a note and put it in the mail slot. Occasionally, I get the Miles College kid or someone else to cover for me. I don't want to miss a business opportunity."

"Thanks. I need to do this."

"You get your butt down there so we can get this monkey off your back. Take all the time you need. But in the meantime, don't forget the dinner party tonight at my house. Yolanda and I are cookin' up some good New Orleans food."

Joe perked up. "Diane and I will be there at six. We'll park in the usual reserved spot in the alley."

CHAPTER 4

DIANE AND YOLANDA

MONDAY—JANUARY 12, 1948

A s Joe drove to Sam's house, Diane asked, "Have you seen Yolanda since we visited her in New Orleans last month?"

Joe glanced at Diane and smiled, remembering the first time he saw her at the White Stag bar in Five Points when he had been in the midst of the prostitute murder investigation. He thought a model for the artist Modigliani had walked in—tall and slim, about five-nine, early thirties. Brunette hair cascaded down to her shoulders, framing her beautiful, narrow face. A godsend, she had pulled him out of the depressive state he had been in since his wife left him almost a year ago.

"No. But I've seen a lot of Sam recently," he said.

Diane's voice dropped to a whisper. "Did you talk to Warren's minister?"

"You really want to talk about this?" Joe asked. He knew Diane had married Warren right after she graduated college. The marriage lasted for a little over a year. Although their marriage was not pleasant, she had been horrified to learn that her ex-husband was a murderer.

"Yes. Did you find out anything that helps explain Warren's actions?"

"I went to his Pentecostal church a week after his suicide and met with the minister. He was a nice man and cooperative, but he couldn't add much to what we already knew. I asked him about the apparent religious aspects of the murders and Sam's 'kiss of salvation' theory. I know you had a hard time believing it was true when I told you. The minister said he had given an impassioned sermon sometime around June last year that focused on Christ's forgiveness of sinners based on the 'kiss of salvation' concept. I asked him if Warren had ever talked to him about the sermon. He said no. We'll never know for sure about the demons Warren was dealing with. I showed you the notes he wrote on the back of his will describing the shame he felt about what he had done. I think that's the closest we'll get to any understanding."

Diane didn't respond.

"You all right?" Joe asked.

"Yes. Thanks for telling me." She sat quietly for the rest of the drive.

As Joe pulled into the alley behind Sam's house and parked in his garage, Joe explained to Diane why this clandestine action was necessary.

She giggled. "How exciting!"

Joe said, "It's good to see you smiling again. But I wish we could park out front."

Looking chagrined, she said, "Me too, Joe. I didn't mean to sound flip."

"I know. We live in a repressive world." He took her by the hand and led her to the back door.

Sam opened the back door before they got to it. "C'mon in."

Yolanda stood by his side, well dressed as always, a stunning Creole woman about forty, who operated a successful interior design business in New Orleans. Her light brown skin glowed with a tan patina.

"We have a treat for you two tonight," Sam said. "We'll start with a Vieux Carré, the famous New Orleans cocktail Yolanda's butler made for us when we were there last month. And Yolanda has prepared a dinner worthy of her cook."

Diane couldn't contain her delight. "I wish Frederick and Pearl were here to help. Frederick is so refined and gracious. And Pearl, besides being such a good cook, is such a jolly person to be around."

"I'll tell Frederick and Pearl what you said. I'm sure they'll be pleased," Yolanda said.

"Are you in Birmingham for business or pleasure?"

"Both. Marcus Gilbert and his wife have more interior design work for me. She's never happy with the way things are. I'm not either, but for a different reason. Although I find their taste atrocious, I don't dictate my taste to them." Yolanda smiled. "Not complaining, they're great clients, and I get to spend time with Sam."

Sam served the cocktails as if they were the elixir of life. "Only one to a customer. These things are loaded. Generous amounts of rye whiskey, cognac, vermouth, and Bénédictine."

"It may be potent, but it's delicious. A toast," Joe said. "Here's to two beautiful ladies, and the two best private eyes in Birmingham."

"Hear, hear!" everyone chimed in.

"And remember, ladies," Joe added, "everything Sam and I are doing as partners business-wise is top secret. Not to sound overly dramatic, but leaks about what we're doing could be fatal."

"Are you serious, Joe?" Diane asked.

"You bet I am," he answered. "Don't forget where we live."

"Joe's right," Sam said. "Marcus Gilbert called me after Jack Ritter's article appeared in the *News* announcing Joe's resignation. Marcus asked if I would be working at Joe's new detective agency. I told him no, but Marcus has a sharp mind. He smells and sees things most others don't. He's the colored Stanford Ramsey. We have to watch those two."

Diane looked confused. "I know Stanford well, but where does Marcus fit in all this?"

Joe picked up for Sam. "Marcus is the wealthiest colored man in Birmingham. He owns a number of legitimate businesses and controls most of the illicit activities in the colored community. Stanford, one of the wealthiest white men in Alabama, is Birmingham's Machiavellian prince. City government employees, including the police, are in his hip pocket. Neither Marcus nor Stanford are to be underestimated or trifled with, as I learned."

"Sam told me you were taking a leave of absence from the police department. Why did you decide to resign instead?" Yolanda asked, trying to get caught up on Birmingham politics.

"The prince reneged on me. I guess, in a way, I asked for it. Mahogany Hall was built and operated by Stanford as his personal pleasure dome. Yolanda's butler, Frederick, found out for us who was sending the prostitutes from New Orleans to Birmingham for use at Mahogany Hall."

Yolanda nodded.

"After Warren's suicide, I asked Stanford to stop the operation, especially transporting women from New Orleans to satisfy the sexual appetites of his buddies. He tacitly agreed, and also agreed to support my leave of absence. A week after Warren's suicide, my sidekick, Brendan O'Connor, and I went to take a look at Mahogany Hall to see what was going on. The hall was being demolished. The guys working the job even showed us around. I'm not sure, but I suspect the word of our visit got back to Stanford, and he put the kibosh on my leave."

No one said anything.

Joe finally broke the silence. "Sam, you were right. This drink is loaded, just like I'm starting to feel. Enough of this kind of talk. We came here to enjoy ourselves. Can't wait for Yolanda's New Orleans dishes."

Sam and Yolanda jumped up, and she said, "Good idea. Dinner is served."

CHAPTER 5

MONTEVALLO, ALABAMA

SUNDAY—JANUARY 25, 1948

JOE LEFT ON A COLD, OVERCAST SUNDAY MORNING for Montevallo, his hometown thirty-five miles south of Birmingham. The town of two thousand was the cultural center of Shelby County because of the Alabama College for Women with an enrollment of about seven hundred.

Joe drove carefully as the frost had just started receding with the temperature creeping up into the low forties. He wanted to arrive before noon so he could have lunch with his mother, Elizabeth. But for his father's death here twenty-four years ago, he missed the small town flavor of the place, and held dear childhood memories of his white and colored friends. His mother had been teaching English literature at the college for more than thirty years. Joe still chuckled about the ongoing town angst over the choice years ago of Columbiana, eighteen miles to the east, as the county seat of Shelby County. Most of the court cases his father handled were held in the Columbiana courthouse.

Although it was a short drive, Joe always knew he was almost to Montevallo when he drove past his favorite Burma-Shave signs.

TO BE OR NOT TO BE
THAT IS THE CRUCIBLE
IF YOU HAVE YOUR FOOT TO THE METAL

PLEASE EASE IT OFF OF THE PEDAL
OR YOU WILL SURELY DISAPPEAR
W. SHAKESPEARE
BURMA-SHAVE
NO BRUSH—NO LATHER

Joe grinned as he passed the signs, remembering his mother's story. It was rumored a student in one of her Shakespeare classes had coined the verse and sent it to Burma-Shave.

He burst through the front door and looked around the hallway, living room, and dining room, remembering his youthful days and the joy of coming home. His mother's design taste had not changed and reflected her Boston roots, an eclectic mix of Early American and Shaker furniture accented with Oriental rugs, many of which were showing wear. He shouted, "Mom, I'm home."

ELIZABETH, IMMEDIATELY RECOGNIZING THE GAME, played along and called from her study, "Joe, have you been down by the river with your friends?"

"Yes, ma'am."

"Well, go clean up for lunch right now," Elizabeth said as she came out of her study. Pausing, she couldn't help but admire her handsome son. He looked so much like his father, over six-feet tall and lean, dark brown hair, and the signature McGrath aquiline nose.

She ran to Joe, and hugged him. "How's the new private investigator?"

"I'm doing fine, Mom. Are you ready to go to lunch?"

"Yes. We're going to the faculty dining room. You can drive."

Joe drove toward the campus, only a few minutes away. "Mom, do you still walk to the campus often?"

Elizabeth arched her eyebrows as if offended. "Yes. I'm not that old, young man."

"Of course you're not," he said, laughing. He drove onto the college's brick-paved streets lined with oaks, maples, dogwoods, and well-tended lawn areas. The mostly red brick campus buildings were lifeless amongst the drab grays on this midwinter day. "The campus looks good, don't you think, Mom?"

"Only if you like gray," she said. "I can't wait for spring when the trees will be full and color returns to our realm."

When they entered the dining room, Elizabeth couldn't help but notice that several men turned to admire her. Now sixty-three years old, she was a good-looking woman with a slim figure, graying hair, and a beautiful face that belied her years. Her dress, conservative and attractive, befitted a college professor. Their luncheon conversation centered on Joe's investigation of his father's murder.

"Do you really think it's a good idea? So much time has passed," Elizabeth said.

"It'll be tough, possibly dangerous, but I have to try."

Elizabeth felt resigned to Joe's determination, but said, "Honey, I don't want you wasting your time. Where will you start? Many of the people you probably want to interview are dead—the District Attorney Hobart Conroy who prosecuted the case, the county sheriff, and others. Of course, some are still alive and are in their mid-forties and up."

"It's always hard to get started. I'll want to review Dad's files. Where are they?"

"All his files are in boxes in the attic, along with two boxes of Uncle Andrew's papers."

Joe put his fork down. "I didn't know we had any of Uncle Andrew's stuff. What's in his boxes?"

"I don't know. One of them might be interesting. A few weeks after the trial ended, Andrew brought a box here from his office and put it in the attic. Someone had searched his office and taken a few unimportant files. Fortunately, they weren't able to open the safe where he had kept the more important documents. After Andrew died, an officer delivered the second box. At the time, I wasn't interested in opening them," Elizabeth said, obviously embarrassed.

"Don't worry, Mom," Joe said, picking up on her consternation, "I'll go through all the boxes carefully, starting this afternoon."

"Good," Elizabeth said.

"I'd also like to talk to Judge Wilberforce. Is he still alive?" Joe asked about the presiding judge in the trial.

"The judge is not doing well, not well at all. He has terminal cancer and spent months with doctors in Birmingham to no avail. He's now at his daughter's house in Columbiana. I'll call Anne when we get home and see if you can talk to him. Dad never spoke unkindly of him, and said he was a fair judge. Some people said otherwise. Do you remember?" Elizabeth said.

"Vaguely. Uncle Andrew did tell me he had talked to the judge. He said the judge was polite but wouldn't answer any of his questions directly. I don't remember Anne."

"I'm not surprised," Elizabeth said. "She's at least fifteen years older than you. She's married to Chuck Holder. He comes from a prominent family in the county. Chuck's grandfather and father had bought land in and around Columbiana for years. Rumors still abound that many of their deals were forced on people under questionable circumstances. They developed commercial buildings in the city and became gentlemen farmers on the other land, including overseeing poor white and Negro sharecroppers. Chuck and his two sons manage all of it today. Anne is Columbiana's society queen. She controls all the important women's clubs and big social events."

"I do remember the Holder name. When you call Anne, any time is fine with me."

JOE GOT THE BOXES OUT OF THE ATTIC and stacked them in the dining room. Some were dated. Ten boxes were labeled Peter McGrath, Joe's father's name. Andrew's two boxes had dates—September 26, 1923, and simply 1935. He started with his father's first box. He spread everything out on the dining room table and went through each piece of paper. He organized the papers into one of three stacks: not pertinent, possibly pertinent, and pertinent. Nothing appeared useful in his father's first box as it predated his murder by twelve years. He was trying to decide whether or not to skip the older boxes when his mother came into the dining room.

"Joe, Anne said you could talk to the judge tomorrow morning at nine. She wants you to keep it short and not ask anything that might upset him."

"Thanks. I suspect it'll be a waste of time, but I have to try. I've found a few references to the Klan in Dad's papers. How's the Klan been behaving in Shelby County?"

"The last Klan meeting I attended was uncharacteristically quiet," Elizabeth said, laughing at herself. "Actually, it seems they've been quiet lately."

"Well, I still gotta check them out."

"Joe, don't use crude contractions."

He smiled sheepishly. "Yes, ma'am. It can be hard to avoid them when you do my kind of work."

"Oh, I'm just being a silly schoolmarm. How would you like to go to a performance of *The Tempest* being staged by the college thespians tomorrow night?"

"I'd love to. 'O brave new world, That has such people in't.'"

"Miranda. Act 5. Scene 1. Try this. 'We are such stuff As dreams are made on, And our little life Is rounded with a sleep,'" Elizabeth said, challenging Joe.

"Easy. Prospero. Act 4. Scene 1. Lines 156 to 158."

"Bravo. You even know the line numbers. I forgive your 'gotta.'"

Joe bowed. "Thank you, sweet lady." He then told her how he had won a Shakespearean game in Birmingham that led to Warren Abernathy's arrest.

"Deception, intrigue, obscure clues, murder. How Shakespearean! Perhaps you were meant to be a detective," Elizabeth said.

CHAPTER 6

THE JUDGE

MONDAY—JANUARY 26, 1948

IT TOOK JOE TWENTY-FIVE MINUTES to drive to Columbiana, a town of seventeen hundred. Anne Holder's house was in the town's best residential section, a tree-lined street featuring large houses, but none matched the Holder's large Colonial-style mansion. Joe knocked.

A colored maid opened the door, "Yes suh, can I help you?"

"I'd like to see Mrs. Holder. She's expecting me," Joe said, just as a white, plump middle-aged woman pushed the maid aside and said, "I'll take care of this, Agnes."

"Yes, ma'am."

"Good morning, Mrs. Holder. I'm Joe McGrath." She was just over five-feet tall and dressed as if ready to attend an important social function. Her face, a network of age lines, caught his attention. Her lips were pinched, which matched her dour expression.

"Good morning," she said in an aloof tone. "Follow me, please. The judge is quite ill and near the end. Please don't ask him difficult or pressing questions." She opened a bedroom door. "Dad, Joe McGrath is here. You remember him. He's Peter and Elizabeth McGrath's son."

Turning to Joe, she said, "Just call if you need me."

Joe regarded the judge for a moment—a shriveled skeleton of a man, unshaven with thinning gray, unkempt hair, propped up in bed on two pillows. "Hello, Judge Wilberforce. Thank you for taking the time to see me."

"Hello, young Joe," the judge said in a weak voice. "It's high time we talked. It's been too many years."

"I'd like to ask you a few questions about my father's last days in your courtroom. Is that all right?"

"Yes, I'm having one of my better days. Ask me any questions, Joe. I'll tell you what I remember."

"Yes, sir. Please tell me if you're getting tired," Joe said, trying to imagine what the judge looked like on a bad day. "I've never really understood what the trial was all about. Can you tell me?"

"Well, I remember that," the judge said. He looked straight ahead, not at Joe, as if watching a memory unfold. "A colored boy named Jackie Simmons was being tried for the murder of one of the Pidd boys. Did you know them, Joe?"

"No, sir."

"Just as well. There wasn't a good one in the bunch." The judge coughed and cleared his throat. "The father, Otis Pidd, some called him Old Man Otis, occasionally worked odd jobs in town. He never married. Darryl was born with his first woman. The twins came along about eight years later with another woman. She didn't hang around long. Otis and his three boys sharecropped a piece of Holder land. Jackie Simmons sharecropped another Holder piece next to the Pidd's. That's where the trouble started."

"What trouble?" Joe asked.

"Otis went to Sheriff Foley with Jackie tied up in his car and said Jackie had shot his oldest son, Darryl, over a dispute about crops on the property line between them. Jackie was arrested and charged with murder."

"How did my father defend him?"

"Very well. When he cross-examined the two surviving Pidd boys, their testimonies were erratic, but they insisted Jackie shot Darryl."

"What were the surviving boys' names, Judge?"

The judge's lips parted in a smile. "Dwight and Dwayne. Can you imagine naming twin boys like that? Crazy boys. No damn good. Folks just called them D-Wight and D-Wayne, or if referring to both boys, the D-Dumbs. They must have been about twenty years old then."

"Your memory's sharp, Judge."

"I suppose. Otis was the better witness for the prosecution. He testified he'd driven up to his home when he heard gunshots and continued driving toward them. He found Darryl lying on the ground, and Jackie was off to the side with a gun near his feet. Peter's cross-examination couldn't move Otis off his story." The judge paused and gasped in pain.

Joe stood. "Are you all right, Judge Wilberforce?" He lifted the judge's head and shoulders, fluffed his pillows, and gently laid him down. "Do you want to stop?"

"Thank you, Joe. No, I'll be all right. These moments come and go. Where were we?"

"Did Dad put Jackie on the witness stand?"

"Of course. He had to. There were no other witnesses to the event. Jackie told quite a different story. He said he was working a piece of land near his home with a mule and plow when he heard all kinds of shouting and cussing coming from the Pidd place."

"How far was Jackie from them?" Joe asked.

"Around a hundred yards. He said he walked toward the three boys and saw them fighting each other like tomcats."

"Did Jackie call them boys in the courtroom?"

"No, he was a smart colored. He knew better. He called them Mister Dwayne and so forth."

"What'd Jackie say then?"

"He said when he got near the three boys, things started happening real fast. Darryl had Dwayne down and was beating on him. Dwayne pushed Darryl off, jumped up, and pulled a gun out of his pocket. He shot Darryl two times. Jackie said Dwayne turned and saw him just as Otis drove up. Dwayne threw the gun at Jackie's feet and yelled to his father, 'Poppa, that black son-bitch done shot Darryl.' Otis and Dwight took Jackie to town. Dwayne stayed with Darryl's body."

"What happened to the gun?"

"That was interesting," the judge said. "Jackie testified that Otis made him pick it up and place it in a dirty old rag that Otis held out. He gave the gun to the sheriff when they got to town."

"Pretty smart on his part. Now the gun had Jackie's fingerprints on it."

"I didn't say they were all dumb, just the crazy twins."

"Did the DA do a cross?"

"You bet he did. He called Jackie a liar, a cheat, and everything else you can imagine. To his credit, Jackie stayed calm and stuck to his story."

"Did you believe him?"

"That's why we have juries. I will say that knowing the Pidds as I did, I found Jackie's testimony credible."

"Were there any Negroes on the jury?"

"Now, Joe," the judge said, sounding as if he was lecturing a law student, "we've had to consider coloreds as jurors since the Supreme Court's Scottsboro Boys decision in the '30s. The four coloreds considered for Jackie's trial were excused by the DA using his preemptory challenges."

"What happened after Jackie's testimony?"

"On your father's last day in the courtroom, he got a chance to do a recross after the DA put Otis on the stand to repeat his accusations. I still think it was a stupid thing the DA did. Why give the defense another shot at your best witness?"

The judge paused again, more in thought than in pain, and continued, "This time your father did a good job poking holes in Otis's testimony. Otis yelled at the jury something like 'If y'all let that darkie go 'cause of this here fancy lawyer's talk, you're a bunch of chicken-livered cowards. That coon killed my son.' People were getting so hot-headed in the courtroom, I recessed for the day as soon as Otis got off the witness stand."

"Did you see my father after that?"

"Yes. When I got into my car after court recessed, I saw him talking to two men in overalls. I didn't recognize them. That was the last time I saw him alive."

"How did the trial go after my father's murder?"

"Fast, once it got started almost four weeks later. We had to wait a while out of deference to your father. We also had trouble finding an attorney to represent Jackie. No one in Shelby County would take his case. We finally found a guy in Selma who took it for an unreasonably high fee in my opinion. And believe me, he did a poor job. It was over in three days, two and a half really. Jackie was found guilty and executed."

"What was the new attorney's name?"

The judge paused in thought. "Oh, I remember. Jason Partlow."

"Is he still alive?"

"I have no idea."

"How old was he?"

"In his thirties, I guess." The judge finally turned his head and looked at Joe from the hollow sockets holding his eyes. "There's one thing concerning your father's murder that I still don't understand. They never found his—"

Anne opened the door and said, "Dad, it's time for your medications and some rest. Mr. McGrath, I'll show you out."

Joe realized Anne had been listening. "Judge Wilberforce, thanks for your time and help. I never knew the details of the trial as you just described them. Rest easy."

"Goodbye, Joe. Nice seeing you."

At the front door, Anne said, "The judge's memory is not good. I don't know what he told you, but take it all with a grain of salt."

"Thank you, Mrs. Holder."

He drove to the courthouse to get a copy of the trial transcript. He wondered: *Is Anne trying to hide something and, if so, why?*

CHAPTER 7

THE COURTHOUSE

MONDAY—JANUARY 26, 1948

JOE DROVE TO THE CENTER OF TOWN, around the circle where the old county courthouse still stood, and headed up North Main Street into the business district. He passed a row of brick buildings, utilitarian in design, which included a grocery store, drug store, barbershop, shoe repair shop, law office, and library.

The new county courthouse was several blocks up Main Street. Joe easily found a parking place.

"Good morning," Joe said to the young courthouse records clerk. "My name's Joe McGrath. I'd like to get a copy of a trial transcript." Joe put her at about twenty-five. Cute, dark brown hair, short, nice figure. Desk nameplate said Kelly. She had an attractive face, set off by a slightly upturned nose.

"Yes, sir," the young lady said. "Do you have the trial number and date?"

"I don't have the trial number. My father, Peter McGrath, was the defense attorney in the case. He was defending a colored man named Jackie Simmons who was charged with murdering Darryl Pidd. The last day my father was in the courtroom was August 21, 1923. He disappeared that day and was found murdered a few days later."

The records clerk gasped. "Oh, my goodness. I'm sorry. . . . I'll look through our files."

"If it helps, the trial resumed three or four weeks later. Simmons was found guilty and executed."

The young lady nodded.

Fifteen minutes later, the clerk came back with a portly, elderly gentleman. "Mr. McGrath," she said, "this is my boss, the Clerk of the Court, Carlton Teague."

Teague reached out to shake Joe's hand and said, "Mr. McGrath, Miss Kelly told me about your request. I knew your father well. He was a fine man. Those were tragic days in this courthouse and county. I was a junior records clerk here at the time. I'm sorry to say that the only remaining transcript we have of that trial is the three-day period following your father's murder."

"What happened to the rest of the transcript?" Joe asked.

"Since the trial broke into two distinct phases because of your father's murder, the DA requested that the transcripts be kept in two separate folders."

"Isn't that unusual?"

"Yes. But Judge Wilberforce agreed and instructed us to do so."

"So what happened to the transcript of the first part of the trial?" Joe asked.

Teague took a breath, looked uncomfortable, and said, "Several weeks after Simmons was sentenced, someone broke into the records vault over the weekend and stole all copies of the first transcript."

"Why do you suppose the first transcript was the only one stolen?"

"I'm not sure. Maybe the first folder was thought to be the entire transcript."

Joe paused, placed a hand to his chin, looked at Teague, and said, "Well, I trust someone investigated this. . . . What'll we call it? Robbery? Destroying court documents? Thwarting justice?"

"How dare you insinuate such things?" Teague said, his voice trembling. "Sheriff Foley did a thorough investigation. He was unable to determine who did it."

"Did Foley look for fingerprints in the courthouse after the break-in?"

"I suppose so."

"Any evidence of a break-in? Broken windows, tampered locks, doors pried open? Anything of that nature?"

Looking more agitated, Teague said, "No, I don't think so."

"Well, how did they get in? Was it an inside job?"

"No, goddamn it! We did all we could at the time."

"Did you check to see if the DA, the lawyers, and others with an interest in the trial might have a copy?"

Teague, struggling to contain himself, said, "We haven't had the transcript for years."

Joe said calmly, "Thank you, Mr. Teague." Looking at Miss Kelly, he added, "I'd like a copy of the transcript you do have."

She turned to Teague for guidance.

"Susan will have it for you tomorrow," Teague said.

Knowing Teague's explanations laughable, Joe hurried to his car. He couldn't wait to get back to his mom's to check Uncle Andrew's files.

JOE SPREAD ALL THE CONTENTS of Uncle Andrew's box dated September 26, 1923, on the table and started looking through the documents. He found the entire transcript in two folders as Teague had explained it was organized. The transcripts were date-stamped September 21, 1923.

Joe sat in his father's old chair in the living room and was overcome with feelings of grief and loss as he thought about how much he missed his father.

Wiping his eyes, he started reading the first transcript and came to the part where Jackie testified in his own defense. His testimony closely matched Judge Wilberforce's description, except for one item. Jackie testified that Otis handed him the dirty rag and told him to pick up the gun and wipe it clean. He then told Jackie to hand him only the rag, which required Jackie to hold the gun in his bare hand before he handed it to Otis.

He read the part about his father's cross-examination of Otis Pidd. It matched Judge Wilberforce's description well. He then read the last few entries in the first transcript with increasing interest.

MCGRATH: Your Honor, the defense
                      has one additional witness
                      we'd like to call.

CONROY:	Your Honor, I object. The prosecution has not been advised of any additional witnesses.
MCGRATH:	This will be a hostile witness, Your Honor.
THE COURT:	Gentlemen, I'd like to adjourn for the day. Please approach the bench.

A CONSULTATION TAKES PLACE.

THE COURT:	The Court is adjourned until nine a.m. tomorrow, at which time Mr. McGrath's request will be considered.

When his mother returned home, Joe set the transcript down, wondering about the identity of the hostile witness.

Joe looked up from his father's chair as his mother kissed him on the cheek. "Joe, you look so much like your father. Maybe you're a little taller and more handsome. Oh, listen to me." She laughed. "A silly old mom."

Joe stood and hugged his mother. "You won't believe this. Someone apparently broke into the courthouse a few days after Dad was killed. They stole the trial transcript that covered the time Dad was in the courtroom, but didn't take the one covering the last few days of the trial."

"I never heard about that. Did they find out who did it?"

"No. I asked Carlton Teague, the Clerk of the Court, some pointed questions. All his answers were vague. He eventually got angry. I think someone in the courthouse was complicit in the theft or possibly was the thief."

"Why would someone steal only part of a trial's transcript?"

"Good question. No clear answer. When I got back from Columbiana, I immediately went through Uncle Andrew's box dated September twenty-sixth. And there was a copy of the entire transcript. I just finished reading the first part, which is the stolen part. I found something right before the court adjourned the day Dad disappeared that may explain why the transcript was stolen. Dad told the court he wanted to call a new hostile witness, but Judge Wilberforce put off both Dad's request and the DA's objection until the next day. Did you hear about it?"

"No. Andrew never mentioned anything like that." Her brow furrowed in thought, she added, "I mean, he told me about a lot of people he talked to. Some said they knew nothing, others were evasive, but Andrew never described anyone as hostile."

"Well, something to pursue. We'll see," Joe said.

"I hope your meeting with Judge Wilberforce was more productive," Elizabeth said.

"It was going well until Anne Holder interrupted us just as he was about to tell me something important. Great start on the investigation."

"What was the judge trying to tell you?"

"He said there was something about the case he didn't understand. He started to explain when Anne interrupted."

"Of course, I'm not sure, but one thing that comes to mind is the car. It was never found and might have provided some clues."

Startled, Joe said, "You and Uncle Andrew told me the car had been crashed beyond repair. I always thought that was why he gave us a new car." Joe continued in a sharp tone, "Why did you lie to me?"

"Honey, our big concern was to help you get over the terrible trauma and lead a normal life. We decided not to tell you things we thought might make it worse for you." Clearly hurt, Elizabeth added, "Maybe it was not the right decision, but we thought it best at the time."

Chagrined, Joe said, "Mom, I know. I'm sorry if I sounded otherwise." He paused. "The transcript also had some other disquieting things in it."

"What?" she asked, still upset.

"I had no idea the way Dad and his client were treated in the courtroom. Often, Judge Wilberforce had to stop the proceedings to restore order. The DA constantly insulted Dad and was especially hard on his colored client. Judge Wilberforce usually upheld the DA's objections and overruled Dad's. And a few times, the judge objected to Dad's line of questioning even though the DA had said nothing. It's strange, the judge I talked to today doesn't sound like the judge in the transcript."

"How so?"

"If I had read this transcript before I went to see the judge," Joe said, "I would have expected to meet an awful bigot. And yet, today he seemed helpful and thoughtful about the case."

"Perhaps a man who knows his death is imminent reflects on his life, wishing he had done some things differently."

"Possibly. But based on the man portrayed in the transcript, I doubt Dad could have won this case."

On the verge of tears, Elizabeth said, "He was so determined and principled."

Joe put his arms around her. "I know, Mom. And that's why I have to pursue this."

She sighed and smiled. "I'll fix a light supper. *The Tempest* starts at seven."

CHAPTER 8

OLD FRIENDS

TUESDAY—JANUARY 27, 1948

AT THE BREAKFAST TABLE, Elizabeth took a sip of coffee and said, "Joe, didn't you love the performance of the actress who played Ariel last night?"

"Yes, but I particularly enjoyed the young lady who played Caliban. And her make-up and costume were great. Isn't it a hoot? In the Shakespeare productions at your college, all the parts are played by women, unlike Shakespeare's day when men played all the parts. What do you suppose Shakespeare would think?"

Putting on airs, Elizabeth said, "I'm quite sure Mr. Shakespeare would have thought highly of our productions."

"Me too. Say, have you seen or talked to Hank or Adam recently?" Joe asked, referring to his best childhood buddies: Hank Moore, a colored boy, and Adam Paige, a white boy.

"Not directly. But I hear Hank's construction business is doing well, and Adam's the best lawyer in town. He reminds me of Dad in so many ways: industrious, honest, and fair to everyone," Elizabeth said.

"Not surprised. I'll call them. Maybe we can have lunch."

"I know they both would like to see you. What are you going to do today?" Elizabeth asked.

"I have to go back to the courthouse in Columbiana. Carlton Teague is having a copy of the trial transcript made for me. I want to see what Teague and his records clerk, Miss Kelly, have to say and how they treat me. I'll also stop and see Sheriff Cate if he's in. I met him a couple of years ago. Seems like a nice guy."

"Well, I'm off to the college. Young women are waiting for my second lecture on *King Lear*—or at least, I hope they are."

Joe called Hank and Adam. They agreed to meet for lunch at Schaeffer's, a restaurant in an old plantation-style house on the southside of town. The owners allowed whites and coloreds to eat together if they sat at picnic tables in the backyard.

"Here's the transcript, Mr. McGrath. I'm afraid we'll have to ask you for five dollars," Miss Kelly said, blushing. "I'm sorry it's so much, but we made a special effort to get a copy for you."

Joe knew Teague was gouging him but decided not to argue. He handed her the money. "Did Mr. Teague say anything else about our talk yesterday?"

She glanced around nervously and then motioned for Joe to lean over the counter. "He was very upset with you," she whispered. "I won't repeat what he said. It was awful. He had the transcript retyped. I'm not sure, but I don't think it matches the original."

Joe stepped back and spoke in a normal voice, "Thank you, Susan." He reached out and took her hand. "You've been very helpful. Maybe we can meet for coffee soon."

She blushed again, even brighter.

"Joe McGrath, haven't seen you in a while," Sheriff Cate said as he stood to shake hands. "What brings you to town?"

"Some changes, Harold. I resigned from the police department and opened my own private investigation firm in Birmingham," he said, eyeing Harold who had put on a significant amount of weight since Joe had last seen him. His reddish face was bloated, and his belly hung over his belt like a huge ham. Joe couldn't help thinking, *Well Harold, now you do look like a small town, Southern sheriff.*

"So you're a private eye," Harold said, grinning. "Come to town to check us out?"

"Yeah, I heard you ran a stop sign on Milner Street. What you gotta say for yourself?"

"Guilty as charged. You gonna turn me in?"

"We'll let you off this time. . . . Actually, I'm looking into my father's murder. I was young at the time and have never understood why the killers weren't found. I know my Uncle Andrew tried hard to identify them but had no luck."

Harold closed his office door. "Joe, I had been a deputy sheriff for about a month when your Dad was killed. Sheriff Foley didn't involve me in the case. I guess because I was wet behind the ears. But from where I sat, Foley didn't work the case very hard."

"Do you know why?"

Harold paused. "He was angry at your father for representing Jackie Simmons. He made that clear to everyone in the office several times. Some folks said Foley was cozy with the Klan."

"Was he a Klan member?"

"Don't know. Maybe."

"Is the Klan still active?"

"They sure haven't gone away. But it's been quiet lately."

"What's become of the Pidd family that used to sharecrop on the Holder property?" Joe asked. "Jackie was found guilty and executed for killing Darryl Pidd."

Harold leaned back in his chair, looking pensive. "Yeah, I remember all that. Otis died in a truck accident a few years after the trial. Dwight and Dwayne are as ornery as ever and stick a plow in the Holder land every now and then. But they spend most of their time tending moonshine stills in the woods and selling the shine around this county and nearby dry counties. They're in and out of county jails all the time when one of their stills gets busted or for drunkenness or just plain craziness. They're worthless pieces of shit."

"I'm surprised they haven't been tossed into a state or federal prison if they work moonshine so much."

"They must have a guardian angel. I don't know why or who," Harold said, winking at Joe. "You'll have to guess who. Do you think the Pidds had anything to do with your Dad's death?"

"I don't know. I've been reading the trial transcript. Otis Pidd made it clear on the witness stand what he thought of Dad. And I suspect most of the people in the courtroom shared Otis's opinion."

"I wasn't there, but you're probably right. You know, Joe, things have gotten better here since the '20s."

"Good to hear. Can I depend on your help if I turn up anything?"

Harold looked unsure. "I'll do what I can, Joe."

Joe got in the car, his mind on their conversation. *Harold's like everybody down here. He'd rather forget the past, but no problem, things have gotten better.*

THE THREE FRIENDS WORE HEAVY JACKETS to deal with the cool, dry weather and sat outside at Schaeffer's, using a picnic table covered with a black and white checkered oilcloth. They were talking about old times when the waiters served coffee and plates heaped with fried catfish, hushpuppies, coleslaw, and potato salad.

"Can either of you set a decent trout line yet, or are all the catfish in Shelby County still safe from you two?" Hank asked, alluding to their youth when he had taught them how to toss the weight-laden line. He laughed at the memory. Taking a bite of catfish, he added, "I suppose some colored kid hooked these on his trout line this morning."

Playing the fool, Adam said, "Oh no sir, I can't throw that line no how, no way. It always end up in some gosh darn tree branch."

Joe added to the banter. "I reckon I do bettah than that thar Adam. Hell, he didn't have 'nuf sense not to take a bite outta that apple."

After much laughter and catfish, Joe told Hank and Adam about the changes in his work situation and explained why he was in Montevallo. He added, "Since I've been here, I've talked to four people who were close to the events back then. They were mostly evasive or didn't want to talk much. And according to the trial transcript, Dad wanted to call a hostile witness on his last day in the courtroom. Haven't been able to find out who it was. What's going on? I would have thought after all this time that people might be more open about his murder."

Hank and Adam looked at each other. Hank spoke first. "Joe, I remember those days as if they happened yesterday. It was awful. Adam and I wanted to help, but we didn't know what to do."

"That's true," Adam added. "What can we do to help now?"

Hank nodded.

"You guys are the best. But I don't want you taking risks," Joe said.

"Believe it or not, things have improved a bit since our fathers' days," Adam said. "Lynchings have dropped significantly. I don't remember the last one in Shelby County."

"Based on the reactions I've gotten so far, this may prove to be pretty dangerous," Joe said.

"Don't worry, I won't run around with a bullhorn shouting, 'Who killed Peter McGrath? Who was the hostile witness?' Lawyers are good at digging up information, just like you cops," Adam said.

"And I can talk to some folks in the colored community who were around at the time. You never know what people heard or saw then. And they sure wouldn't have shared it with Sheriff Foley. He was bad news," Hank said.

"Don't mention my name," Joe said. "The fewer people who know I'm nosing around, the better."

Hank and Adam nodded.

Joe decided to tell them about Sam Rucker. He didn't mention that Sam was his partner in the new detective agency, only that they worked together. He added, "Sam's a colored private eye who will be coming with me to Montevallo next time. He's a smart cookie. Hank, can you help him get his bearings in the colored community?"

Joe noticed Adam and Hank's looks of amazement at the mention of Sam.

"Sure, I'll be glad to help," Hank said, averting his gaze from Joe.

"Who did you talk to? We don't want to double up on them unless you say so," Adam said.

Joe told them the names of the four people, and asked, "Adam, did you ever appear in Judge Wilberforce's court?"

"Just once. In 1936, the first year I practiced law here, I was a junior attorney and briefcase carrier in my father's law firm. We represented a colored man who was sued by the Holders. They claimed they had a signed contract to purchase the colored guy's property. The price on the contract was ridiculously low. We presented a solid case showing the contract had been forged, but Wilberforce lived up to his reputation as being tough on coloreds and found for the Holders."

"And Wilberforce's daughter, Anne, is married to Chuck Holder," Joe added.

"Right, and for that reason alone, Judge Wilberforce should have recused himself from the case. Joe, you haven't spent much time here since you went off to college. You have to remember one thing. This county's a tale of two cities. Folks in Montevallo are more open and liberal because of the college. Can't say the same about Columbiana."

Joe left the restaurant, delighted to have seen his old buddies. He now knew he could trust them with his life.

CHAPTER 9

THE TAINTED TRANSCRIPT

TUESDAY—JANUARY 27, 1948

AFTER LUNCH WITH HIS BUDDIES, Joe went back to his mother's home. He removed the second part of the transcript from Andrew's box and placed it next to to the copy Miss Kelly had given him.

He read each page of both transcripts carefully, comparing them line-by-line. The incompetence of the new defense lawyer, Jason Partlow, immediately struck him. Partlow never made an objection to the prosecution's many ridiculous assertions. His cross-examinations were weak and summarily useless. Once or twice, Judge Wilberforce even had to step in and suggest objections for the defense.

Joe stretched to relieve the tension in his neck and turned to the last few pages in the manuscripts, the closing statements. He was about to conclude that Miss Kelly was mistaken. The new copy of the transcript had not been altered. The prosecution presented the first closing statement as was customary.

Joe read District Attorney Conroy's closing statement in both copies of the transcripts, and saw that most of the last paragraph had been deleted from the new copy. Using a ruler, he carefully underlined the deleted passage in Andrew's copy.

        Now I know you gentlemen are from
        around here. And I know you will

be able to consider fairly all the
evidence and testimony you've heard.
I say this because just before y'all
were sworn in, you remember what
Peter McGrath said before the twelfth
man was selected. Now I grieve for
Peter's family and hope they find the
scoundrel who did him in. But y'all
got to remember what he said about
you. He said he was concerned that a
jury made up of too many Columbiana
folks could not, I repeat, could not
reach a fair and impartial verdict
in this case. That's what he said,
gentlemen. I know for a fact that
folks in Montevallo were awful upset
when Peter agreed to represent this
here murderer Simmons. I also know
for a fact that one prominent man in
Montevallo was particularly upset.

Y'all have to do your duty for Shelby
County and find this here colored
killer, Jackie Simmons, guilty as
charged and sentence him to die in
the electric chair.

That was the end of it. Jason Partlow declined to make a closing
statement for the defense, leaving Jackie Simmons to the will of the
jury.

Joe stood and paced around the dining and living rooms. Though
the DA's statement had cited facts not established during the trial, it
appeared neither Partlow nor Judge Wilberforce had objected, as they
should have. Even if Partlow had objected, Wilberforce must have
overruled him. And Carlton Teague had certainly been willing to
break the law by altering an official court document in order to hide
something.

Joe stopped pacing and wondered, *Why had Teague seen fit to
delete that passage? Who is he trying to protect? How wide is the net of*

persons apparently complicit in Dad's murder? I have to see if we can find Partlow. Maybe I'll go see—

"Hi, honey. You look deep in thought," Elizabeth said.

Joe, startled, turned around. "Oh, hi Mom. I didn't hear you come in."

"You look preoccupied."

"I just read the rest of the transcripts, including the copy I got today from the courthouse of the last part of the trial. It's mind boggling."

"How so?"

"Carlton Teague altered the copy of the transcript I got this morning."

"My God," Elizabeth said, taking a seat in the living room. "Isn't that against the law?"

"Sure is." Joe said. He read her the altered passage and explained the issues and the questions it raised. "Any idea who this 'one prominent man in Montevallo' might have been?"

"Andrew talked to so many people. And as I told you about the hostile witness issue, he never mentioned anyone in that context. There were numerous prominent Montevallo men back then. The mayor, several businessmen, some clergymen. Some men at the college. The president, some faculty members. I just don't know."

"I never thought of the college as a source. Is there someone at the college when Dad was killed who you can even imagine may have been involved?"

Joe noticed his mother frown and her body stiffen, if not by the question, at least by its implications.

"No, I can't imagine that, Joe," she said sharply. "The ivy walls make for a pretty cloistered environment. However, truth is, I don't pay a lot of attention to a person's underlying character. For better or worse, I keep my head buried in my books and my students. You'd best ask that question of others."

CHAPTER 10

A PROSPECTIVE CLIENT

WEDNESDAY—JANUARY 28, 1948

THE NEXT MORNING JOE PACKED his overnight bag. He had decided to drive back to Birmingham later in the day. As he walked downstairs, Elizabeth saw him with the bag in hand.

Looking disappointed, she asked, "Are you leaving today?"

"Yes, Mom. I intended to stay the whole week, but I'm getting antsy about the new business. I gotta—" He smiled. "I have to see how Sam's doing. Sally's going to join us next Monday."

"Can you have lunch with me? I'll come home."

"Sure. I hope to see Raymond Chapman this morning. He's still the Montevallo police chief, isn't he?"

"Yes. I have to run. I'll be back just after twelve."

"JOE, LONG TIME, NO SEE. HOW YOU BEEN?" Police Chief Chapman stood and shook hands. A spit-and-polish cop, he wore a starched uniform with sharp creases that fit like a glove.

"Nice to see you, Raymond," Joe said. Average height, trim with not an ounce of fat on him, reddish hair cropped close to match his cop persona, his ramrod posture reminded Joe of an Army master sergeant he knew. "Doin' fine. I visit every now and then to see my mother."

"I heard about the murderer you nailed in Birmingham recently."

"Yeah, that was a tough one." Joe told Raymond about his new detective business and added, "I'm doin' some background work on my father's murder."

"Big order, Joe. I think most folks around here would like to forget it. I doubt many will tell you more than you already know."

"What do you remember about his murder?"

"I went off to Auburn for my freshman year a few weeks after it happened. I was pretty much out of touch with Montevallo until your Uncle Andrew hired me as a junior cop in 1933. I remember talkin' to you briefly at his funeral two years later."

"I remember. Did my uncle ever say anythin' to you about the case?"

"Not much. He said Sheriff Foley was a pain in the ass during the investigation. Didn't think he put out much effort, even though he had primary jurisdiction in the investigation."

"I always thought my uncle had prime responsibility."

"No, Andrew said your father's body was found just outside the city limits, so it was county and Foley had jurisdiction. Andrew still worked on the case and took me with him a couple of times when he thought he had leads on the location of your dad's car. Never did find it, but Andrew kept lookin' until he died."

"Any idea what happened to the car?"

"Maybe someone drove it out of the area and sold it, or just ditched it. Who knows? It might be in a lake or pond."

"I suppose it could be in any of those places. Have you heard any talk that might be connected to Dad's murder?"

"Mum's been the word, Joe. As I said, I think most people want to forget it."

"I won't. Got to run. Thanks. Nice talkin'."

"Don't be a stranger."

BY THE TIME JOE GOT BACK to his mother's home, it was nearly lunchtime. He sat in the living room and thought about the last few days. *It sure as hell isn't going to be easy. Need to find out more about the Pidds and Anne and all the Holders. The car might be the key. Maybe Miss Kelly can be helpful. Need to talk to Sam.*

He had the operator place a call to his new office number.

"McGrath Detective Agency. Sally Bowers speaking."

"Sally, it's Joe. I thought you wouldn't join us until next Monday?"

"I had unused vacation days." She laughed. "So I'm on vacation here in the new office. Sam and I have been getting things organized."

"Well, welcome to the payroll if we can find any."

"Good news on that front. I think we have our first client—Kendall Forrester, the owner of Dominion Insurance. He read about our firm in Ritter's column and then saw the ad you put in the *News* announcing the firm's opening. Joe, you won't believe how Sam dealt with this white man. By the time Forrester left, he was eating out of Sam's hand."

"Not surprised to hear it. Let me talk to Sam."

"He's over at his other office right now. I expect him shortly."

"Okay." Joe told Sally about Jason Partlow and the role he had played in the trial. "See if you can find out if Partlow's still alive and how to contact him. Start in Selma. That's where he lived when the trial took place. I'm leaving Montevallo after lunch. Should be back midafternoon."

JOE STIRRED A POT OF MUSHROOM SOUP FOR LUNCH while Elizabeth made two tuna fish sandwiches.

"Are you satisfied with your work here the last few days?" she asked, as they ate.

"Satisfied is not the right word. Try confused, perplexed, angry. But haven't set any trout lines yet. Someone will take one of those baited hooks."

"Trout lines?" Elizabeth smiled at Joe. "Was Hank still kidding you and Adam about your fishing skills yesterday?"

Joe hunched down and acted like a little boy. "Yes, Mama. But we keep tryin'."

"Well, good metaphor. When am I going to see my granddaughter again? You and Jane both have birthdays in February."

"Yes, she'll be eleven. How fast they grow up. . . . I'll talk to Mary," Joe said, not excited about talking to his estranged wife. "Jane and I will try to come see you soon. Hopefully, Diane can join us."

"If it's easier, Joe, I can come to Birmingham for a weekend. Any progress with the divorce?"

Joe had taken a bite of his sandwich and waved his hand to indicate he'd answer shortly. He sipped iced tea and said, "My lawyer filed the papers with the court. He may have it done before year-end. I sure hope so. I'd like to settle this and move on."

"Well, one year for a divorce in Alabama is quick."

As Joe prepared to leave, he said, "I'll let you know, but I plan to return in a few weeks with Sam to continue the investigation."

"Good, I'm looking forward to meeting him. There is another person you should talk to." Elizabeth paused.

Joe waited, observing his mother's wary and somewhat quizzical expression as if she were reluctant to proceed.

Elizabeth finally said, "Archie Hamilton. He was one of your father's best friends. He's a local farmer and lives west of town."

"I'll try to talk to him next time I'm in town." Joe gently took Elizabeth's hand. "Mom, you've been my only anchor since Dad was killed. I know what I'm doing now is not easy for you. I love you and really appreciate all the help you're giving me. And you're here alone most of the time. Do you want me to stop the investigation?"

She held his hand tightly, fighting back tears, and said, "No."

"Please tell me if you do."

CHAPTER 11

BACK TO BIRMINGHAM

WEDNESDAY—JANUARY 28, 1948

JOE GOT BACK TO BIRMINGHAM AT TWO O'CLOCK. Sally was at her desk arranging files when he walked in.

She smiled. "Hi, Joe. Right on time. Sam's here now."

"Hi, Sally, having you here makes the office look complete."

He was pleased with the improvements in its appearance. Diane had come over last week and directed a rearrangement of the office furniture, which utilized the space more efficiently. She also helped them hang prints of famous artists she had bought for the office as gifts, including works by Thomas Cole, Claude Monet, and J.M.W. Turner. She had said their tranquil appearance would put prospective clients at ease. Joe and Sam had laughed after she left, but they later came to realize she was right.

Sam was at his desk poring over papers. He looked up, a curious twinkle in his eyes, and called out, "Well, lookie who's here. How'd things go in Montevallo?"

"Slow. Dead ends and stonewalling."

"Fill me in."

Joe slumped down in a chair and told Sam all about his meeting with Judge Wilberforce: the trial, the Pidds, Jackie Simmons, Jason Partlow, and Anne Holder. Joe added, "He was about to tell me something important when Anne interrupted. I'm sure she's protecting him or herself, or both. My mother thinks he was going to mention Dad's car. It was never found after his murder."

"Hmm, is that all?"

"I wish." Joe mentioned the reticence of the sheriff, and launched into a lengthy explanation of what he called the transcript fiasco and its implications. A hint of despair in his voice, he added, "It's gonna be tough, Sam."

"Unlike your cop days, Joe, when you had your badge and legal authority," Sam said, "now you have to work around the edges in the weeds and shadows."

Joe was skeptical. "Why don't you write the handbook for private eyes?"

"Nope, it's more art than science. You should start thinking that way in Montevallo. And don't get the whole community riled up before you get to first base."

Joe nodded, but he was upset. It was not the first time he had felt this way when Sam was obviously right. Joe had to change the subject. "Sally told me about Kendall Forrester and Dominion Insurance. What's the job?"

"Maybe a good one. He visited the office yesterday without an appointment. You know his company, don't you?"

"Sure. The largest insurance company in northern Alabama."

"Sally is one smooth operator. Forrester asked for you. She said you were out of town for a few days, and suggested he talk to me. She said I worked for you. And here's the hook. She told him I was the colored guy who used to write a column for the *Birmingham World* newspaper and now ran a colored private investigation firm on the side."

"Yeah, smooth." Joe smiled. He wasn't surprised. "What happened?"

"He said he'd read my articles and heard about my investigation firm. So we talked after he did the usual white guy thing when he first saw me. You know, the startled look of surprise or even fear. Hell, you did it the first time you saw me."

"Sam, you know damn well you're quite a sight with your height and build."

"And color," Sam added, sarcastically.

"Thanks for reminding me," Joe said, smiling. "Sometimes I forget."

Sam played along. "You sure you ain't color blind?"

"Lemme think about it. Yep, could be. So once Forrester realized you weren't going to throttle him, how did it go?"

Sam said, bugging his eyes out for effect, "Now don't you worry, Mista Boss Man, I played the subservient colored to that white man. Yes suh this, and no suh that. We got along jus' fine."

"For Christ sake, you're a ham." Joe shrugged and shook his head. "What's the job?"

Sam smiled. "He wants to consider signing us to a long-term contract to do investigative work for his firm."

"Good. Let's get a Coke. I need one after the drive." They went to the pantry and got drinks from the refrigerator.

They sipped the Cokes, and Joe said, "Did Forrester say why he wants our help? He has insurance investigators on his staff. The police department has an arson investigation guy. I never thought he was very good."

"He mentioned both. But he said they've had a number of high profile, expensive claims. He needs guys like us to do investigative work on the q.t. He added that he didn't mind paying legitimate claims, but, and here I'll quote him, 'I'll be goddamn if I'll pay bogus ones. And you'd be surprised how many of those claims are by wealthy whites.' "

"So where are we with him?" Joe asked.

"He wants to meet again when you're here and discuss money and the contract arrangements."

"How about that? You reeled him in."

"Yep. I can play the back office darkie better than most."

"You can play any goddamn part you want. And I don't mean just Othello," Joe said, laughing. "Back to money. What do you think we should ask for? You're the expert in pricing this kind of work," Joe said.

"I'd ask for a fixed monthly retainer, say three hundred bucks. When he has us on a job, we'll charge for our time by the hour. In addition, direct out-of-pocket expenses plus ten percent to cover some of the overhead."

"Yeah, I like it. How much per hour?"

"Five dollars an hour for you and three for me. Brendan and anyone else we bill at four. If Forrester balks, we suggest a lower rate for bigger jobs. Or if he uses us frequently, we can cut the rates a buck an hour."

"I don't like it. You and I should have the same rate."

"Joe, you know coloreds don't get paid as much as whites. A big client like this will want an itemized invoice for each individual. Name, time, rate, dollars. If I'm shown at the same rate as you or Brendan, it could cost us some business or worse. We have to play the game."

"I still don't like it," Joe said, getting agitated.

"Look, it's not time for a crusade," Sam said, turning even more serious. "We have to get this business off the ground. Let's show clients what we can do. Then maybe we push for some changes."

"But everything's split fifty-fifty between you and me, right?"

"Yep, just like our contract says."

"Right. Sam, I gotta get something off my chest."

"I know."

Joe was startled by Sam's comment. "Twice today, I've found myself getting angry with you. And only because you're right. I know it's the Southern thing about the white guy always being right. But I can't seem to shed it."

"You're shedding it and don't even know it," Sam said. "If I thought for a moment you were a racist cracker, I wouldn't have anything to do with you. We got work to do . . . partner."

Joe felt a sense of relief that had eluded him from the start of their conversation. "Right. Let's get on with it." Joe called Sally into his office. "Sally, please call Mr. Forrester's office and arrange a meeting with him at his convenience. Tell him I'm back in the office."

"Where do you want to meet, Joe?" Sally asked.

"Wherever he'd like."

Joe told Sam about the people he'd met and interviewed in Montevallo. When Sally walked back in, they were talking about the importance of trying to locate Joe's father's car.

"Mr. Forrester will be here at eleven tomorrow morning. He said he'd like Sam to be in the meeting," Sally said.

Sam started laughing. "Kemosabe, maybe white man like Tonto."

Joe grinned.

CHAPTER 12

KENDALL FORRESTER

THURSDAY—JANUARY 29, 1948

J OE EYED KENDALL FORRESTER who appeared to be in his fifties. Modest in height and overweight, dressed in a double-breasted brown suit. He smelled of aftershave, and his lean, narrow head and face were decidedly mismatched with his rounder body.

"I need two things," Forrester said, looking resolutely at Joe. "First, an exclusive contract. Don't want you to do this kind of work for anyone else. Second, a confidential arrangement. We can't control all leaks, but keep it quiet. That'll make you more effective to me. Can you accommodate me?"

Joe caught Sam's nod out of the corner of his eye and said, "Yes."

"Good. Joe, call me Kendall, please." A smile spread across his face, better balancing his proportions. "How would you like to proceed?"

Joe wanted to call Forrester out for ignoring his partner. But he knew Sam would tell him to forget it, just get the contract, so he handed Forrester a copy of the cost provisions. "Kendall, Sam works for me in this office while still maintaining his own private investigation office in the colored business district."

Kendall read the sheet and nodded. "Makes your operations even more attractive to me. Besides Dominion, which works the white community, I own Grinnell Insurance. Do you know Grinnell, Sam?"

"Sure do. My ex-girlfriend works there. I thought colored folks owned Grinnell."

"We keep the ownership quiet and let folks believe what they will. It's better for business that way. . . . I can tell you're bothered by that," Kendall said as Sam stared hard at him. "We pay the manager and staff very well compared to other colored businesses."

"Glad to hear it," Sam said, trying his best not to sound sarcastic. "Grinnell's office is a few blocks from mine. I have two policies with them. Home and office."

"Thanks for the business. Anyway, both firms write residential and commercial fire and life policies. I want you to work with both whites and coloreds. And, Joe, you have connections to Birmingham's law enforcement community. All represent assets to me. Once we nail down the contract, I have a job for you." Kendall coughed and pulled out a handkerchief to cover his mouth. "Excuse me. A lingering cough. I had two policies on a warehouse on the Southside that was destroyed by fire on Friday, July 4, 1947. It came to be known as the Fourth Fire. The policies were held by Stanford Ramsey and Marcus Gilbert."

Joe couldn't help laughing. Sam stood and turned around to hide his expression.

"Did I say something funny?" Kendall asked, looking perplexed.

"Sorry, Kendall. Sam and I have had recent experiences with Ramsey and Gilbert. Yes, I remember the Fourth Fire. Do you, Sam?"

Sam nodded as he sat.

"Let's talk about the fire and Ramsey and Gilbert after we agree on contract details," Joe said, unconsciously straightening his tie. "We need a confidentiality clause about the work we do, similar to the one you requested. Equally important, we'd like you to agree to hold in confidence anything you hear from us concerning our other work in both detective agencies and in my past work as a cop."

"No problem," Kendall said.

"Good," Joe said, shooting a glance at Sam, "The only other clauses we need are payment terms and a cancellation clause for both parties."

"I suggest monthly payments. You submit a hand-delivered invoice to my office at the end of each month. I'll have a check hand-delivered to your office within fifteen days. Either party can cancel the contract with a thirty-day notice. If you agree, I'll have the contract drawn up for your review and signatures."

Sam nodded.

"Draw it up, Kendall. Let's go," Joe said.

"Glad to see you two work so closely together," Kendall said with a knowing smile. "I'll write you a check for three hundred dollars for next month's retainer." He wrote the check and handed it to Joe. "I'll make the contract effective February second."

"Thanks, Kendall," Joe said, sliding the check over to Sam to look at. "I'm sure you heard about Warren Abernathy's suicide last November when I tried to arrest him for the murders of three colored prostitutes."

"Of course. Couldn't believe it. I knew Warren. A little eccentric, but I would have never guessed he could do something so atrocious."

"Yeah, a shock to a lot of people. Let's take a break. C'mon in our cozy pantry. We've got coffee and Coke, and donuts if you're hungry."

Joe asked Sally to join them. They got their drinks. Kendall was the only one to take a donut. They stood in the reception area by Sally's desk, talking about the labor unrest rocking the city's iron and steel production companies.

Back in the conference room, Joe picked up where he left off. "There's something you should know about our relationships with your clients. Sam and I worked together on the prostitute murders."

"Interesting. Tell me more."

"Have you ever heard of Mahogany Hall?"

Kendall looked startled. "You know about Stanford's pleasure palace?"

"Know about, seen it, and know it no longer exists," Joe said.

"What? You must be kidding? That was Stanford's playpen to keep his minions in line."

"He'll have to come up with something else. How much do you know about the playpen, Kendall?"

Kendall laughed. "If you're asking me if I've been there, the answer is no."

"I wasn't. Just want you to know where I'm at with Stanford. After Warren's suicide, I pressed Stanford to stop using the place for his sex parties, especially with colored ladies from New Orleans. He not only stopped importing the gals from New Orleans, he had the place demolished. I'm sure he squelched my request for a leave of absence from the police department. That's why I resigned and opened this business."

"I'll be damned. This is getting better and better."

Joe frowned, a perplexed look on his face. "Whaddaya mean?"

"Stanford and I get along like oil and water. I can't stand the man—his pretensions, his ridiculous home he calls a Scottish castle, his iron fist on everything political in the city. Stanford thought Mahogany Hall was such a big secret. Hell, most people knew about it and just kept their mouths shut, not wanting to alienate him. So where's Marcus in all this?"

"I'll explain, Mr. Forrester," Sam said. "I've known him for years. We're members of the same church. I've done several jobs for him. He controls the colored community like Mr. Ramsey does the white. Marcus uses his money for control while Mr. Ramsey uses his for political clout. Marcus pays off the cops and most white officials to look the other way."

"Does he pay you off, Sam?"

"He's tried, but I won't accept his bribe money. I call it honor. Some call it stupid."

"Sam, I like a honorable man. How does Marcus fit in with Stanford?"

"In many ways, I suspect. But the one we know about has to do with Mahogany Hall. Marcus managed the movement of the New Orleans prostitutes to the hall. The ladies were escorted on Southern Railway to Birmingham. His men then took them in a bus, blindfolded, to the hall. One night, we followed the bus and worked our way through the woods to near the hall and saw a number of white men arrive."

"How many?"

"Not sure. Thirty to fifty."

Kendall looked amused. "I'll bet a roll call of the men there that night would have made an interesting story in the Sunday *News* society pages."

"Probably, right," Sam said, grinning at Kendall. "Might have even made the front page. But not exactly my area of expertise."

Kendall stood and walked around the table, laughing, not as if amused but pleased. "Goddamn, this is better than I could have ever imagined. You two are the perfect guys to help me."

"What do you want us to do with the Fourth Fire?" Joe asked.

"Dominion has a number of polices in place on properties Stanford owns. He—"

Joe interrupted Kendall. "Did Stanford have a policy with you on Mahogany Hall?"

Kendall sat down, chuckling. "Good question. Yes. But I doubt we'll see a claim on it based on what you've told me. If he does make a claim, I now have enough to frame a denial. So you've already earned your keep."

"Glad to accommodate. But I doubt that's what you had on your mind about this job." Joe rubbed his chin, wondering where this was going.

"Absolutely right. Stanford rents properties to Marcus, like warehouses and office buildings. Marcus, in turn, has taken out policies with Grinnell on the equipment and furnishings in those properties. He also has policies with Grinnell on properties he owns outright. My companies are carrying a high amount of risk between those two."

"Have you had any significant claims from them?" Joe asked.

"Three in the last five years, including the Fourth Fire. That's where y'all come in. Ramsey owned the warehouse. Gilbert leased it and used it. My investigators weren't allowed into the warehouse until early Sunday morning, July sixth. We were told it was too dangerous."

Sam, confused, asked, "Isn't that unusual?"

"Damn right. We normally get in a building along with the cops and coroner. Just before my guys went into the warehouse on Sunday, a young officer handed them a copy of the coroner's report and the police report. The cop told my guys the fire wasn't arson, and said the colored guard died of asphyxiation in a room he used for breaks. Although we suspected arson, my investigators and the independent experts we hired couldn't find conclusive evidence. We paid both claims. I want you to start nosing around and see if you can find anything, I mean anything, pointing at foul play. Here are copies of the police and coroner reports, and our internal report on the claims." Kendall handed the files to Joe.

Joe stared at the file folders, realizing the problems this case would present. "I assume you know that Stanford's got Police Chief Big Bob Watson in his hip pocket. The arson cop is one of Big Bob's right-hand men. I thought homicide might get involved, but after our guy reported it wasn't arson, homicide wasn't called in."

"Yeah, I know about Stanford and Big Bob," Kendall said. "But if it was arson, it would have been murder, right?"

"DA makes the final call. Probably hard to prove it was first degree. Maybe second. Certainly manslaughter. We have to find conclusive proof that the arsonist acted on behalf of Marcus or Stanford. Tough hurdle," Joe said.

"I know. Can you get on it right away?"

"Yes, we'll get started," Joe said. "We have other things going on. Sam and I will be working a job in Montevallo, my hometown, every now and then."

"I understand," Kendall said affably. Pounding the table for emphasis, he added, "Just give me my money's worth. And one other thing. As I mentioned before, your work has to be done discreetly. I don't want people to know you're nosing about."

Sam and Joe looked at one another and laughed for a moment but dropped it, not wanting to upset Kendall.

"Kendall, this is an area where Sam and I are real experts. Someday we'll tell you the shenanigans we played to work together on the prostitute murders."

"I look forward to hearing those stories."

AFTER KENDALL LEFT THE OFFICE, Joe turned to Sam. "Between now and Monday, let's do some digging into Kendall's background and reputation."

CHAPTER 13

OPEN FOR BUSINESS

MONDAY—FEBRUARY 2, 1948

J OE UNLOCKED THE OFFICE DOOR and felt like this was the first day on a new job. *Okay, don't be silly, McGrath. Get to work. But first things first.* He went into the pantry and made a pot of coffee.

As the coffee brewed, he was rereading the contract Forrester had sent Friday afternoon, when the office door opened.

"Good morning, Sally. Welcome to the official start of a new career."

"Hi, Joe, I brought some Hershey's Kisses. We'll have to share them with everyone else."

When she put the jar on her desk, Joe played a game they had perfected at police headquarters. "Sally, do you have a kiss for me today?"

"Joe, you know I always have a kiss for you."

Joe took a candy from the jar. "Thanks for the kiss. As soon as Sam gets in, I'm going to review Forrester's contract with him one more time. If we're okay with it, I'll sign, and I want you to get it hand-delivered to his office."

"Will do. I've got some information on Jason Partlow. Called the Selma Police Department and talked to a sergeant I know from our police days. He hadn't heard the name, but he asked one of their captains who was in the department in 1923. He knew of Partlow and said the last he'd heard of him, he had moved to Montgomery in about 1946. I'll check some sources in Montgomery today."

"Go get 'em, Sally."

JOE AND SAM SAT IN THE CONFERENCE ROOM WITH THE CONTRACT on the table. "Turn up anything interesting on Forrester?" Joe asked.

"Nope. Everything matched pretty well with what he told us," Sam said. "Talked on the q.t. to the Grinnell Insurance office manager. At first he was reluctant to talk about Forrester, which I understood. He's the guy's bread and butter. He finally loosened up and said he seldom saw or talked to Forrester, but that he paid well and treated folks fair and square. What'd you learn?"

"I called Franklin Pierce, the white guy Ramsey turned his back on and insulted. He said—"

Sam chuckled. "Yeah, your Shakespeare game buddy."

"Hardly my buddy, but that's the guy. Anyway he said Forrester was one of the few wealthy men in town who stood up to Ramsey. I'm ready to sign. You okay with it?"

"Yeah, let's get busy and put some money in the bank."

Joe signed the copies of the contract and handed them to Sally for delivery to Forrester.

"Where do you think we should get started on this? I could talk to some guys over in the police department, but I don't think it's a good idea," Joe said.

"You bet it's not. You talk to the wrong guy, it'll get right back to the chief and then to Ramsey. Game over."

"Well, where do we start?"

Sam, rubbed his chin, said, "I'll talk to Eddie 'Pops' Johnson, the old colored pimp who tipped us off to Mahogany Hall. He shorted Marcus, and he's lucky Marcus only dumped him. He was on hard times. I found him a job. He owes me."

"Sounds like a start. Let's see where it leads us," Joe said.

"Go to Montevallo this week if you want to."

"I'll let things cool off for a few weeks. As you suggested, I don't want to get the community riled up. I'd like you to go with me next time. I got a colored buddy in Montevallo from my childhood days. He can help you get your feet on the ground."

"Yes suh, master."

Joe's feigned anger quickly faded to a smile. "Stop it, goddamn it."

CHAPTER 14

EDDIE "POPS JOHNSON

WEDNESDAY—FEBRUARY 4, 1948

I T WAS ALMOST DARK, as Sam drove carefully toward Eddie "Pops" Johnson's home in North Birmingham in a heavy rain on a cold, windy day. Since Pops didn't have a phone, Sam had called him at the junkyard where he worked. When told Pops was off today, Sam decided to take a chance in hopes of catching him at home.

He parked in front of a small, wood-paneled house. The yard was overgrown and paint peeled off the wood siding, which was patched with tarpaper. The threadbare curtains were drawn tight.

Sam huddled under his umbrella, fighting to keep it pointed into the wind so it wouldn't splay open. He slogged through the water flowing down the street at the curb and knocked on the door.

"Who's dat?" a gruff voice asked.

"Sam Rucker, Pops. I'd like to talk."

Pops opened the door just enough to peer up and down the street as if looking for someone, even in the heavy rain. Seeing no one, he opened the door completely. "C'mon in, Sam. Wet enough for you?"

"It'll do. Still worried about Black Bronco?" Sam said, referring to one of Marcus Gilbert's top pimps and strong-arm men.

"I never stop worryin' about that asshole after what he done to me."

"Has he given you any more trouble?"

"Nah. Haven't seen that black bastard in over three months. I's jus' always on the lookout."

"Glad to hear it. Let me know if he comes acallin'. How you been doin'?"

"Can't complain. Shit, wouldn't do no good anyways."

Sam smiled at the old guy. He put Pops in his late fifties and knew he was single. The house was a mess, papers and clothes strewn everywhere, dust accumulated on most of the furniture. Looking through to the kitchen, Sam saw dirty dishes and pots and pans stacked in the sink and on countertops. There were several used paint cans positioned around the house catching drips from the leaky roof.

"Things goin' all right at the yard?' Sam asked. "They treating you okay?"

"Yeah, it's goin' okay. They's good people. It's good work. First time I's worked for an honest livin' in a long time, thanks to you. Hey, I's started goin' to church again." Pops, giggling like a kid, added, "I done met me a lady friend. Whatcha say to that?"

"I say that's great. No offense, Pops, but why don't you get your new lady friend over here to help you clean up the house?"

Pops laughed so hard he started choking. He settled down and said, "Well, you a mind reader, Sam. She comin' over this weekend to help me. She be takin' good care of me." He flared his nostrils like a stud horse ready to perform.

Sam couldn't help laughing. "Pops, you be sure you do some house cleanin' so you don't scare your new lady friend off. If you want, I know a guy who could help you with some outside house repairs when the weather gets better. Whaddaya say?"

Pops looked taken aback. "Sounds right nice. What's goin' on, Sam? I know you don't come here to talk about my love life and my house, 'specially on a day like this."

"You're a smart man, Pops. I got a problem. Hope you can help me."

"What's up?"

"The warehouse fire on the Southside last July fourth. Marcus used the warehouse, and a colored man who worked there was killed. You hear about it?"

"Yeah, I heared 'bout it. I knowed the guy what was killed, Willie Thompson. Good guy."

"The cops and the insurance company ruled out arson as the cause. Marcus got a big insurance check," Sam said.

Pops looked angry. "You sayin' somebody killed Willie on purpose?"

"Maybe, if the fire was arson."

"Shit," Pops said. He rubbed his eyes as if upset or thinking. "You knows I was just a pimp, Sam. I ain't done nuthin' like that."

"I don't believe you had anything to do with the fire. I just wanna know if you heard any interesting talk about it."

Pops seemed bewildered and remained silent.

Sam worried he had pushed him too far.

Pops finally said, "I was hurtin' after the fire. I knowed Willie real good. Had a wife and two kids. Folks said he mighta set the fire. I don't believe it. He was a smart guy, knowed his stuff."

"Who said Willie mighta set the fire?"

"Black Bronco and some others. Now this here afore I got in trouble with Marcus. I 'members after the fire, Black Bronco sayin' the Boss Man—that's what we call Marcus—gonna be gettin' a big payout soon. Later, I hear Black Bronco sayin' stupid Willie be alive if he doed his job right."

"Interesting. Of course, the payout could have been for a number of Marcus's little games. Black Bronco's comment about Willie could mean several things too. Hear anything else?"

Pops looked spent. "No. That's all I 'members. You think they kilt Willie?"

"Don't know, Pops. Sorry to drag you through this."

"It's okay," Pops said, shaking his head as if to clear his mind. "Sam, I owes you big time. You wants me to ask around 'bout this?"

Sam smiled at Pops, but said firmly, "Pops, don't you go near Black Bronco or any of Marcus's people. Don't ask anybody about this. If Marcus finds out you're asking questions, your days may be numbered. Do what you're doin'. Enjoy your lady, clean up your house and repair it, and work hard at the yard. You're a good man, Pops."

He was clearly relieved. "Thanks, Sam. You done me right, and I's know it."

CHAPTER 15

THE REPORTS

THURSDAY—FEBRUARY 5, 1948

J OE STOPPED AT THE COPS' DINER and bought a dozen donuts for the office. He was in a hurry since he had to meet Sam at eight thirty. Joe kept waiting for Helen to appear and call out, "Hey, Big Dick," until the cashier told him it was Helen's day off.

In the office, Joe got a couple of cups of coffee and several donuts and took them into the conference room where Sam was waiting.

"Well, bless my bones, white boy's serving colored boy," Sam said.

"Gotta keep you happy. This is in lieu of this month's paycheck. What'd you learn from Pops?"

Sam handed Joe his notes. "Read these first."

Joe went through Sam's notes quickly and asked, "Have you looked over the reports Forrester left with us?"

"Only the summaries," Sam said.

"Read the details when you get a chance. There are interesting things in both reports that add some credence to what Pops told you."

"Yeah? Like what?"

"The reports pretty much confirm what Forrester told us," Joe said. "The police report says the fire was caused by an electric arc in a wire bundle near the room where Willie Thompson's body was found. No evidence of arson. Coroner's report says Thompson's cause of death was asphyxiation. The fire occurred early Friday morning, but Forrester's investigators weren't allowed into what remained of the building until Sunday morning. Their report says the body had already been removed by the coroner, and the room Thompson used had been cleaned up. Cops don't usually do a cleanup, so maybe they got someone else to do it. Forrester's investigators confirmed an electric arc occurred. But they were unsure if it was the cause of the fire since the area around the wire bundle had also been cleaned up. They found no other evidence of arson. Case closed. Insurance policies paid."

"You know the coroner pretty well, don't you?"

"Yeah. Frank Cutler and I go back a ways," Joe said.

"Will he talk to you in confidence?"

"Maybe."

"We need something to hang onto here," Sam said. "If we find proof of arson, it doesn't help Forrester unless we can find a link between the arsonist and either Marcus or Stanford."

"I'll call Cutler. Have to move carefully with him. He gets real fidgety if he senses trouble for himself."

Sally stuck her head in the door. "Joe, Brendan O'Connor's on the phone."

"Thanks, Sally."

Joe grabbed the conference room phone. "Hey, Brendan. Sam and I were just talking about some new business."

"Hi, Joe. You won't believe it. Goddamned department canned me."

"What happened?"

"Someone must have found out I was going to work for you. You're not too popular here. At one of Chief Watson's cop meetings last week, he said something like, 'I reckon y'all heard Professor McGrath has opened a detective agency. I s'pose he thinks he gonna solve our crimes for us. I'm glad to be done with the smart-ass.' I swear he was lookin' at me when he spoke."

"Who fired you?" Joe asked.

"Dick Oliver called me into his office Tuesday and told me Wednesday was going to be my last day. When I said I'd prefer to work until the end of the month as I had requested, he said since I was going to work for you, I might as well start right away."

"Do you want to start now?"

"Can I wait until February sixteenth? I want to spend next week in Mobile. I'm overdue a visit to see my parents and friends."

"Sure. Don't worry, you'll hit the road running with us."

Joe hung up. "Brendan was canned Wednesday, Sam."

"Yeah, I heard most of what he said. Obviously, the cops don't think kindly of you or your new line of work."

"Doesn't surprise me. Watson and I never got along. Oliver's better, but he takes the safest and least threatening path. I'm sure Watson ordered him to do it."

"If you talk to Frank Cutler, I hope you can trust him," Sam said.

"Me too. Let's get some lunch."

"Okay. Know a good place in Chicago?"

Joe felt confused, then laughed. "Sorry. My mind was on Brendan and I plumb forgot where I was."

Sam laughed but shook his head. "Joe, I never forget where I am."

CHAPTER 16

FRANK CUTLER

MONDAY—FEBRUARY 9, 1948

JOE TOOK A SIP OF HIS BEER and glanced at his watch: 6:21. Maybe Frank was going to be a no-show. Joe had called his old buddy Thursday afternoon, but he was unable to meet until Monday. Joe hadn't seen him in over two months and was relieved when Frank walked into the White Stag, an English-style pub in Birmingham's Five Points district.

"Hey, Frank, I'm over here," Joe called out. Though the pub wasn't crowded, he'd grabbed a table in the back corner for privacy.

His short, chubby friend walked over, and Joe chuckled to himself, realizing for the umpteenth time that Frank was the last guy you would pick out as a coroner. His round, cherubic face always had a smile, and he was a fun guy at a party. Yet in the autopsy room, he was all business and worked with a dexterity that belied his small, pudgy hands.

"Good to see you, Joe. Sorry I'm late. Got hung up in the office at the last minute. Do you know you're the talk of the police department?" Frank said.

"So I hear, and it's not all good."

"Like I've told you before, you were always the odd man out as a boy in blue."

"Can't argue," Joe said. "What'll you have? I'm drinking an English beer, a pint of bitter."

"Hmmm. Never had one. I'll give it a try."

Joe motioned to the waiter and ordered one for Frank.

"Glad we could get together. It's been too long," Joe said.

Frank took a sip of his bitter. "This is good. Nice call."

"How's the autopsy business?"

"Couldn't be better. Death's the perfect job security, and folks can't outsmart it. The detective agency doin' okay?"

"It'll do for the first few weeks. Things will pick up."

"Hope so. You said you wanted to talk about something. What's up?"

"You're my best friend in the law enforcement community. Can we talk in complete confidence?"

Frank hesitated. "Yeah, I guess so."

"I need better than guess so."

"Is this something I should be concerned about?"

"I'm not sure."

"All right, on one condition. If things get too uncomfortable for me, I'll say so. You know I don't like to be in the limelight."

"Fair enough." Joe smiled and continued, "Do you remember the warehouse fire on the Southside last summer on July fourth? It was a Friday. Colored night guard was killed in the fire."

"Yeah, remember it only too well."

Joe sensed a note of caution in Frank's voice. "You did the autopsy, right?"

"Wrong. Took advantage of the holiday and went on vacation the week the fire happened."

"Didn't know that. Where'd you go?"

"Bayou la Batre on the Gulf Coast. Great fishing and eating trip. You been there?"

"Nope. But who does autopsies when you're on vacation or sick?"

"Office policy requires a licensed MD to perform autopsies. We have a list of six Birmingham MDs to call on. My assistant, Gerhard Mueller, helps them."

"Well, who did the autopsy on the guy killed in the fire?"

"It's a long story. When I got back in the office on Tuesday after my vacation, Mueller told me about the fire. He said the DA wanted the autopsy done immediately, and Dr. Scott, one of the MDs on our list, was called in to do it. Scott determined the cause of death was asphyxiation. The cops ruled out foul play or arson. In fact, Scott also did one other autopsy while I was in Bayou la Batre."

"Why didn't Mueller do the autopsies?"

"He wasn't a fully licensed MD in Alabama. He was supposed to work under my supervision for a year before being licensed."

"I read the report on the colored guy's autopsy. There was no mention that Scott did it. Mueller signed as coroner's assistant, and you signed as coroner." Joe pulled the report Forrester had given him out of his briefcase and handed it to Frank.

"That's not my signature. Where the fuck did you get this?"

"I can't tell you how I got it. Somebody must've forged it. Mueller?"

Frank looked confused. "I have no idea. Possibly Mueller."

"You didn't ask him about it?"

Regaining his composure, Frank said, "How could I have asked him based on the copy you just showed me? It's the first time I've seen it. It's dated Saturday, July fifth. I wasn't even in Birmingham."

"Have you seen the autopsy report written by Mueller and Scott?"

"I'll answer that in a minute. What do you know about Mueller?"

"I've seen him working with you on a few autopsies. I know he joined you early last year. He's German. I've talked to him a few times. Speaks pretty good English. Seems quiet and unassuming."

"I wish that was all. Joe, have you heard about the German rocket engineers the Army brought here after the war?"

"Yeah. The V-2 guys who leveled London. They're at Fort Bliss, Texas. Chief engineer is Wernher von Braun."

"Mueller and von Braun are cousins. I suppose he insisted Mueller be brought to the states with him."

"Jesus! Is a rocket engineer your assistant?"

"No," Frank said, laughing. "He was a medical doctor in Germany."

"Maybe von Braun wanted to get him out because of what he did in Germany. Some horrible stuff happened there."

Frank shrugged his shoulders.

Perplexed, Joe said, "I always wondered how Mueller found a job in an Alabama coroner's office."

"What I'm about to tell you is off-the-record. I could get in deep shit real quick if certain people found out."

Joe nodded.

"Two weeks before Mueller started working for me in January 1947, I got a visit from three men. Jefferson County Sheriff Wilcox and two guys who identified themselves as Army special agents. They closed my office door. Said the meeting was top secret and that I could not tell anyone about it. I agreed, unsure what else to do."

"Why are you telling me?"

"Because you're my friend. Because I trust you. Because I've got to get some of this shit off my chest. Hang on, it gets worse."

"Did you get their names?"

"Yes, but I'm not going to tell you. One of the men said that Alabama Senator John Sparkman was working with the Army to relocate von Braun and his engineers to the Redstone Arsenal in Huntsville."

Joe whistled in amazement. "When?"

"They weren't specific. One of the agents did most of the talking. Wilcox sat silent the entire time. Any questions I asked were ignored or answered with a simple yes or no. The agent told me Mueller was von Braun's cousin and a medical doctor. Mueller and his family were already in Birmingham. He'd been provided a furnished home with a maid and a car in the Glen Iris neighborhood. He'd report to work as my assistant the week after the agents' visit. I was told to oversee his work and ensure he was ready to become a fully licensed MD in the State of Alabama in a year."

"What a package. He got treated better than most of our troops who served overseas," Joe said.

"I thought about that too. Half in jest, I asked the agents if Mueller was a Nazi. They were not amused and both immediately answered no. As the three got up to leave, the agents reminded me to keep my mouth shut."

"Does anybody else know about this?"

"Don't think so. Wouldn't be surprised if some Birmingham and state muckety-mucks know."

"Goddamn, that's a hell of a story."

"There's more," Frank said, pausing.

CHAPTER 17

FRANK'S TRAPPED

MONDAY—FEBRUARY 9, 1948

J OE SENSED FRANK was deciding where to go next.

"On Tuesday, after Mueller told me about the fire and autopsy findings, I pulled his personnel file," Frank said. "I had to write a six-month evaluation of his performance for the state licensing board. In the file was a copy of a license dated January 26, 1947, granting Mueller the right to work as an MD in Alabama, the date he started working for me. I immediately called the licensing board in Montgomery, and they confirmed Dr. Mueller was fully licensed in the state. They added it was no longer necessary for me to send them any evaluations on Mueller. "

"Judas Priest, how did that happen?" Joe asked.

"I have no fuckin' idea. Whoever did it, Mueller now had cover."

"Why didn't they do this when they moved him to Birmingham? "

"Don't know. You think that's bad. The other shoe drops. I found a copy of the autopsy report in Mueller's file. He had signed it as my assistant and dated his signature July 5, 1947. My real signature followed his, dated July 8, 1947. It looks like I signed the report as a form of approval the day I returned from my vacation. I checked the file in the office where the original autopsy reports are kept. It was signed in ink and was identical to the one in Mueller's file. I checked with other people in the office, and their copies matched Mueller's."

"Son of a bitch," Joe said, shaking his head in disbelief. "First, someone botched your signature and now they get it right. Is that all?"

Snickering in disgust, Frank said, "Almost. I called Dr. Scott and asked him if he did the autopsy on the guy killed in the warehouse fire early Friday morning. He said, and I quote, 'What the hell are you talking about, Frank? Sure, I know of the fire, but I had nothing to do with the autopsy.' I apologized and told him I must have misunderstood my clerk, adding that I knew he did one for us earlier that week. Pretty lame, I know. But Scott seemed to buy it."

The two men sat and stared at each other until Frank turned away.

"Did you look at the body and confirm Mueller's findings?" Joe asked.

"Whoa," Frank said, clearly agitated. "Getting close to the limelight. Who hired you to work on this?"

"Can't say. My client asked to remain anonymous. Most people who hire a detective agency want it that way."

"So I do all the talking, but you don't tell me a damn thing," Frank said, raising his voice.

Several people sitting at the bar looked over at the two men.

"Quiet down, Frank. I will tell you this. By the time the insurance investigators were allowed into the warehouse on Sunday, not only was the body gone, the room where it was found had been cleaned, including what remained of the room's walls and ceiling."

Frank looked surprised. "I did take a look at the body just before the family arrived to claim it Tuesday afternoon. Apparently, they had a hard time making arrangements with a funeral home for the pick-up. Not only was the body covered with third- and fourth-degree burns, it had a severe skull fracture on the right side of the skull, probably from a blunt object."

"So whoever clobbered the guy was left-handed, or he was struck from the rear," Joe said.

"Probably left-handed."

"How can you be sure?"

'Not absolutely sure, but the angle of the skull indenture indicates he was hit from the front."

"What if the family makes a stink about the body's appearance?" Joe asked.

"Get real. A colored family's complaint against the coroner's office is going nowhere."

"Okay, but you could lose your license and more, if all this ever gets out. Why didn't you challenge Mueller, or tell the cops or the licensing board about it?"

"Goddammit, Joe, what can I do? It seems all those people were involved in the cover-up." Frank's shoulders and face sagged as if all was lost. "I've had this recurring nightmare since all this started. I'm a puppet. All the puppeteers are standing over and around me holding onto the strings. They're looking at me with awful, malevolent expressions. You can guess who they are."

Joe listened as his friend described his nightmare, realizing what a poor mental state and difficult position he was in.

"If I try to step right, the one to the left pulls a string and dangles me in the air until he puts me back where I was," Frank continued. "When I try to step left, the one on the right pulls me back. When I try to escape even harder by leaping forward, all of them pull me way up and back, and I disappear in a dark hole. I can't get out. I wake up, shaking and sweating. My wife's concerned about me. I tell her it's nothing, just a bad dream."

"How can I help you?" Joe asked.

"I'm a cautious man. I just want to do my job, keep my head down, and retire early. Can't wait to move to Mobile to be near good fishing, golf, and Mardi Gras. It's too dangerous to do anything. Think about the people involved. Senator Sparkman, Army special agents, Sheriff Wilcox, maybe the FBI. I knew Stanford Ramsey owned the warehouse. He's probably in on it. Maybe Chief Watson. Maybe the governor. List goes on. They've got me cornered. I'm a small fish, and I want to stay that way. You're not gonna put me at risk, are you, Joe?"

"Of course not. But if I can find a way to expose some of what happened without putting you in jeopardy, is that okay?"

"I suppose so, but I don't see how you can. No more questions or discussion. You put the pieces together, Professor," Frank said, casting his eyes down.

"When I can, I'll tell you more about what we're doing. Want another bitter?"

Frank looked up, forcing a smile. "Sure."

CHAPTER 18

JOE AND SAM'S DILEMMA

WEDNESDAY—FEBRUARY 11, 1948

JOE CONTINUED MULLING OVER what Frank Cutler had told him on Monday. Glancing at the clock, he hoped Sam, who spent yesterday in his office in Scratch Ankle, would be in soon. Just as Joe reached for the phone to call him, Sam walked in.

"Good mornin', Boss Man. How's it goin'?" Sam said.

"Well, if it ain't Sam Rucker. Nice to see you, partner. Shake up any business for us over in the Ankle yesterday?" Joe asked.

"As a matter of fact, I got us three clients," Sam said, looking pleased with himself. "Small potatoes. But they'll add a bit to our meager pot. I left Dave Williams to man the office and start working on the cases."

"Who?"

"Dave Williams, a senior at Miles College. Works part time for me."

"Name's familiar."

"Should be. He's the kid who worked the front desk at the New Home Hotel the night the first prostitute was murdered last September. You interviewed him."

"I remember. Nice kid. Articulate. Well dressed and good looking. Worked midnights while going to school. Obviously very motivated."

"He's the kid I want to bring on after he graduates this year. He and Brendan will make quite a team."

Joe couldn't help laughing. "They sure will. Shit, we'll either set this town on fire, or it'll set fire to us."

"Don't worry, by then we'll be experts in arson investigations."

"Right. I need to tell you about my meeting with Frank Cutler on Monday. Some of this stuff is unbelievable."

"Yeah? Try me."

Joe explained his meeting with Frank in detail. He added no analysis or comments. Sam sat quietly, nodding his head occasionally.

"Well, what do you make of all that, Mr. Private Investigator?" Joe asked.

"Willie Thompson was murdered. The fire was arson."

"I'm with you there. Why?"

Sam paused, collecting his thoughts. "Six things. First, Black Bronco told Pops that Marcus was about to receive a big payout. Second, later Pops heard him say that Willie would still be alive if he'd done his job right. Third, Cutler's description of the body. Fourth, somebody cleaned up Willie's room before the insurance investigators were allowed in. Fifth, Black Bronco is left-handed. Sixth, somebody went to a lot of trouble to set the paper trail straight."

"What was Willie's job that night?" Joe wondered and then answered his own question. "Was he supposed to set the fire or at least help them set it? If so, maybe he did it so poorly, Bronco just took him out. Or maybe he wasn't even supposed to be there, got confused about dates, and when they found him, Bronco killed him. No witnesses. Lots of what ifs."

"Always are. Do you believe everything Cutler told you?"

"Yes. Can't think of a reason he'd make it up."

"Why didn't Mueller just sign the autopsy report on Saturday, July fifth?" Sam asked. "By then, knowing his license was backdated to January 26, 1947, he could have signed as the MD who performed the autopsy."

"Yeah, I've been thinking about that. Here's a scenario. Mueller forged Frank's signature on the autopsy dated July fifth. Someone realized what a botched job Mueller had done and decided to set things right and added a twist. Both the license and autopsy report were altered before Frank got back in the office on Tuesday. It would've taken several people to do all that. Someone with excellent handwriting and copying skills. A safe, reliable contact in the licensing department in Montgomery. And someone in the coroner's office to change the copies in the files, probably Mueller."

"Okay," Sam said. "Two questions. First, why were Forrester's investigators given the copy with the botched signature? Second, what was the twist?"

"First one. The person who caught the botched signature didn't catch it until later in the day Sunday or maybe not until Monday morning. Forrester's folks were given what was thought to be the valid autopsy report. When the copies of the botched reports were destroyed, the copy Forrester had was overlooked. Maybe because the young cop failed to mention he had given it to Forrester's people."

"Okay. What's the twist?" Sam asked.

"The twist goes in another direction and explains why Mueller didn't sign the autopsy report as you suggested. I admit it's more improbable, but whoever's running this show wants to keep a tight noose around Frank's neck. And it's working. He's a basket case emotionally. He has nightmares and thinks his career's in jeopardy."

"I agree, it's improbable. However it developed, one of the Army agents must have watched Mueller like a hawk to be able to react so quickly. Are you sure it's Cutler's signature on the autopsy report that's now in the files?" Sam asked.

"No, I haven't seen that report. I'll see if Frank will give me a copy. When I left the police department, I kept some files from recent cases, including copies of autopsy reports I know Frank performed and signed. We can compare the two reports. Whaddaya make of all the Mueller, von Braun, Sparkman, and Army special agent stuff?"

Sam laughed. "Great story. We oughtta write a book." Turning serious, he said, "If the Army and others are Mueller's guardian angels, there's no way we're going to be able to get close to them. And I don't think we need to. They've got Mueller's license covered now. We'd never be able to tie him to the murder, even as an accessory. Actually, we have a bigger problem. Everything we know comes from two guys who are vulnerable if we use their information the wrong way."

"We've also got another problem," Joe said. "Assuming Willie was murdered, if we can't tie the arsonist to Marcus or Stanford, it won't help Forrester."

"You're not gonna like this, Joe," Sam said, shaking his head, "but I don't give a shit whether or not we can tie it to Marcus or Stanford.

There's a chance we can tie it to Marcus, but I doubt we'll be able to tie anything to Stanford. What I'd really like to do is nail the asshole who murdered Willie. Best bet, Black Bronco or someone he knows."

"If we could do that, the whole thing might start to unravel. How do you propose going about it?"

"Right now, I have no idea. Let me think about it."

"While you scratch your cranium, I want to help Frank out of the impossible corner he's in. The poor guy is going nuts. I think I'll write an anonymous note to Jack Ritter. If anybody can shake the trees and get any loose fruit to fall out, it's Jack."

"Might work, but risky," Sam said.

"I'll keep the note short and sweet. Only a few choice morsels. No names. I'll type it and mail it from somewhere well outside of Birmingham."

"Let's both mull this over for a while."

Sam's reticence bothered Joe. He thought about challenging Sam, but chose to ignore it for the moment and said, "Okay. But we need to give Forrester an update. At least we can report some progress."

"What do you propose we tell him?" Sam asked.

"First, let's talk about what we don't tell him. No mention of Frank or Pops. Nothing about the German engineers, and the Army's plan to move them to Huntsville. Nothing about Mueller's license or the signature on the coroner's report."

Sam looked skeptical. "Not much left, Joe. Why bother talking to Forrester now?"

"I want him to know we're working the problem. We can tell him what we've learned from two independent confidential sources. The fire was most likely arson and Willie Thompson was murdered. We'll say we aren't prepared to draw any conclusions until we verify what we were told, adding we can't yet tie the arson to either Marcus or Stanford. Think that's enough or too much?"

"It's okay. It'll give us a chance to see how Forrester reacts and size up the man we're working for."

"Good. I'll have Sally call his office and make an appointment. Probably best to ask him to come over here."

CHAPTER 19

FORRESTER'S REACTION

FRIDAY—FEBRUARY 13, 1948

E ARLY FRIDAY MORNING, Joe and Sam talked while they awaited the arrival of Kendall Forrester.

"You're gonna love this story, Sam," Joe said. "Late yesterday afternoon after you left the office, a good-looking white woman, maybe forty, forty-five, came in. Mrs. Samantha Browning. She wants us to tail her husband, Ralph, and record his comings and goings. She thinks he's having an affair."

"Well, lordy lordy, good to hear white folks do mess around," Sam said. "Did you agree to work with her?"

"Oh, yeah. She looks and smells like money. Lives in Mountain Brook. She gave me what we need to get started and a five hundred dollar cash retainer."

"Great. The lady is serious."

"You don't know how serious. She was wearing a skirt that came down to only the top of her knees. As she reached for her purse, she lifted her right leg so I could see everything. She didn't have any panties on. She said, 'Mr. McGrath, it's going to be a pleasure to work with you.' "

"And what did you say to her, Don Juan?"

"We're very experienced in this sort of thing and will do our best to assist her. We signed an agreement. We're required to tail her husband and see if there's any proof he's having an affair."

"You cad. Wait 'til I tell Diane about our new client."

Joe threw his head back, laughing. "You keep your goddamn mouth shut, Sam Rucker." Joe took a deep breath and stopped laughing. "Look, you game to go with me to Montevallo next week? I'd like to get you involved. Leave Tuesday morning and probably come back Friday. I'd like us both here Monday when Brendan starts. We can get him going on the new job."

"Sure, I'll go. Do you think Brendan's ready?"

"I'll prep Brendan on what we've got. He and I did some stakeouts together. He knows the ropes."

"Fine. I'll have Dave Williams cover my office next week."

"Doesn't he still work midnights at the New Home Hotel?"

"No. He quit the first of the year. He's working for me this semester, his last until he graduates. Not full time. He'll work around his class schedule. No problem. He's a hard worker." Sam glanced at the wall clock: 8:24. "Forrester should be here soon."

"One more thing. Frank slipped me a copy of the July eighth autopsy report in the official files. It's the one with his signature that he claims he didn't sign. It matches perfectly with an old report I have that I know Frank signed." Joe handed the reports to Sam.

He compared them. "I'm not a handwriting expert, but whoever did it, it looks perfect."

"Joe, I was surprised when you called and said you had something. It's been only two weeks," Kendall Forrester said.

Unlike the last time he was in their office, he was more casually dressed. Tan slacks. Blue blazer. Nice off-white silk shirt. No tie. But the overweight man with the lean, narrow head still reeked of shaving lotion.

"It's very tentative stuff," Joe said. "Sam and I are going to be in Montevallo on other business next week, so I wanted to tell you what we know and what we don't."

"Good."

"Based on conversations with two confidential sources, it's likely the fire was arson and Willie Thompson was murdered. Sam—"

"Are you sure?" Kendall asked. "This is big."

"As sure as likely means. Sam talked to a colored man, and I talked to a white man. I want to emphasize that our sources' lives could be in danger if their names were leaked."

Kendall sat quietly, mulling over his response. "So either Stanford or Marcus or both took me to the cleaners. Who are the sources?"

Sam responded immediately. "Mr. Forrester, a good colored man with a wife and two children is dead. We want to be sure no one else gets killed. We don't know who the arsonist is, and whether or not he is connected to either of your policyholders. At this time, we think it's best not to tell anyone our sources."

Kendall appeared agitated. "Sam, we have a confidentiality agreement. You telling me you don't trust me?"

"No, sir," Sam said. "At the right time, we'll tell you what we can. With lives at stake now, it's too risky."

Kendall, obviously not happy, rubbed the fat folds of skin on his neck in thought. "What else have you got, Joe?"

"It's more what we don't know at this point. As Sam said, we can't tie anything to Stanford or Marcus yet. We have to verify our arson and murder findings with other sources. We'll pursue it when we get back from Montevallo."

"Okay. Just to protect my financial interests," Kendall said, "I'm gonna cancel my policies with them when they come up for renewal."

"Are many policies renewing soon?" Joe asked.

"Yes, two with Stanford and one with Marcus, both on March first. All we have to do is state that the insurance risk on the properties has become unacceptable."

"I understand your risk, Kendall. But I don't think now's the time to cancel policies."

"Why not?"

"If you abruptly cancel three policies, it sends up a red flare. Stanford and Marcus will put the lid on all their folks. Nobody will talk to us."

"I agree. Bad idea," Sam added.

"And if I hold off?"

"Maybe we'll find something tying the arsonist or murderer to one of them." Sam said. "Maybe we won't."

Kendall shook his head. "Joe, I need to talk to you . . . alone."

Without hesitation or comment, Sam left the room and closed the door.

"Is this talk necessary in private?" Joe asked.

"Yes. I've got two issues with you."

"Okay. Let's have 'em."

"I feel cornered. I'm at risk while you and Sam are off doing work for another client. And even if you can prove arson, I may have no recourse."

"What's the second issue?"

"I'm not used to being talked to like that by a colored man."

"I think Sam is your real issue. If your financial interests were your main concern, why didn't you cancel the polices soon after the fire last year?"

Kendall didn't answer.

"Two weeks ago, we signed an agreement, and I told you we had work to do for other clients. You seemed to understand. Sam's speaking straight with you is all that's changed."

Kendall paused, staring at his hands. "You're right. I do like the arrangement with your two offices. And I thought Sam's color wouldn't bother me. I was wrong."

Joe thought a moment about how to reply. "Sam and I started working together closely last fall. I had a few issues with him, and I reacted as you have. It's hard to shed our ingrained prejudices."

"Don't lecture me, Joe."

"I'm not, and I won't. But humor me for a moment. Imagine you hadn't met Sam. What if I told you a guy in my office was from a well-known Birmingham family, father a noted Birmingham minister, studied for a while to be a minister himself, got a degree in criminology from the University of Chicago, well-spoken, smart as a whip, and a nice guy to boot. What would you think?"

Kendall smiled, "I'd think you have one helluva partner. Sam's your partner, isn't he?"

"He works for me. We have a business agreement concerning our two offices."

"Nice arrangement. I take your point."

"Are we still doing business?"

"Yes, for now I just hope you can find some linkages after you get back from Montevallo."

"We'll try," Joe said. "But remember, if we find a link to either Stanford or Marcus, we have to decide how to go forward with the information in order to recoup your losses."

"Understand, but do your damnedest. I've got to get going."

The two went into the reception area where Sam sat.

Kendall turned to Sam and offered his hand. "So long, Sam. I just had to get some things off my chest."

Sam shook his hand. "Goodbye, Mr. Forrester. We all have heavy things on our chests."

After he left the office, Sam asked, "Is he still a client?"

Joe smiled. "He'll be all right."

CHAPTER 20

BRENDAN COMES ON BOARD

MONDAY—FEBRUARY 16, 1948

A T SIX FORTY-FIVE, JOE RAN UP THE STAIRS to the fourth floor. He knew it was a lame excuse, but he always patted himself on the back for getting some exercise. He wanted to arrive before Brendan reported for his first day. Joe exited the stairway on the fourth floor and saw Brendan waiting patiently at the office door.

"Well, I'll be damn. How long you been waiting, Brendan?"

"About twenty minutes. Didn't want to be late for my first day on the job, boss."

"Welcome aboard," Joe said, giving Brendan a bear hug. "Let me open the door. We'll get you a key and all that sorta stuff immediately. C'mon in. Sally and Sam should be here soon."

JOE SIPPED ON HIS FIRST CUP of steaming coffee, savoring its flavor and smell as much as he enjoyed watching his three colleagues at the conference table doing the same.

"So Brendan, you ready for the private eye life?" Sam asked, breaking the coffee reverence.

"Ready as I'll ever be. Can't wait to get my teeth into something."

"Don't worry, eager beaver," Joe said, "got you an assignment." He told Brendan about the new client. When he said that she suspected her husband was messing around, he noticed Sally roll her eyes in disgust.

Joe pushed a file across the table to Brendan. "I want you to start tailing her husband tomorrow. All the details you need to know are in the file. Be extra cautious. Don't tail too close, especially in light traffic. If you lose him, it's okay. Just pick him up later or start again the next morning. Keep a log of all his comings and goings. Addresses, time-in, time-out, pertinent notes. Read the file carefully. We'll talk this afternoon."

"Didn't you forget an important item, Joe?" Sam said.

"What?"

"The lady's interesting entreaty."

Joe laughed. "I don't think that's necessary. But I do have something else. Brendan, do you have access to another car?"

"No."

"Sam, can Brendan use your car while we're in Montevallo?"

"Sure."

"Brendan, Sam and I are going to Montevallo in the morning for the week to work on finding my father's murderers. I told you about that, didn't I?"

"Yes. I still can't imagine how I would have handled something like that."

"It was tough, believe me," Joe paused, his mind drifting for a moment. "Anyway, drive Sam's car to your apartment tonight. Leave your car in a safe parking lot downtown near the office. Alternate cars each day, or even during the day, if possible. Okay?"

"Sure," Brendan said.

"When we get flush with cash, we can talk about buying an office car for this sort of thing."

"Yeah," Sam said, snickering, "and a trip to the moon on gossamer wings."

"Get me a ticket. Anything else?" Joe said, looking around the room.

"Yes," Sally said. "On Saturday, I finally got in touch with the sergeant I know at the Montgomery Police Department. He'd been on vacation. I asked him if he knew Jason Partlow." Sally paused.

Joe knew she was playing it for effect and went along. "Well, what did he say?"

"He laughed and said all the cops and court officials in Montgomery know Partlow. He's an ambulance chaser and is in and out of court with frivolous liability claims and two-bit hoodlums, when he's not on a bender."

"Did you get Partlow's contact information?" Joe asked.

"Of course. Here're his work and home phone numbers and addresses." Sally handed Joe a piece of paper.

Joe looked at Sam and Brendan.

"Gentlemen, if you need to know the whereabouts of anyone, ask Sally to get on it. I swear," Joe said, holding up his right hand as if taking an oath, "she knows police and court staff in every town and city in the state. Great work, Sally."

She smiled coyly. "You're welcome."

"Joe, you should go to Montgomery while we're in Montevallo and talk to Partlow," Sam said.

"It's sixty-five miles," Joe said. "I could get down there, interview him, and be back in a few hours. We'll see how it goes. Sally, take our new sidekick and get him office keys, and fill out the paperwork we need to get him on the books. Brendan, you can use the spare desk in the room Sam and I use. It'll be cozy, but we have an extra desk in the conference room if you find us too annoying."

SALLY WATCHED BRENDAN COMPLETE the required federal and state forms. She had been immediately disarmed by his youthful enthusiasm and college-boy face with its light, ruddy complexion scattered with freckles. He was medium build and height, and his reddish hair always seemed in need of a comb.

Brendan handed Sally the forms. Scanning the documents to ensure they were complete, she noted his birthdate and realized he was only twenty-six years old.

"Thanks, Brendan," Sally said. "Looks fine. I haven't seen you since the department put you back on night patrol duty. It's wonderful to have you working with us. Are you happy with the move?"

"You bet. Joe's my mentor. Learned a lot from him . . . and Sam. We'll make a great team. But truth is, I'm sure the department would have canned me anyway. Anybody close to Joe was on the chief's black list."

Sally was surprised. "Do you think I was on it?"

"Of course not. The chief's not that dumb. Besides, you were a valuable employee and are also too charming."

Sally smiled. "Do you always talk to older women that way, Brendan?"

"No," he said, returning the smile, "only to you and my mother."

"Well, it's nice to be included with your mother. Now let me explain where everything is and discuss our office procedures. Don't worry, there aren't many."

As Sally showed Brendan around, a concerned look formed on her face. "Brendan, be careful. I know Joe or Sam wouldn't say it, but I think this kind of work is more dangerous than being a policeman."

CHAPTER 21

ADAM'S APPLE

TUESDAY—FEBRUARY 17, 1948

T HE NEXT MORNING, Joe picked up Sam at his house at eight o'clock, and they headed south on Highway 31 toward Montevallo.

"Think the young guy's ready to go?" Sam asked.

"Oh, he's ready to go, but I know what you mean. I think he'll do fine. We have to give him a chance. I gave him my mother's phone number and told him to call if he has a question. He'll also keep Sally up to date."

"Good. How do you see us handling things in Montevallo?"

"I called my childhood friend, Hank Moore. He owns a construction company in the colored community. He said he has a room you can use in his house. Normally, I know Mom would want you stay with us, but I think it's better this way, don't you?"

"Yeah. We gotta play the game if we want to get anywhere with this," Sam said.

"Afraid so. Hank suggested you come over to his construction office this morning. I'll drop you off there. He's been talking to some old timers and has a few lined up for you to meet. He'll fill you in, but said not to expect too much. He'll also show you around town. Here are his home and office addresses."

Sam put the note in his shirt pocket. "Sounds like a start."

"I'll meet with my white lawyer friend, Adam Paige. He's been quietly talking around."

"Can you trust these guys, Joe?"

"Absolutely. Don't worry. I'll pick you up at Hank's tonight at six. Mom's invited you to dinner. She wants to meet you."

"Do we have to play back door games like we do at my house?"

"No. I know it's not the way we agreed to work, but my mother said, 'Joe, don't you dare bring Sam in by the back door. Our front door is open to everyone.'"

"Well, bless her heart. I don't even have to meet her to know I'm going to like her."

"I've got a bone to pick with you, Sam," Joe said, his voice a sharper tone.

"Let me guess. You're upset because I brought up the lady's interesting entreaty in front of Sally and Brendan, right?"

"No, goddamn it," Joe said, his anger building. "Frank Cutler. He's one of my best friends. I want to help him. Now! The fuckin' feds are playing him like a marionette. In the meantime, you want us to drag our feet."

Sam briefly took his eyes off the road and looked at Joe with a steady gaze, and said calmly, "I'm not dragging anything. I don't want either of our friends to get hurt. As long as we keep quiet or move carefully, I'm sure they'll be all right."

Joe felt his anger subsiding. "I'm worried Frank won't be all right. I'm concerned about his mental state." Joe told Sam the details about Frank's recurring nightmare. "He feels completely cornered and doesn't see a way out, except to do nothing."

Sam shook his head. "Awful. I'm not an insensitive man. But if you tip off the press with an anonymous letter, someone in Marcus and Stanford's camps, or those protecting Mueller, will finger Frank or Pops as the source."

"I'll grant you the Army agents might think of Frank. I doubt Pops will come to anyone's mind. He's been out of the picture for quite a while."

"Probably right. How about we do this? When we get back to Birmingham, you draft your letter to Ritter. We'll review it together. If we're both okay with it, you send it."

"Sounds good. Thanks," Joe said, "Sorry about the outburst."

"I'm glad you want to help your friend and not just let it go. That's the easy way out."

They nodded at each other and drove the rest of the way in silence until they approached the Burma-Shave signs with the faux-Shakespearean quote purportedly written by one of Elizabeth McGrath's students. When Sam saw them, he burst out laughing.

JOE HAD NEVER BEEN IN ADAM'S OFFICE. He realized that even small town lawyers did much better than cops or private eyes. Adam's office had a spacious reception area where two women worked. The first woman, a young attractive blonde, was behind a counter obviously meant for visitor check-in. The other woman, an older lady with short brown hair, sat at a large desk and seemed to be important. He had no idea what she did.

Approaching the first woman, he said, "Good morning, I'm Joe McGrath. I have an appointment with Adam."

"Good morning, Mr. McGrath. I'll let Mr. Paige know you're here." She called Adam, and he came out of his office in a flash.

"Joe! Good to see you. C'mon in."

Adam's office was even more opulent than the reception area. A large desk sat in the center of the room surrounded by several cabinets and bookshelves, all made of black cherry. The cabinets held law books and a scattering of fine china and crystal. One cabinet displayed several golf trophies.

"Looks like your practice is doing well—and your golf game," Joe said.

"Can't complain. You still play? Maybe we can play a quick nine while you're here."

"Haven't played much since we were teenagers. I wouldn't give you much competition."

"We'll have to see sometime. Did Sam come with you?"

"Yeah, Hank's going to show him around and get him started. Mom's having him over for dinner tonight."

"Nice," Adam said.

"You said you talked to a few people."

"Actually, quite a few. I'd mention your father's murder as an aside when in meetings or on the golf course. Occasionally, I even talked to guys I ran into on the street. I gotta tell you, the most common reactions were 'Let sleeping dogs lie' and 'Why dredge up that old story now?' "

Joe shrugged his shoulders in disappointment. "Thanks. Maybe all this work will go nowhere, but I'll keep at it for a while."

"Don't look so hangdog. There was one guy who didn't react too negatively. I think you should talk to him."

"Good. Who?"

"George Noggin. He runs the Chevy dealership his father started. George's about fifty-five and knew your father. Speaks highly of him."

"I knew the Noggins. Did he mention the hostile witness?"

"I didn't ask directly. Too leading. I did ask if he had attended the trial. He said no."

"How do I get in touch with George?" Joe asked.

"Here's his phone number. When you call him, mention my name. It's best to be up front with him."

"Thanks. I'll call him today. My mother suggested I talk to Archie Hamilton. I vaguely remember him. Do you know him?"

"Well, if you want to talk to a crazy, radical guy, he's your man," Adam said.

"He's a farmer. Right?"

"Yeah. Grows some crops, raises cattle, trains and boards fine horses. Lives about six miles west of town. Calls his place Shoal Creek Farms and Stables. Acts like a racist redneck. Wears coveralls and chews tobacco. Talks like a hick. I think he does it for effect. But he's no dummy. Earned a B.S. degree in agriculture from Auburn. But watch out for his politics. He's as liberal as they come. Runs his farm like a commie commune. I wouldn't believe a goddamn word he says. He's really out in left field."

"Christ, you sure I'm in Shelby County? Don't worry, if I talk to him, I'll be cautious," Joe said, thinking, Goddamn right, I'm going to talk to him.

Joe added as he got up to leave, "Hey, later this week, how about the four of us, you and Hank and Sam and me, meet for lunch at Schaeffer's?"

"Okay. I'm not in court this week. Shouldn't be a problem."

Joe left Adam's office with a restless feeling in his stomach.

CHAPTER 22

SAM MEETS MONTEVALLO

TUESDAY—FEBRUARY 17, 1948

J OE DROVE FROM ADAM'S BUILDING back to his mother's. He wanted to see if he could get in touch with Archie Hamilton. He looked through the local phone directory and found his number.

"Shoal Creek Farms and Stables. Archie Hamilton speakin'."

"Mr. Hamilton, this is Joe McGrath. I'm the son—"

"Well, I'll be goddamned. I knows who you are, Joe. Elizabeth and Peter's son, right?"

"Yes sir, that's right."

"Whatcha doin' in Montevallo? No more sirs. Call me Archie."

"I live in Birmingham, Archie, where I worked for years as a homicide detective with the police department. I recently left the department and opened a private detective agency."

"Good plan. You don't gotta work for that dimwit Big Bob Watson. What an asshole. You down this way workin' on a case?"

I'm liking this guy already, Joe thought. "Yeah, and visiting my mother as well," he said. "I'm trying to learn more about my Dad's murder years ago."

Archie said nothing. Joe could hear him breathing.

Archie finally said, "Very interesting. Peter was one of my best friends. I was distraught over his death. How can I help you?"

Joe heard a distinct change in Archie's speech. He no longer spoke with a pronounced Southern drawl and his grammar was perfect.

"If you have time today, I'd like to meet and talk," Joe said.

"After I finish the morning chores, I have to come into town on business. Do you know Julie's Café on Main Street?"

"I've seen it."

"How about eleven?" Archie asked.

"I'll be there. Thanks."

Joe got to Julie's Café just before eleven. A few patrons gave him a hard look, as they did most strangers. No one seemed interested in talking to him.

He ordered a cup of coffee and was sipping it, when a man walked in the café you couldn't ignore. Probably in his fifties. But it was his height, about six foot four, which first caught Joe's eye. Solid as a rock, he reminded Joe of Sam. He wore clean, but well-used, blue coveralls over a cotton collarless workman's shirt, and a pair of scruffy boots. His gray hair fell loose from a sweat-stained straw hat around a sun-creased face, not handsome but pleasing except for the obvious chaw of tobacco in his jaw.

"Archie Hamilton?" Joe asked.

"Hiya, Joe. Figured it was you. Look like your dad." He grabbed a chair at the table and swung his leg over the top as if mounting a horse. "Say, do you know Stanford Ramsey? Bigwig in Birmingham. He's bought several horses from me. Haven't seen him in a few years. Does he still run the city?"

"Pretty much, and he's the city's biggest wig. Yeah, I know him. He doesn't realize it, but he helped me solve a murder case recently."

"I reckon Stanford can't help you down here. So you've come to town to nose around concernin' Peter's murder? Long time ago."

"Yep, most folks won't talk or have little to say."

Archie turned his head to the left and leaned over a spittoon, and let loose with some tobacco juice. "Not surprised. Probably more skeletons in the closet than we can imagine."

"What do you remember about it?"

"Mostly how much I miss your father. Like I told you, he was a good friend. Honest and trustworthy to a fault. But he didn't realize the hatred swirling around him."

"Did you attend any of his last days in court?"

"Yes, a few."

"Dad tried to call a hostile witness his last day in court. Were you there?"

"Yes."

"Do you know who the hostile witness was?"

"No. But mighta been Karl Merkel or Wilson Riley. Both are dead. Karl was the Piggly Wiggly store manager. Maybe Klan. Wilson, a service station owner, had a racist chip on his shoulder as big as an oak tree."

Joe couldn't help laughing. "Nice metaphor." His gut told him Archie was holding back, just throwing him crumbs. He decided it best not to press him. Maybe later. Continuing to make light of the situation, Joe smiled and added, "So the identity of the hostile witness is a big mystery?"

Archie smiled back. "Yep. I guess you got a mystery to solve, private detective," he said, emphasizing the word private. "Excuse me, I gotta go to my next appointment."

Archie stood, took a few steps toward the door, and looked back. "Call me if you wanna talk some more."

Joe sipped his coffee. *Hmmm, is that an invitation to talk in private? Maybe too many ears in here.*

AFTER LUNCH IN A COLORED CAFÉ, Sam and Hank walked along Main Street in Montevallo's six-block white business district. Earlier in the day, they had toured the colored district. As they approached the only movie theater in town, they could read the marquee, *The Treasure of the Sierra Madre.*

"I want to see that film. I like Humphrey Bogart. Tough guy," Hank said.

Sam paused, looked at the two-story theater, and said, "I like Bogart too. Colored people sit upstairs, I suppose?"

"That's the way it is," Hank said, as a white man walked up to them.

Sam looked him over: forties, unshaven, long unkempt hair, and a vivid red scar two-inches long just below his right eye. He wore filthy blue jeans covered with patches.

"Who da big darkie with you, Hank? I bet ya boys up to no good," the white man said.

"This is my friend, Sam, Mr. Dwayne. He's from Birmingham."

"I don't give a shit whar he's from. Y'all get outta here, now," Dwayne said as he stepped toward Hank and gestured with his fist.

Sam moved between Hank and Dwayne, who jumped back in fright. Sam glared at Dwayne, when he saw a tall, older white man approaching. He wore coveralls and a soiled, straw farmer's hat. Sam thought, *Goddamn, here comes another redneck.*

"Hey, Hank. Everythin' all right?" the white man asked.

"Mr. Dwayne just stopped to have a little conversation with us, Mr. Archie," Hank said.

"Looks like more'n that to me. Whatcha doin' over here, Dwayne? Can't find enough coloreds to harass over in Columbiana?"

"I be over here on bidness, and it ain't none of your bidness," Dwayne said.

"It's my business what goes on in my town. You over here workin' a new still in west county?"

"Ain't got no new stills, Mr. Hamilton. I jus' wants these colored boys to get off this here white sidewalk. They knows bettah than to walk along here."

"Well, how the hell they s'posed to get to the theater or the stores?"

"They oughtta use the alleyway and side entrances what's for coloreds."

Archie stared hard at Dwayne and spit a load of tobacco juice near his feet. "Dwayne, take your sorry ass back to Columbiana where you belong. We'll take care of Montevallo."

Sam thought there was going to be more trouble when Dwayne glared at the three men as if he was going to say something. Instead he stomped away.

"Good riddance," Archie mumbled. He turned to Sam and looked him in the eyes, something few men could do. "Don't believe I've seen you in town before. I'm Archie Hamilton," he said, offering his hand.

Sam shook his hand. "Sam Rucker, Mr. Hamilton. Thanks for the help."

"You from around here, Sam?"

"No, sir. I live in Birmingham. Down for a few days to see Hank and some friends."

"Welcome to Montevallo, Sam."

CHAPTER 23

WHO'S DWAYNE?

TUESDAY—FEBRUARY 17, 1948

JUST BEFORE SIX O'CLOCK, Joe parked in front of Hank's home, a two-story craftsman style house in a well-kept colored residential neighborhood in Montevallo. Hank and Sam were sitting in a swing on the porch.

As they walked toward his car, Joe asked, "Did Sam behave himself, Hank?"

"He did just fine, 'til we had a run-in with a white moonshine operator and redneck," Hank said. "He tried to chase us off a downtown sidewalk. He's a real asshole. He and his brother operate stills and sell white lightning all over the county. They can't hold down a regular job, but I'm told their hooch is pretty good stuff. Some of their best customers are colored. So they take our money with one hand, then punch us in the face with the other."

"What was the guy's name?" Joe asked.

"Dwayne Pidd," Hank said.

Joe couldn't believe it. "How old was he?"

"Not sure. Maybe fifty, sixty," Hank said.

"He's probably not that old," Sam said. "A lot of racist rednecks look like hell but aren't as old as they appear."

"Is his brother named Dwight?" Joe asked.

"Yep, cracker number two, his twin brother," Hank said.

"Goddamn, my Dad's colored client in 1923 was accused of killing Darryl. He was Dwayne and Dwight's older brother. The colored guy testified he saw Dwayne shoot his brother. Christ, if any more D-names were involved in this, who the shit would know what was going on? So what happened today?" Joe said.

Hank laughed. "You tell him, Sam."

"Not much." Sam grinned. "Just when it looked like it might get nasty, an older white man walked up. Nice guy named Archie Hamilton. He told—"

"You're kidding? I just talked to him this morning," Joe said.

"Well, about one o'clock, he told Dwayne to get his ass back to Columbiana," Sam said.

"Did you talk to Archie?"

"He introduced himself. Asked where I was from. Told him Birmingham."

"Is that all?" Joe asked.

"Christ, Joe, this sounds like an interrogation. What gives?"

"Sorry. Trying to figure out if he's put us together."

"Doubt it. But it'll happen soon enough in this small town, especially if we're seen driving around together."

"You're right. But let's go now. It's almost dark. Hank, I won't keep him out late. Us youngsters gotta get our sleep."

It was less than a mile from Hank's house to Elizabeth's, but like in all Southern towns, it was a short leap from one world to another. Joe drove at a modest speed in hopes of avoiding attention. For several blocks, his was the only car on the road until he noticed another car pull out behind them from an intersection and continue to follow them at a discreet distance.

"A car's been following us for several blocks," Joe said. "Help me keep an eye on it."

Sam looked back. "Got it. Only one headlight working."

They were two blocks from Elizabeth's house when the car turned.

"Car turned right," Sam said. "Black Ford sedan. Looks like shit. Couldn't read the license plate. Probably two white guys."

"Okay. Mom's house is on the next block."

CHAPTER 24

BRICK, STRING, NOTE

TUESDAY—FEBRUARY 17, 1948

J OE WAS PLEASED TO SEE HOW WELL his mother and Sam got along. She had been eager to meet him, and Joe knew she came home early to prepare dinner, although she normally worked until five o'clock grading papers.

"Miss Elizabeth, that was a wonderful meal. The roast beef was delicious," Sam said.

"Thank you, Sam. I do wish you'd call me Elizabeth."

"Yes ma'am, I know you asked me to earlier. But I think we better stay with Southern protocol while Joe and I are working together."

"Protocol. Is that what you call it?" Elizabeth said, her voice rising in pitch. "It's racism. That's what it is."

"Enough, you two," Joe said, clearing the table.

"I apologize, Sam," Elizabeth said. "I get testy about these things sometimes."

"So do I, Elizabeth, I mean Miss Elizabeth," Sam said.

They both laughed.

She got up and said, "Joe, I'll finish cleaning up and get the coffee and dessert. Then I have to do some prep work for tomorrow's classes."

Joe winked at Sam. "That's Mom's way of saying we need time to talk alone. She knows her courses upside down and inside out."

"Can't be too prepared, Joe."

"Right. Speaking of that, I want to fill you in on my two conversations this afternoon. First guy I talked to was George Noggin, who owns the local Chevy dealership. Nice guy. Said some nice things about my father and uncle. When I asked him if he had any idea who might have killed my father, he listed the obvious, the Klan, disgruntled clients, a loose nut. I don't know why, but I think he was holding out on me."

"He sounds like most of the people you've already talked to," Sam said.

Elizabeth came back from the kitchen with coffee and dessert. "Here, you two youngsters enjoy this while I go—"

In rapid succession, the sounds of glass shattering, furniture falling and breaking, ended with a loud thud reverberating through the living and dining rooms.

Sam ran to the living room windows facing the street and saw a man jump into the front passenger seat of a black Ford sedan as the car, engine roaring and tires squealing, pulled away from the curb. Joe stood in front of Elizabeth to shield her if there was more to come.

"They're gone. Same black Ford that followed us," Sam said, surveying the damage. A single windowpane was shattered. A lamp on a side table by the front window was on the floor, its beautiful Tiffany lampshade in pieces. In the center of the living room floor, lay a small red brick with a piece of paper tied around it.

Sam picked up the brick, untied the note, and read it. When Elizabeth and Joe came into the living room, he handed the note to Joe. He read it aloud. "mcgrath you and that thar afican jungle bunny git outa town rit now. next time ifn youall don't you aint gonna like what hoppen." Joe looked at his mother. "At least we know this note wasn't written by one of your English major students."

Elizabeth, her face paler than usual, managed a weak smile as Joe put his arm around her and helped her into a chair.

"Where can I find a broom and dust pan, and some cardboard and tape?" Sam asked.

Joe kept his hand on his mother's shoulder. "In the kitchen to the right is a storage closet. I think you'll find everything in there."

Sam found what he needed, cleaned up the broken glass, and put what was left of the lamp back on the table. He cut out a piece of cardboard the size of the windowpane and taped it in.

"That'll keep cool air out until you can get the pane replaced."

"Thanks, Sam," Joe said. "Mom, I'll help you to your bedroom."

"Young man," Elizabeth said, her voice stronger, "where are your manners? We have a dinner guest. You and Sam sit down and enjoy dessert and coffee. I'm going to my study. We mustn't let hoodlums like this intimidate us. Your father certainly never did."

She stood, her face less pale, and walked resolutely toward her study.

Joe and Sam returned to the dining room table. Joe freshened their coffees.

"Joe, your mother's a strong woman," Sam said.

Joe nodded and smiled, and murmured almost inaudibly as if letting Sam in on a big secret, "Yes."

"You know the cat's out of the bag. Someone has already put us together. Any idea who?" Sam asked.

"No, this seems out of the blue. Dwayne Pidd maybe. I'll try to find out what kind of car he drives. I'll report this to the police. I know the chief. Maybe they can help identify the car."

"You think that's a good idea?"

"One way or another, everyone around here will hear about what happened tonight. No sense trying to keep it quiet."

"You're right. But if it was Dwayne, how did he put us together?"

"Don't know. Someone must have told him. Let me think about it. Okay, where were we before the sideshow started?" Joe asked.

"You had mentioned George Nuggin, or someone with a name like that. You thought he might be holding something back from you. I said he sounded like most of the people you had talked to."

"Right. George Noggin. He seemed like everybody else, until Archie Hamilton came along, the fella you met this afternoon. He's a horse of a different color."

Sam chuckled. "Joe, this sure as hell ain't the Land of Oz."

Joe grinned, somewhat sheepishly. "Hamilton might be helpful. A character but an interesting guy. He knew my father well and spoke highly of his honesty. Of course, a lot of people have said those things about him. Archie said Dad had a blind spot for the animosity and hatred some had for him. He was in the courtroom on Dad's last days."

"Did he know who the hostile witness was?"

"Said he didn't. But he threw out a couple of names: Karl Merkel, manager of the Piggly Wiggly grocery store, and Wilson Riley, a service station owner who, and I quote Archie, 'carried a racist chip on his shoulder as big as an oak tree.' They're both dead."

"I'll tell you something else about Karl Merkel in a minute. Archie have anything else?" Sam asked.

"No. He had to go to another meeting before he took time to save your ass. But he did drop what I took to be a hint. He wanted to talk in private. What did you hear about Merkel?"

"Before Archie helped us out, Hank had two older colored guys come to his office to meet with me. First, I met a retired Baptist minister. The only interesting thing he said was that when white folks go at one another, colored folks stay out of the way."

"Sound advice, I suppose," Joe said.

"Damn right it is, Joe. The other guy, Oscar Bird, was more helpful. Around the time your Dad was murdered, Oscar's son, eighteen-year-old Odell, worked for Karl Merkel at the Piggly Wiggly. The boy liked to go out fishing at night. Oscar told him it was dangerous. Odell said he enjoyed the quiet and solitude. Anyway, a few days before your father disappeared, Odell went fishing one night at about ten o'clock. The moon was nearly full."

"Have we got another moon-related murder on our hands?" Joe asked.

"I don't think so. From here on, Oscar's telling me what his son told him. Odell got close to the lake he wanted to fish when he saw a faint glow above the trees in the distance and heard some muffled voices. He worked his way through the trees and up a rise toward the lights and sounds. While still in the trees, he saw a clearing full of men in white sheets and hoods standing in front of a burning cross."

"A Klan meeting," Joe murmured.

"Sure wasn't a Halloween party. Odell was about to skedaddle when a car drove up and Karl Merkel got out. He put on different colored robes. I guess he was the Grand Dragon or something. The kid realized the pickle he was in. He stayed in the trees and lay down until the Klan finished and cleared out."

"Smart kid," Joe said.

"There's more. After Merkel robed up, he took control of the meeting. Odell couldn't hear much of what they were saying. Probably

Klan gibberish and racist trash. Odell was getting sleepy when he heard Merkel yell out something like, 'That fuckin' McGrath. He gonna get what he's got comin' for defendin' that coon.' Soon after that, the meeting ended. Odell hurried home and told Oscar what happened."

"Did Oscar or Odell ever tell anybody about this?"

"No. Oscar said this was the first time he'd ever mentioned it. He had told Odell to keep his mouth shut or they'd be next."

"Can we talk to Odell?"

"I wish," Sam said. "A couple of years after your father's murder, Oscar and Odell had a huge argument, and Oscar threw him out of the house. Odell went up north. Oscar got a few letters, then nothing. He has no idea where he is."

"Damn."

"Hank's rounded up a couple more guys for me to talk to tomorrow. What are you gonna do?"

"Hope to talk to Judge Wilberforce about the hostile witness. But I don't know if he's still alive. If he is, his daughter might not let me see him. I'll call in the morning," Joe said, feeling disappointed.

"Hey, this hasn't been a bad day," Sam said. "Hooked up with Archie. Got some names to work with. You never know. Something will pop."

Elizabeth walked into the dining room. "Finished my work. I'm going upstairs to read a while before I go to bed. Joe, will you take care of the broken window?"

"Yes, Mom. First thing in the morning. Don't worry about it."

"Good," and she added with emphasis, "Mr. Rucker, it's been a pleasure meeting you. You're welcome here any time. Please return soon. And you two watch yourselves. This is dangerous business you're pursuing."

Sam stood up. "Thank you, Miss Elizabeth. I look forward to seeing you again soon."

"Mom, I'm going to drive Sam back to Hank's house. I'll be back soon. And don't worry. As Scarlett said, 'After all, tomorrow is another day.' "

"Oh God, Joe. Don't use that awful last line from that dreadful book."

"Well, Mom, it didn't do too bad in book sales or at the box office."

"Hmmm," Elizabeth mumbled as she turned and left the room.

After she was out of earshot, Sam couldn't control his laughter, "After tonight, I understand you and your family much better."

ON THE DRIVE BACK TO HANK'S, Sam said, "After what happened tonight, you sure you want to go on with this? What about your mother?"

"Tough questions. Let's keep going for now. I'll talk to Mom, but I know what she'll say."

"What?"

"It's up to me, and we must not be intimidated by hoodlums."

Joe dropped Sam off and on the way back to his mother's, he thought about the evening. *Who the hell tipped off the brick throwers?*

CHAPTER 25

JUDGE WILBERFORCE REDUX

WEDNESDAY—FEBRUARY 18, 1948

J OE SLEPT LATER THAN USUAL. When he got downstairs, his mother had left for school, and there was a note on the kitchen table. She reminded him to get the window fixed, and apologized for her outburst about *Gone with the Wind*, conceding it had several passages of literary merit. Joe smiled, knowing she was just being nice. He agreed with her opinion about the novel.

After a quick breakfast, he made a phone call.

"Montevallo Police Department. Officer Jeff Davis speaking."

"This is Joe McGrath. Is Chief Chapman available?"

"No, sir. He'll be in later this mornin'. Can I help you?"

"I want to file a report. Tell the chief I called. I'll come in after lunch. That okay?"

"Yes, sir. He should be here. I'll leave him a note."

Joe looked through the Montevallo telephone directory and found a window repair shop. The broken pane had been replaced by ten thirty. After the repairman left, Joe wrote a note to his mother saying the window was repaired but it needed some additional touch-up paint, which he would do tonight. He attached the paid bill to the note and then dialed Anne Holder's home.

"Hello, Holder residence. Agnes speaking."

"Agnes, this is Joe McGrath. May I speak to Mrs. Holder?"

"She not in. She up in Birminham for a social engagement. She be home 'bout four o'clock. Can I take a message?"

"How's Judge Wilberforce doing, Agnes?"

"Oh, the poor man. He not be doin' too good. He have good days and bad days, mostly bad."

"I'd like to come by and say hello to him. Would you ask him if it's all right?"

The phone was silent, and Joe knew Agnes was deciding what to do since Anne Holder was absent.

She finally said, "I go ask him, Mr. McGrath. Jus' a minute."

Joe doodled on a note pad until Agnes returned.

"He say he be happy to see you, Mr. McGrath. He say he got sumthin' to tell you. When you be comin'?"

"How's eleven thirty?"

"That be fine. He takes his medcines at eleven. Now you can't stay too long, you hear?"

"I understand," Joe said, knowing she wanted to be sure he was gone well before Anne returned.

AGNES SHOWED JOE TO THE JUDGE'S ROOM. Joe was shocked. The man had become considerably more emaciated since his last visit.

"Hello, Judge Wilberforce. Thank you for letting me visit."

"Sit down, Joe. I've been thinking about you and your family. When a man knows he's dying and will meet his Maker soon, he thinks a lot about making peace with himself and those he's wronged."

"Yes sir, I'm sure that's true."

The judge struggled to turn his head so he could look directly at Joe. "Even now, this is not easy."

"I suppose dying never is, Judge."

"Oh, dying's the easy part. I've come to accept that and am more than ready. It's the wronged, Joe. It's the wronged. They weigh on your mind and soul. I wronged your father. He was only doing his job, as a good lawyer should. I also wronged Jackie Simmons. Both of those men might still be alive but for me. Most everybody knew Dwayne Pidd shot his brother, but nobody wanted to step up and say it except your father. He—"

The judge took a deep breath but gagged. After several wracking coughs, he tried to grab a small bowl off his side table. Joe reached over and handed it to him. The judge spit a glob of phlegm into the bowl.

"Should I get Agnes?"

Placing the bowl down, the judge wiped his lips with a cloth. "No. That woman's a saint. You won't believe the things she does for me."

"Are you sure you want to continue, Your Honor?"

"Damn right. This isn't a court of law, Joe. And I sure as hell don't have any honor. I could have handled the trial differently."

"What could you have done?"

"More things than I can count. For starters, I could have granted the change of venue your father requested. I certainly thwarted his objections, most of which were appropriate in fact and law." The judge paused, breathing hard. "I could've reined in the racist circus DA Conroy made of the trial. I could've made a bench objection to the DA's unsubstantiated statements in his closing argument. It goes on and on."

"Why didn't you do any of those things?"

"Joe, you know the answer. I was trapped in the same web as most Southerners are. We fear the colored man—his size, his strength, his sexual prowess. We have to control him with our laws and enforce them mercilessly and unfairly in our courts."

The judge didn't notice, but Joe was looking at him with an expression of respect. "You've been thinking a lot about this, Judge. Have you talked to Anne or anyone else about this?"

A series of pig-like snorts reverberated from the judge's throat. Joe thought he was a having another attack until he realized the judge was laughing.

Catching his breath, the judge said, "You must be kidding, Joe. Anne would just call me a crazy old man who's lost his mind. She can't wait for me to drop dead so she can collect her inheritance."

"What do you want from me?" Joe asked.

"At this time, there's nothing to be done but to ask for your forgiveness." With some effort, the judge lifted his arm and held his hand out to Joe.

Joe took the judge's hand. "I forgive you, Judge. I appreciate your honesty in a moment like this."

"Don't put me on a pedestal, Joe. I don't deserve it, but I thank you. I hope you're never faced with such a need. At least, I can go forward with some sense of peace."

"I'm not a saint either. I fully intend to find the people responsible for my father's murder. Can I ask you a few more questions?"

"Sure. I know you didn't come here to say hello."

"Do you know who killed my father?"

"No. It wasn't me, but my actions certainly fueled the flames of hatred in the community. I can rattle off names of people who might have done it. Some of them are dead. I'll bet you know who most of them are. I hear you've been talking to others in the county."

"Who told you that, Judge?"

The judge made a few of his laughing snorts. "Anne. She's got quite a network."

Joe knew he shouldn't put the judge on the spot, but it was obvious he and Anne didn't get along well. "Did Anne or any of the Holders have anything to do with the murder?"

The judge didn't hesitate to answer. "She and her husband are on my list."

"Anne's a tough lady, isn't she?"

"You don't know the half of it. I want to make peace with her too, but she's not interested in making peace with anyone, especially me."

The judge sighed and turned away and lay back on his pillow. Joe, unsure whether the judge was upset with him or tiring of the conversation, realized he'd better conclude things quickly.

"Who was the guy DA Conroy meant when he said in his closing statement that a prominent man in Montevallo was upset with my father?"

"So you read the transcript?"

"Yes, sir."

"I honestly don't know. There were a number of men he could have meant."

"Well, do you know who the hostile witness was my father wanted to call the last day he was in your courtroom?"

"I would have wronged Peter on that ruling too. I had decided to deny his request the next day. He wanted to call —"

Both men snapped their heads up when the front door closed with a slam.

They heard Anne Holder call out, "I'm back home, Agnes. I wasn't feeling well. Whose car is out front?"

Joe and the judge looked at one another and heard Agnes's reply, "Mr. McGrath, Miss Anne. He talkin' to the judge."

Anne's voice became shrill. "Why did you let that man see him?"

Joe could barely hear Agnes's frightened response. "The judge say it was okay."

Anne flung the door open to the judge's room so hard it hit the wall with a loud thud. "Joe McGrath, how dare you come into my house without my permission. What have you two been talking about?"

The judge spoke up immediately. "Anne, I wanted to see Joe. I needed to ask him for his forgiveness."

"Forgiveness for what?"

"I wronged his father in that trial years ago."

"You didn't wrong anyone. You did your duty. Stop being a silly, senile old man. Follow me, Joe. I'll show you out."

She led him to the front door, saying nothing until she opened it. "You're not welcome here, Joe. Don't ever come back."

Joe doffed his hat as he experienced another slammed door and walked to his car. *Goddamn that woman's timing.*

CHAPTER 26

THE BLACK FORD SEDAN

WEDNESDAY—FEBRUARY 18, 1948

JOE STOPPED AT A COLUMBIANA DINER near the courthouse to have lunch. As he entered the diner, he saw Susan Kelly, the court records clerk, sitting alone studying the menu.

He walked over. "Well, good afternoon, Susan. Late lunch?"

"Mr. McGrath. What a surprise. Nice to see you. Yes, this is late for me."

"I just finished business here and decided to get a quick bite before heading back to Montevallo. Mind if I join you?"

Her eyes darted around the diner. He knew she was checking to see if any other courthouse employees were there. Her boss, Carlton Teague, had gotten upset with Joe when he ordered a copy of the trial transcript.

Apparently satisfied, she smiled. "Of course, Mr. McGrath, please sit down," she said, blushing slightly.

"Thanks. Susan, please call me Joe. What's good here?"

She suggested a grilled ham-and-cheese sandwich with a side of coleslaw, and they ordered. While they ate, they discussed the weather and other inane topics people who don't know each other well talk about.

Over coffee, Joe asked the question that most interested him. "Susan, you were right about the copy of the transcript I was given. It had been altered. Has Carlton Teague or anyone else said anything about it since I got it several weeks ago?"

"No, not about the transcript. But Mr. Teague did tell me to notify him immediately if you ever came back to the courthouse." She smiled. "I don't think accidently meeting you here counts."

Joe smiled back. "Thanks. I'd like to ask a favor. If you hear any talk about the transcript or me, would you call and tell me about it?"

She looked surprised. "Oh. Yes, I'll do that," she said, pausing for a moment. "There's one thing you should know. I didn't prepare the transcript copy you have. Do you remember when Mr. Teague asked me to have it ready for you?"

"Yes."

"Well, right after you left, he told me not to worry, that he would take care of preparing the copy. I think he had his secretary type it up."

Joe pulled out his note pad, tore off a piece of paper, and wrote on it. "Interesting. Here's my work number in Birmingham, and my mother's number in Montevallo. I stay with her when I'm in town. How do I get in touch with you other than at the courthouse?"

She looked pleased and gave Joe her home phone number. "I have to go. My lunch hour is almost up. It was nice having lunch with you."

"I'll pay the check. I know you want to leave before me. Thanks for your help. You're a delightful young lady."

Susan, trying not to blush again, got up to leave the diner, but blush she did.

As Joe drove back to the Montevallo, he couldn't get Susan's pretty face and attractive figure out of his mind. He tried to think about Diane, but Susan kept forcing her out. He was glad when he parked at the Montevallo Police Department to finally be able to let go of her image.

"C'mon in, Joe," Chief Chapman called out from his office. "Jeff told me you wanted to file a report. I heard about the brick tossed through your mother's window. Musta been tough on her?"

"It was. Who told you? I didn't mention it to Jeff."

"Hell, everybody was talkin' about it at Julie's Café this mornin'. You can't keep nothin' quiet in this town."

"Seems you're right," Joe said. "I'm not sure I want to file a formal report, but I do need to talk. We were having dinner when the brick came through the front window."

"Tell me what happened?"

Joe described the evening carefully, but as he explained that Sam Rucker was a colored man his mother invited to dinner and what the note said, Raymond's friendly gaze immediately faded to stern disapproval.

"She had a colored man over for dinner?" Raymond asked as if he had heard incorrectly.

"Sam works for me in my detective agency in Birmingham. I brought him with me to do work in the colored community concerning my father's murder. He's staying with a colored friend."

"That's nice," Raymond said, his words rolling out sarcastically. "But your mother had a colored over to dinner?" Raymond repeated.

"I know most people around here frown on my mother's liberalism, but I didn't think anyone would toss a brick through her window."

"You're wrong, Joe. You can't wave a red flag in front of people and not expect some bad actors," Raymond said, his expression softening. "Well, you got any idea who did it?"

"No. Only name comes to mind is Dwayne Pidd. You know him?"

"Know him?" Raymond let loose with a big guffaw. "Hell, every law enforcement officer in the county knows the Pidd twins. Our jail cells are their second home. If it's not for one of their illegal stills, it's somethin' else. Why Dwayne?"

Joe told Raymond about Sam's encounter with Dwayne in downtown Montevallo. He didn't mention Hank or Archie Hamilton.

"If that's all you got, you know I can't do much," Raymond said.

"Did you know my father was representing the colored guy accused of murdering Dwayne's brother in 1924? The colored guy testified that Dwayne shot his brother."

"Yeah, Sheriff Foley told me about that. Still doesn't cut it, Joe. That was a long time ago. C'mon, you gotta put this behind you. Do you want to file a formal report?"

"No. I gotta get going. . . . One more question. What kind of car does Dwayne drive?"

"He's got a Ford sedan."

"What's it look like?" Joe asked.

"Like shit. It's old and black. Held together by baling wire and tape. Goddamn miracle the car works."

"Thanks, Raymond. See you around."

CHAPTER 27

A HORNET'S NEST

THURSDAY—FEBRUARY 19, 1948

Eᴀʀʟʏ Tʜᴜʀꜱᴅᴀʏ ᴍᴏʀɴɪɴɢ, Joe drove to Hank's house to meet with Sam. They had decided this was the safer alternative.

"Mornin', Joe," Hank said. "Sam told me about the brick and note. Do you think Dwayne Pidd threw it?"

"Mornin', Hank. Yes, pretty sure it was Dwayne," Joe said. "We'll deal with him later."

"C'mon in the kitchen, my wife's cookin' breakfast. Honey, this is Joe McGrath. Joe, Mattie Ruth. She's the best damn cook in Montevallo," Hank said.

"Pleased to meet you, Mr. McGrath," she said, looking askance at Hank. "Don't believe a word he says."

"Nice to meet you, Mattie Ruth. And it's Joe, please." He turned to Sam who was sitting at the breakfast table. "Mornin', Sam."

"Well, Joe, you sit down by Sam," Mattie Ruth said. "I'm gonna serve y'all breakfast. Then I'll be outta here, 'cause I know you two gotta talk business."

"I'm on my way outta here too," Hank said. "I got an early job goin'. But you'll see I was right about Mattie Ruth's cookin'." Hank gave Mattie Ruth a big hug and a loving butt pat.

"Hank, before you go, can you meet us at Schaeffer's for lunch at one today? Adam can make it," Joe said.

"Yeah. I can give Sam a ride."

"That okay, Sam?" Joe asked.

Sam nodded.

"Good. I'll pick you up at twelve thirty," Hank said and left the house.

"Okay, you busy boys, here's your breakfast," Mattie Ruth said as she put plates heaping with soft scrambled eggs, bacon, grits, and buttered toast on the table along with steaming mugs of coffee. "There's more on the stove and hot coffee in the pot. Help yourselves. When you finish, jus' turn the stove off and leave things. I'll clean up later. You can go in the dining room or living room to talk. Now y'all be good. I got errands to run."

Joe and Sam said, nearly in unison, "Thank you, Mattie Ruth."

The two men dove into breakfast as if they hadn't eaten for days, not saying a word to each other.

Joe came up first for air, took a swig of coffee, and said, "Damn, that was good. Hank was right."

Sam wiped his mouth with a napkin and shoved his plate away. "Sure was. How'd it go yesterday, Joe?"

"I got Mom's windowpane fixed. She's still shook, but she wants us to continue the investigation. I visited with Judge Wilberforce for the second time. His daughter, Anne, wasn't there when I arrived. He asked me to forgive him for the way he had treated my father in the trial. It really moved me because I think the old guy was sincere."

"I'm sure he was. My preacher daddy always called those kinda things deathbed confessions," Sam said.

"I asked the judge who the hostile witness was. He was about to tell me when Anne got home and ended my visit. She threw me out of the house, and told me never to come again."

"However she does it, the woman times her entrances perfectly," Sam said, grinning broadly.

"She's also an accomplished manipulator. She treats her dying father like shit. After my graceful exit, I stopped at a diner in Columbiana and ran into Susan Kelly, the records clerk at the courthouse. She agreed to call me if Carlton Teague or someone else at the courthouse said anything about me or the transcript."

"So, we have an ally?" Sam asked.

"Yep, she's a lovely young lady."

"Oh, she's lovely now. My, my," Sam said, coquettishly.

"Get off it, Rucker. She could be of help," Joe said, knowing Sam had nailed him.

"Yes, sir." Sam saluted.

"At ease, corporal," Joe said, smiling.

"Will do. Question. Where are the trial transcripts now? Both the complete one and the altered one Teague gave you. Are they secure?"

Joe immediately got where Sam was going. "In a box at Mom's house. They're not secure."

"Why don't you take them with us to Birmingham and lock them in our safe?"

"Good idea. Made one more stop yesterday to see Police Chief Raymond Chapman."

As Joe described Raymond's reaction to the dinner party, Sam shook his head. Joe wasn't sure if Sam's expression was one of disgust or resignation, as he said nothing.

"Raymond said the Pidd twins were in and out of his jail all the time for operating stills and other shit. When I was here last month, Sheriff Cate told me the same thing. He thought the Pidds had a guardian angel. I suspect it's the Holders. I asked Raymond to describe Dwayne's car. The car he described matches to a T the car that tailed us and pulled away from Mom's house."

"So where are we with this mess?"

"We have a hornet's nest on our hands."

"So who's queen hornet"?"

"Right now, it has to be Anne Holder. She's the only woman we've talked to who is anywhere near the center of all this. She's a tough-minded woman, and I suspect she takes no prisoners."

"I'll buy that. So who are the others?"

"We've got a lot of live male hornets. Anne's husband, Chuck. The lovely Pidd twins. The Clerk of the Court, Carlton Teague. Sheriff Harold Cate. Montevallo Police Chief Raymond Chapman. Dead hornets include Sheriff Foley and Karl Merkel. Some other maybes include George Noggin, and the two men who talked to Dad by his car after his last day in court. Have no idea who they are."

"How the hell do you propose we smoke these characters out?"

"We have a few friends. Besides Susan Kelly, no comments please, there's Hank and Adam. And I hope, Archie Hamilton. I'll talk to him again. But I'll go slow with him until I think we can trust him."

"How you gonna measure it? Give him a lie detector test?" Sam asked.

Joe smirked. "Sure, while I hold a pistol to his head. So what have you got to report, Mr. Smart-Ass?"

Sam smiled. "I saw three other older guys that Hank lined up. They mostly talked about the problems all coloreds have just getting by day-to-day. But one of them mentioned buying moonshine from the Pidds. He said they always charge colored folks more than whites. He thinks the Pidds work with someone else on distributing outside the county. A couple of times he's seen trucks driven by white men headed north toward Birmingham. And before you ask, he said he didn't recognize the men driving the trucks."

"Sam, white men drive trucks toward Birmingham all the time. How the hell would he know what's in the trucks?" Joe asked.

"I asked him that. He said, 'I jus' knows.' Since the Pidds live on Holder property, maybe the Holders are bootlegging the stuff. Then it makes sense. They are the Pidd's guardian angels."

"I like it. We've gotta find the right time and place to put the Pidds up against the wall and get information out of them," Joe said.

"I'd enjoy that immensely."

"Bet you would. I'll try to get in touch with Hamilton again today. Let's go back to Birmingham tomorrow morning. We need to see how Brendan's doing and get back on Forrester's job," Joe said.

"Okay. I thought you were going to Montgomery this week and talk to Jason Partlow?"

"I'll do it next time we come to Montevallo."

ALTHOUGH IT HAD RAINED LAST NIGHT, the day turned sunny and unseasonably warm for February. The four men got some paper towels and dried off the table's oilcloth in Schaeffer's backyard patio, the only place in the area where whites and coloreds could eat together without trouble.

Adam, who had just met Sam for the first time, said to him, "You enjoying our little town?"

"Yes. Most people are very nice," Sam said.

"I heard about the brick and note thrown through Miss Elizabeth's window. Bad apples everywhere."

"Where'd you hear about the brick and note, Adam?" Joe asked.

"Raymond Chapman told me. But you know how fast things spread through town. Any idea who did it?"

"No. Some racist creep, I'm sure," Joe said.

Hank cut in. "Let's order some food. I'm starving."

They talked sports, grumbling about Kentucky's domination of basketball in the Southeastern Conference, between bites of their southern fare. Hank ate fried catfish, Adam had fried chicken, and Sam and Joe had barbeque. All had sides of turnip greens and peas, and washed it down with sweet iced tea.

"Had any luck this week with your investigation, Joe?" Adam asked as the waiter cleared the table,

"Not much. It's mostly see no evil, hear no evil, and sure as hell don't want to talk about it. Sam ran into the same stonewall."

"When are you going back to Birmingham?"

"Tomorrow. We'll be back in a few weeks."

"I know it's tough. But folks just want to forget things that happened so long ago. Can I do something for you while you're gone? I wanna help you anyway I can."

Joe shook his head. "No, not right now. I've got to get my head around which way to turn."

ADAM LEFT SCHAEFFER'S FIRST. He said he had an appointment he couldn't miss. Joe, Sam, and Hank stayed at the table, sipping iced tea.

After Adam was out of earshot, Joe said, "Well, our lawyer friend's a busy boy."

"He does a lot of good work for white and colored folks," Hank said. "He's always on the go."

"So it seems," Joe said. "I'm going back to my Mom's and call Archie Hamilton. I need to talk to him. He may be the guy we need on our side if we're gonna get anywhere with this. But for the time being, mum's the word."

CHAPTER 28

ARCHIE HAMILTON

THURSDAY—FEBRUARY 19, 1948

D RIVING TO HIS MOTHER'S HOME, Joe still wondered how Adam knew about the brick and the note. On Tuesday, only three people knew that he and Sam were together, and that Sam was staying at Hank's house: his mother, Hank, and Adam.

As soon as Joe got to his mother's, he called Archie.

"Shoal Creek Farms and Stables. Archie Hamilton speakin'."

"Archie, it's Joe McGrath."

"Hey Joe. Wanna buy a horse?"

"Not today. Can we get together and talk this afternoon?"

"Yep. How about comin' out to the farm? Things are pretty busy around here."

"Glad to. What time and how do I get there?" After Archie gave him directions and suggested four o'clock, Joe said, "I'll be there," hoping this meeting would prove worthwhile.

Joe crossed the covered bridge Archie had mentioned that spanned Shoal Creek. A black, wooden fence bordered the land to the left. The entrance to the farm was a mile beyond the bridge. The black fence continued well after the entrance. A majestic sign arched over the entrance announcing the farms and stables. On one side of the arch was a logo featuring a rendition of a cornfield, and a logo on the other side featured the silhouette of a horse.

As Joe drove into the farm, the black fencing on both sides of the road extended as far as the eye could see, finally converging to a single point. Joe thought, *This is what infinity must look like.*

Horses to the left appeared to be thoroughbreds, feeding and romping about well-kept pastures. A few men were working with several of the horses. To the right was farmland, some of which was being plowed by crews of white and colored men.

The infinity impression dissipated when Joe saw Archie's home, a two-story neo-colonial. The house was painted off-white with six columns framing the front porch and entry. Stables were to the left of the home, barns to the right, with a number of one-story homes arranged in a semicircle pattern around the main house, all painted off-white. Joe thought the place looked like a famous Kentucky horse farm he had seen in magazine photographs. He started to realize there was a lot more to Archie than he had imagined.

As soon as he got out of his car, Archie came out the front door and bounded down the porch steps to greet him.

"Welcome to Shoal Creek, Joe. How do ya like my little place?"

"Hey, Archie. I like it, but little? How much acreage?" Joe asked.

"Oh, 'bout four thousand, give or take. C'mon in."

The interior did not disappoint. It was tastefully decorated. Painted in a mix of off-white and soft pastels, it was beautifully appointed in early American furniture and the hardwood floors were accented with Oriental rugs.

Archie led Joe into the study, where the main feature was wall-to-ceiling bookshelves except for the windowed wall facing outside. Each shelf had a ladder that rolled side-to-side to access the upper shelves. Joe scanned the room and saw leather bound copies of literary classics as well as several shelves dedicated to Shakespeare.

Archie put his hand on his cheek as he watched Joe peruse the bookshelves, and said, "I like good books, Joe. Have a seat."

Archie pointed toward two chairs facing a coffee table. "Would ya like a drink? Iced tea or somethin' a little stiffer?"

"You gonna have somethin' stiffer?"

"Well, I jus' reckon I will. Got some great Kentucky bourbon."

Joe smiled. He hadn't thought or heard so much about Kentucky in a long time. "Sounds great. Is it good for sipping?"

"Perfect, a man after my own heart, Joe. We gonna get along jus' fine." Archie poured the drinks and handed one to Joe. They clinked glasses. "Whaddaya want to talk 'bout?"

"You've got an incredible place here. The farm. Your home. Did your wife do the interior design work?"

"I wish. She died in childbirth years ago." Archie looked away as if searching for an answer. "Our only son survived, Arthur Jr. He's a doctor and lives in Atlanta with his family. I never remarried."

Joe knew better than to say he was sorry. "I saw a number of smaller houses surrounding the main house. What are they used for?"

"I'm glad you didn't call them cabins or bungalows. Most people do, and they ain't. A lot of my hired hands and their families live in 'em, white and colored."

"Side-by-side?" Joe asked.

"Yep." Archie turned and spit a mouthful of tobacco juice into a spittoon next to his chair. "Excuse me, I'm being a bad host."

Archie went into a small room off his study. Even though he closed the door, Joe heard several spits followed by splashes, followed by several gargling sounds and spitting. A toilet flushed, and Archie came back into the study.

"I have got to quit chewing, Joe. It's a terrible habit, but it is tough to stop. Have you ever used it?"

Joe thought a different man had walked out of the bathroom. There was no bulge in Archie's cheek, and his voice, elocution, and grammar were perfect.

"No. And I don't plan to," Joe said.

"Good. We got sidetracked by chewing tobacco. Where were we?"

"You were telling me about the small houses and the hired hands who live there."

"Oh, yeah. Joe, you are now in an island of equality surrounded by our southern home, a sea of racism and inequality. Here we live and work as equals. Before you ask, I am not a paternalistic southern landlord nor is this an experiment in socialism, or as some call us, a commie commune."

"Adam Paige described your place exactly that way the other day. Shoal Creek must upset a lot of folks around here."

"It does. Most of them now just ignore us. Farm's been this way since my father established it in the 1880s. Don't go around making a big deal about it. Folks work, eat, and play together. We have annual parties either in my house or outside, depending on the time of year. Easter, Fourth of July, Thanksgiving, and Christmas."

Joe grinned and couldn't help asking, "Ever had any bricks thrown through your windows?"

Archie laughed uproariously. "If anyone tried, they know I'd either crack their skulls open or level them with a shotgun."

"I guess you're not a pacifist."

"Or a Quaker. We don't pick fights, Joe. But we'll sure as hell defend ourselves. Yesterday morning, I was in town at the café and everyone was talking about the brick thrown through your mother's window. How is Elizabeth doing?"

"A bit upset, but she's fine. Christ, didn't take long for the news about the brick to get around."

"Small town, Joe."

He decided to take a chance. "Archie, you went into the bathroom one guy and came out another. Who are you?"

"That is the question, Joe. Whether 'tis nobler to be a Southern redneck or a gentleman?"

Taking the cue, Joe said, "God has given you one face, and you make yourself another."

"Aha, I see we could banter with Shakespearean quotes all evening. Your mother told me you were quite an expert. But to the question, Joe. This farm is my livelihood and the livelihood of all those who work and live here. And while we all work together to make it successful, I am the chief salesman. I was born and bred in the South, and I choose to live in its stifling conditions. But I learned years ago, doing business here requires one to bend. I choose to bend to my redneck self in public and especially in business dealings."

Archie paused and smiled. "Son, y'all can't 'magine how folks deal with ya when ya talks like this. Hell, if'n I go to Birminham, Montgumry, or Mobile on bidness, folks thinks they done took me to the cleaners even when I's walk out with the best deal I's ever got."

"I'm gonna check and make sure I have my wallet when I leave," Joe said.

"You be wise to do so," Archie said, laughing. . . . "Okay, enough about me. What did you really come here to talk about?"

CHAPTER 29

THE HOSTILE WITNESS

THURSDAY—FEBRUARY 19, 1948

J OE DOWNED THE LAST OF THE BOURBON and put the glass on the coffee table. He realized he had come to his moment of truth with Archie. After he had been so open, Joe knew he had to level with him, or walk away and forget it.

"Archie, I need your help. No, Sam and I need your help."

"So you and Sam are working together. Thought you might be. Seems to be a fine man."

"He is, period. Sam's my partner in our detective agency, a silent partner since we don't live on an island of equality. When we met Tuesday, I told you I was trying to identify those people involved in my father's murder, but I didn't tell you everything. We were sizing each other up. At least I was."

Archie nodded, then asked, "Yes?"

Joe told him all that had happened since his first visit in January up to the luncheon with Sam, Hank, and Adam. Joe added, "Adam and Hank were my best childhood friends. Until Dad's death, we were always together. Hank and I drifted apart after we started high school. Adam and I remained close friends until we went off to college. I can't put my finger on it, but he seems like a different man today."

Archie had listened carefully, with his head bent to the side, cradled in his right hand. Sitting up straight, he picked up his glass from the coffee table and finished the bourbon. "You're right about child-hood friends, Joe. Hank is a man I would trust with anything. Adam is another matter."

Joe leaned forward, listening carefully.

Archie stood and picked up Joe's glass. "I never heard that story about Oscar and Odell Bird, and Karl Merkel. Interesting. We need a refill. We are headed into dark, difficult territory."

He handed Joe a refreshed drink. They clinked glasses and sipped.

"Damn good," Joe said.

"I wish I could say the same thing about Adam. I know he was a brilliant student."

"Valedictorian in our graduating high school class."

"And tops in his undergrad work at Davidson and then at Yale law school," Archie added. "I was surprised when he came back home for good. With Yale top honors, he could have found a position with a prominent Boston or New York law firm. But I guess he couldn't resist the lure of the family business."

"I don't get it. Small town Southern lawyers, like Adam's father and mine, did okay, but they earned a pittance compared to the big boys up North."

"You're in the dark, Joe. It's not the law. Oh, Adam plays the lawyer game, even takes colored clients and represents them well. But I'm sure it's for cover. Have you ever seen his house and property?"

"No. He does have a nice office."

"Small potatoes. His huge house is on six hundred acres just north of town on highway 17. It's gated and surrounded by a large English-style stone wall." Archie paused and smiled. "Funny story. A year after he moved into the house, an old codger built a junkyard on his own property across the highway facing right at the entry to Adam's property. Adam tried every legal trick he knew to force him to remove it. When that didn't work, he tried to buy it. The old coot wouldn't sell. It's still there. Now, Adam's friends call his place the junkyard. Pissed him off at first. Seems he kinda likes it now."

Joe became impatient with Archie, and said testily, "Very funny. But what's Adam covering up, for God's sake?"

Archie ignored Joe's tone. "Biggest bootlegging operation in Alabama and maybe the South. Folks around here call it 'the opera-tion.' He and his cohorts—you've met a few of them—own or control a number of stills in the area, including the ones operated by the Pidds. Even bigger, they illegally import booze from Cuba, Mexico, and Europe, and I hear they have a sophisticated distribution network throughout the South and beyond. They sell at prices undercutting legitimate distributors and state liquor control boards."

"Damn, Archie, I never heard 'the operation' mentioned by anyone. How did it come about?"

"Slowly. Started forty years ago when a few people organized the scattered still operators, convincing them they'd do better as a group than as individuals. Most folks around here don't like to hear that sort of thing, but the organizers were right. The principals were the Holders, Geoffrey Wallace, and Adam's father, Phillip. You knew him, didn't you?"

"Sure. I spent a lot of time at the Paige's house as a kid. Mr. Paige was always nice to me. Never heard him mention moonshine or bootleg booze or 'the operation.' And Adam never mentioned it."

"Not exactly dinner table conversation, Joe. I doubt Adam knew much about it until he was older."

"Who's Geoffrey Wallace?"

"The hostile witness Judge Wilberforce tried to tell you about. He was a history professor at the college. He's dead now. I'm sure Elizabeth knew him. His son, Damian, teaches history at the college now. He's not involved in 'the operation' as far as I know."

Joe, stunned, couldn't hide his anger and blurted out, "Goddamn, Archie, why didn't you tell me about Geoffrey when we talked Tuesday?"

Archie replied calmly, "Take it easy. You said it earlier. We were sizing up each other. Your father was my best friend. I saw you a few times when you were a kid. At our Tuesday meeting, I had no idea who you really were other than the McGraths' son. I think we both understand each other better now and can work together."

Joe knew he wasn't in a contest with Archie. Yet he felt he was losing, unsure which way to turn but had to keep going.

"I see," Joe said, realizing he could hardly see anything. "Where did 'the operation' go from there?"

"Into the '20s and Prohibition, the group's springboard to greater things. While the New York and Chicago mobs got all the attention, our Shelby County boys quietly built themselves a network that thrives to this day. There's a lot I don't know, but it appeared to me that Phillip and Geoffrey were the brains behind 'the operation.' And Geoffrey lived a quiet life behind the ivy and his professorial duties at the college."

"What prompted Dad to call Geoffrey as a witness?" Joe asked.

"Not absolutely sure. I probably still wouldn't know, if your father hadn't walked up to me in the courtroom his last day alive and whispered in my ear, 'I'm going to call Geoffrey Wallace.' After he said it, he smiled at me as if we were co-conspirators. I'll never forget it." Archie's head drooped, struggling to maintain his composure. "I think your father was going to use him to expose 'the operation' and tie him to the Pidds in hopes of driving a wedge of doubt in the jurors' minds about who shot Darryl Pidd." Archie paused again, still distraught.

Joe realized what an idiot he had been with his thoughts moments ago. Archie cared for his father almost as much as he did. "Thanks. I know it sounds strange, but I feel better. I guess it helps just knowing that."

Archie nodded, regaining his composure. "Yeah, knowing helps cope with the extraneous thoughts haunting us."

"How could 'the operation' have continued for so long without people's knowledge? It doesn't make sense. Hell, you know so much about it. Why didn't they take you out?"

"Good question, but the answer makes sense." Archie jumped up, obviously feeling better, and pulled a book from the bookshelf. "Our homegrown bootleggers are not like the Mafia, going around killing folks right and left. Do you know the early nineteenth-century author Catharine Sedgwick?"

"Yes, she and Lydia Child were the two best American women authors of that period."

Archie laughed. "Well, you certainly know more than just Shakespeare." He handed Joe a leather-bound book. "*Live and Let Live.* The title of Sedgwick's novel says it all about Shelby County folks. Couple that attitude with the jobs 'the operation' has created and well-placed bribes with cops, politicians, important businessmen, and arm-twisting—and things move along smoothly and quietly. I've heard talk of a few dust-ups now and then, but apparently nothing 'the operation' couldn't handle."

"So that's how your farm is perceived—live and let live?" Joe asked.

"Pretty much. Look Joe, we're not crusaders out to convert the world to our way of living. We don't go around shouting about how we live. If some folks want to try it, fine. If not, also fine. We don't look for trouble. If it comes our way, we deal with it."

"Does live and let live mean you won't work with me to find my father's murderers?"

"No. Joe, you've been a breath of fresh air, blown in here to try and right a grievous wrong. I absolutely want to help. What can I do? When do we start?"

"I've brought you up to date on what we've done and what we know. You've given me incredible insights to this community, Adam, Geoffrey Wallace, and others," Joe said. "Sam and I are going back to Birmingham tomorrow. We've got business in our detective agency we need to deal with. We'll be back in a few weeks. We should let Adam be for the time being. Unless you have a better plan?"

"No, I agree. But is there anything you'd like me to do?"

Joe smiled. "Yeah. Stick a wad of chewing tobacco back in your jaw and put on your good-old-boy persona, and just listen to folks and find out if you hear or see anything interesting."

Archie stuck a finger in his jaw and grumbled. "Yes suh, I's can do that. I gits on it rite away. If'n I hears sumthin', y'all be hearin' from me."

The two men laughed, had another drink, talked Shakespeare, and compared favorite authors.

As Joe got up to leave, Archie said, "You enjoyed the bourbon, right?"

Playing Archie, Joe said, "Sho'nuf. That's mighty fine hooch."

Archie got a bottle from his liquor cabinet. "Here. Enjoy the hooch."

"Thanks. I'll put it to good use."

Joe was about to get in his car to leave when he turned to Archie and asked, "Do you know my mother well?"

Archie paused for a moment. "Yes, Elizabeth and I have been good friends for a long time. She's the finest woman in Montevallo."

Joe touched his hat, smiled, and nodded goodbye.

CHAPTER 30

THE PROMISED LAND

FRIDAY—FEBRUARY 20, 1948

As Sam put his suitcase in the trunk of Joe's car, he noticed a small box and asked, "Is that the trial transcripts?"

"Yep. C'mon, let's get going. It's almost eight o'clock," Joe said.

Hank had suggested they use a back road over to Highway 31 in hopes of avoiding traffic and prying eyes. Once Joe was driving northbound on 31, he said, "Well, pardner, we safely outta the badlands yet?"

"Oh, I s'pose we'll be gittin' back to the promised land soon. But I can't wait to get back down here and get hold of the Pidds," Sam said, holding up his huge hands.

Joe snickered. "If you ever get those meat hooks into them, they'll rue the day.... I talked to Archie late yesterday afternoon." Joe briefed Sam on the meeting, told him about Archie's communal-style farm, and even mentioned the parting comment Archie made about his mother.

Sam, laughing playfully, said, "Well, I jus' reckon Miss Elizabeth might have a boyfriend." Turning serious, he added, "So Adam's a man to watch. Figures. What's up with Geoffrey Wallace's son Damian?"

"Archie doesn't think he's involved in 'the operation.' Seems he's just a college professor. Let's try to wrap our heads back around Kendall Forrester and the warehouse fire."

"Okay. And we have to see what progress Brendan's made on the lady-with-no-panties investigation."

Joe faked a grimace. "You shoulda been a comedian, Rucker."

"Too easy. I need a hard problem."

"I'll give you one. I've decided not to write a letter to Jack Ritter. You're right, too risky. So here's the problem. Where do we turn with the warehouse fire?"

"We gotta flush out Stanford Ramsey and Marcus Gilbert without casting suspicion on Pops Johnson and Frank Cutler. We told Kendall we had to verify our information with other sources. I don't think we should. It'll only broaden the network of people who know we're pokin' around. Increases the chances that Stanford, Marcus, or the Army agents and others might think Pops or Frank are our sources. Agree?"

Joe nodded.

"Idea. First let's review what we know based on Frank. Correct me if I'm wrong. January 1947, two Army special agents visit him in his office unannounced. Tell him conversation is top secret and to keep his mouth shut. A German doctor named Gerhard Mueller, the cousin of German rocket guy Wernher von Braun, is being assigned to Frank's office to work as his assistant. Frank will supervise his work and report his progress to the Alabama state board that oversees physician accreditation. Goal is to get Mueller fully accredited in a year, early 1948. Right so far?"

"Yep," Joe said.

"Frank's on vacation the week the warehouse fire occurs in the early morning hours of July fourth, a Friday. He doesn't return to Birmingham until late in the evening on Monday, July seventh. Back to work on Tuesday, July eighth. The cops and the DA, probably under pressure from Stanford and Marcus, have Mueller perform an autopsy on Willie Thompson, the guard killed in the fire. Mueller writes the autopsy report, signs it as coroner's assistant, and someone, probably Mueller, forges Frank's name as coroner. The report is dated Saturday, July fifth. How am I doing?"

Joe said, "Fine. Keep going."

"Kendall's arson investigators finally get into what's left of the warehouse on Sunday morning, July sixth. They are given copies of the autopsy report with Frank's forged name on it—that's the one we have—and the police report, which says the fire was not arson. Kendall's guys doubt the police report but can't find conclusive proof otherwise. A substantial amount of cleanup work had been done before they got in on Sunday." Sam paused.

"And?" Joe asked.

"Between Sunday morning, July sixth and Tuesday morning, July eighth, someone realized the problem with the July fifth dated autopsy report and was able to get Frank's correct signature forged and the date changed to July eighth. All copies in the files were replaced except for the one Kendall has and gave to us. Whoever engineered this was also able to get a state approved MD license for Mueller, apparently post-dated January twenty-sixth, into the office state licensing board files. That's the day Mueller started working for Frank. No wonder Frank feels cornered by forces he can't control. Who wouldn't?"

"No one I know. Any more?" Joe asked.

"Willie's parents had problems making arrangements with a funeral home, so the body wasn't picked up until late Tuesday afternoon, July eighth. Frank had time to take a look at the body. The autopsy report stated that Willie died of asphyxiation and the body had only minor burns. Actually, the body was covered with third- and fourth-degree burns and had a skull fracture caused by a blunt object. The blow likely came from a left-handed person. The so-called official autopsy report is trash. Frank's signature was forged, and the cause of death and description of the body were blatantly incorrect, outright fabrications. That's it on Frank. A couple of things on Pops."

"A plus so far," Joe said. "Uh oh, what's this?" Joe asked turning to the left.

He caught a glimpse of a dark green, late model car passing them at a high speed. He was pretty sure the driver was a white male and the only person in the car. "Think he was tailing us?"

"We'll know soon enough if he slows down and tries to hassle us," Sam said. "I think he's just in a hurry. You weren't even driving the speed limit."

"Yeah, you're mesmerizing me with your monologue."

"Don't let me put you to sleep. Where was I?"

"Pops."

"I'll be short and sweet with Pops. He overheard Black Bronco say soon after the fire that Marcus was going to get a big payout, and that

Willie would be alive if he wasn't so stupid and had done his job right. Don't forget, Black Bronco is left-handed. He's the kind of guy Marcus would assign to the warehouse job. That's it."

"Which way do we turn now? You said you had an idea."

"Yeah. Remember how Stanford reacted when you told him you knew about and had seen Mahogany Hall, and you asked him to stop transporting colored prostitutes from New Orleans for his fun and games?" Sam asked.

Joe nodded and smiled, feeling pretty sure he knew where Sam was headed.

"Stanford not only stopped transporting girls from New Orleans, he had Mahogany Hall demolished. There was little backlash from either him or Marcus. Now I'll admit he probably squeezed you out of the police department, but I think you were more than ready to punch out." Sam paused.

"Yeah, it was time to go," Joe said.

"I think the same strategy will work here. It's best you lie low and let me approach Marcus. After he and I do our usual pas de deux, I'll tell him I've heard something that might interest him. He'll ask what, and I'll tell him there is credible info floating around that proves the warehouse fire was arson, and Willie Thompson was murdered. He'll wanna know the sources. I'll play dumb and say it's just talk on the street. I'll add that I know he got a fire insurance payment for his loss, and suggest he might want to return the money to head off any further talk or suspicion."

"He'll hit the fan, Sam."

"Of course he will. He'll accuse me of bribery and blackmail, but here's what I think will happen. After we go back and forth a bit, he'll say something like, 'I's gonna think 'bout it,' or 'Git your ass outta here.' As I leave, I'll tell him I also heard Black Bronco killed Willie Thompson."

"Well, since you're now the oracle able to predict the future, what'll happen next?" Joe asked, as he stopped at a traffic light on the outskirts of Birmingham.

Sam closed his eyes as if in deep concentration. "I'm getting a picture. After Marcus stomps around for a while, he'll call Stanford and tell him what I said. I'm not predicting that conversation, except to say your name will come up and they'll finally agree to pay the insurance payment back to Kendall's company. Their game is power and money. Stanford will realize that I was delivering a message and the best way to put things to bed is to return the insurance money. A loss of small potatoes compared to the bigger consequences. And Stanford will tell Marcus to take care of the Black Bronco situation."

"My, my, isn't that a lovely scenario? And what if the shit hits the fan?"

"They'll come after you and me. Maybe some threats. Maybe they'll push people to boycott our detective agencies. There might be both, but I think Stanford will hold things in check. If the things I told Marcus quiet down and don't reappear, all will return to normal. I've got one other prediction. Wanna hear it?"

"Christ, I can't wait," Joe said, looking incredulous.

"The Army agents will surely hear about this, likely from Stanford. Realizing some of their plan could unravel, they'll make a move to minimize damage. Since their priority is to move von Braun and his people to Huntsville, they'll quietly relocate Mueller to some other state. Don't worry about Frank and the autopsy report. They'll tell Frank that Mueller is being reassigned and leave it at that. They won't be worried about the autopsy report. Mueller's gone, Willie's in the ground, Frank's petrified and will keep his mouth shut. They don't know Frank looked at Willie's body. Even if they did, it's Frank's word against the autopsy report he's already supposedly signed. The only way to disprove the autopsy report is to exhume Willie's body. Won't happen. The colored mortician who handled the body sure as hell didn't and won't go to the cops. Frank is still boxed in."

They were almost in downtown Birmingham.

"I gotta think about this," Joe said. "You want me to drop you off at your home?"

"No. Let's go to the office. We've got work to do. Besides, Brendan's been using my car."

The green car was still on Joe's mind, but he let it go, figuring Sam was probably right.

CHAPTER 31

BRENDAN'S SUCCESS

FRIDAY—FEBRUARY 20, 1948

WHEN SAM AND JOE WALKED INTO THE OFFICE, Sally was at her desk. "How did things go in Montevallo?"

"Other than a brick though my mother's living room window, just fine," Joe said.

Sally looked stunned. "Oh my, is everything all right?"

"Yes, just some racist creeps flexing their muscles the only way they know how," Joe said, placing the box on Sally's desk. "There's some files in this box related to my father's death. Please put them in the safe."

"Right away."

"Is Brendan in yet? We'd like to talk to him about our lady client with the wayward husband."

"He should be in soon. He may have something interesting."

"Can't wait. Sam and I will be in our office when he gets here."

Joe looked up from his desk and saw Brendan walk in. "Hey, Brendan, let's meet in the conference room. We wanna hear about Samantha Browning, the lady-with-no-panties."

"How the hell did you know about that?" Brendan asked.

Joe laughed at his youthful sidekick. "Tell us what's been gong on with her."

Brendan blushed, and Joe thought about Susan and wondered why he always seemed to make younger people blush.

"Last Tuesday morning, I was on my stakeout at the Browning's house." Brendan pulled out his notes with a flourish. "Mr. Browning left for his office at 8:23 a.m. and he—"

Sam, smiling at Brendan's youthful enthusiasm, said, "Brendan, just give us the highlights unless you think a detail is essential."

Looking a bit chagrined, Brendan continued. "Okay. He spent the morning in his downtown bank where he's a vice-president. Just before noon I followed him to the Rhodes Park Apartments on Highland Avenue South and Twenty-Ninth Street South. He parked right in front. I got lucky and found a spot close to his. After he entered, I hustled over to a window next to the front door. He was the only person waiting for the elevator. As soon as he got on, I went into the building. The elevator stopped on the fourth floor. I checked the mailboxes in the foyer. Ten on the fourth floor. Two had women's names. I wrote the names down, got back in my car, and waited. Forty-five minutes later he came out and drove to the bank. He went home after work. End of his day."

"Good work," Joe said. "Well, well, I doubt Mr. Browning had only finger sandwiches and tea for lunch. Did you take the office camera if the opportunity for a photo came up?" Joe had purchased a Kodak Ektra 35 mm camera for a steal from a buddy.

"Yeah, but I didn't take the flash. I figured it might tip off the subject."

"Good thinking. The flash is also difficult to use on that camera. What else?"

"On Wednesday morning, he parked at the bank and then walked over to the Tutwiler Hotel. I thought he might be meeting the lady. I went into the hotel lobby. The Events Board showed an all-day Banking Seminar in several of the meeting rooms. On a nearby table was a program for the day. Browning was shown as a morning and afternoon panel group participant, and he was giving the keynote speech at the luncheon. I went back to the office for a while."

"Quiet day, huh?" Sam asked.

Brendan looked embarrassed. "Yeah. Until she showed up. Mrs. Browning came into the office at ten. Joe, she asked for you. Sally explained you were out of town for the week and suggested she talk to me. I told her I was working on the case, and that her husband was at an all-day conference at the Tutwiler. She said she knew all about it. I didn't mention any other details, especially what I learned yesterday. I thought it best to wait until you got back to talk to her."

"Good," Joe said. "Brendan, you looked like you were . . . I guess embarrassed. Was there a problem?"

"She got up and closed the conference room door." Brendan paused. "Joe, I think the lady was coming on to me. She pulled her chair out and sat facing me with her skirt pulled up a bit and slowly uncrossed her legs so I could see—"

Joe jumped in. "Straight up her legs, and she had no panties on."

"Right," Brendan blurted out. "Damn, I mean she's a good looking woman, but she could be my mother for Christ sake."

Joe and Sam couldn't help laughing. Sam said, "Sorry, Brendan, but it is funny. Joe got the same look when she first came to the office. Friendly advice. Don't ever get caught in that flytrap. On your own time is fine. But women clients or co-workers are a big no-no."

Brendan smiled sheepishly. "I'm not a kid, Sam. I know better. She asked me to meet her for a drink. I told her I was way too busy with my work since you were out of town. She got up slowly and gave me another good look. She asked Sally to call her when you got back and left."

"You handled it well, Brendan. Any exciting things happen yesterday?" Joe asked.

"Yes. But first, on Wednesday I used the time Browning was at the conference to case the apartment building. I wanted to see if I could find out which apartment he visited on the fourth floor. I took a few pictures. I figured he'd be going back soon. Detail alert," Brendan said, smiling. "On Tuesday, it took Browning eleven minutes to drive to the apartment using Twentieth Avenue South to Highland Avenue. I tried it by starting on Twentieth assuming I was following him, but then I cut over to Twenty-Fourth, which is a straight shot to Highland Avenue. I sped a bit and got there in seven minutes. I walked up the stairs to the fourth floor. The door is at the far end of the hall. If I cracked the door open, it opened inward, and I could see the elevator. One of the two women whose names I had, lived in the unit down the hall from the elevator. The other one was just to the right of the stairwell door. More dicey, but at least there was a large, leafy plant between the door and the stairwell door."

"Maybe the woman he's having an affair with was married and lives in another unit," Sam said.

"Yeah, I knew that was possible, but I figured this would work."

"Pretty good plan," Joe said. "Some risk. But minimal. I assume there's more?"

Brendan couldn't suppress a big grin. "Yep, the plan worked perfectly. On Thursday, Browning got in his car at noon and started driving south on Twentieth. I followed him for a few blocks, cut over to Twenty-Fourth. His car was nowhere to be seen when I got to the apartment. I hustled up the stairs to the fourth floor and waited with the door cracked for about five minutes. Like clockwork, he got off the elevator and knocked on the unit next to the elevator, number 402. He went in. I saw the woman's face, but I didn't take a picture. Too risky. The occupant's name is Rebecca Koch. Later I searched the *Birmingham News* archives and found her picture. Same woman. Seems she's a socialite."

Joe looked perplexed. "Where have I heard the name?"

"You gotta read the society pages more often like Brendan does," Sam said. "Several years ago, she and her wealthy husband were all the news over a contentious divorce. I guess this is where the lady settled."

"Ah so, thank you, Hedda Hopper. I remember. Her ex is the president of the bank Browning works in," Joe said, pausing in a reflective moment. "Think there's any connection?"

Brendan looked confused, but Sam got it immediately. "Maybe. But we oughtta stay away from trying to establish more than we were asked to do. The lady wants to know if her husband is having an affair. Just tell her he likely is and with whom. End of case."

"You're right, Sam. Brendan, you can stop following Browning around."

"Will do. I also took pictures of Koch's apartment door. It has her name on it, and I got one of her mailbox. Then I found a place to stand in some brush near the front of the apartment. I got a picture of Browning as he walked out of the building."

"Excellent. Here's what I want you to do. Write a report detailing everything you told us. Get copies of the photos you took and include them in your report with a notation of the date, time, and exact location of each photo. Also include a copy of the photo you found in the newspaper. Make it clear we were unable to observe the couple having sex. Sign it and leave a space for my signature. I want to get Mrs. Browning in here next week to close this case out."

"I've taken the photos to a lab. I'll pick them up tomorrow."

Joe went to the conference room door. "Sally, join us please. I'm sorry you had to hear all that chatter."

Sally came in with her notebook, looked at the three men, and shook her head. "Joe, after all my years with the police department, I've heard it all and more. What can I do for you?"

"Sorry, Sally," Joe said. "Didn't mean to be condescending. Please call Mrs. Browning. Tell her I'm back in town and would like to meet with her in the office. Monday's fine at any time. Let's go back to work."

As they walked out of the conference room, Joe said to Sam, "I'll think about your suggestion concerning Stanford and Marcus over the weekend. We'll talk Monday."

CHAPTER 32

MRS. BROWNING

MONDAY—FEBRUARY 23, 1948

JOE GOT TO THE OFFICE EARLY MONDAY MORNING. After brewing a pot of coffee, he sat enjoying his first hot, aromatic cup of the day, continuing to mull over Sam's suggestion.

Sam and Sally arrived moments apart. Mrs. Browning was due at eleven.

Sam grabbed a cup of coffee and joined Joe. "Well, Boss Man, where do we go with my proposal?"

It always annoyed Joe when Sam called him Boss Man. "Cut the Boss Man crap. We're partners. . . . I'm with you on your plan. Let's do it. When will you talk to Marcus?"

"Good," Sam said, ignoring Joe's testiness. "I'll see him as soon as possible. Any big concerns?"

"Same as before. Don't want Pops or Frank to get burned. Hope Stanford and Marcus don't come at us with guns blazing."

"Always possible. I don't think it'll happen. I'll call Marcus this morning. How do you want to handle Mrs. Browning?"

Joe relaxed and smiled. "Well, I think I'm in for an interesting meeting. She started with me, and I think it's best I handle it. I'll tell her what we've found out. Should be the end of it."

"Don't bet on it. I think the lady's got more on her mind."

"Oh, you of the dirty mind, go call Marcus and do something you can handle."

"Will do, Boss Man," Sam said, raising his hands palms up, entreating forgiveness. "Just kidding."

BRENDAN HAD THREE COPIES OF THE REPORT, which he and Sally had worked on over the weekend. He and Joe reviewed it and signed it.

When Mrs. Browning arrived Joe showed her into the conference room, closed the door, and offered her a chair. As he sat down next to her, she positioned her chair facing directly at him. She wore a short, almost translucent, light blue silk skirt.

"Did you have a pleasant trip, Joe?"

"I was in Montevallo visiting my mother. She teaches English literature at the woman's college."

"Oh, how nice," she said in an offhanded, disinterested way. "I had a talk with Brendan O'Connor on Wednesday. He's a naïve young man. I don't think he understands older women. Do you understand me, Joe?" She moved around in the chair so her skirt slipped even higher.

"Yes, I understand you very well, Mrs. Browning. We have concluded our investigation and here's our report." He handed her the report and continued, "Mr. Browning is probably having an affair with a woman named Rebecca Koch. She lives in the Rhodes Park Apartments, unit 402, on Highland Avenue. It's all documented in the report along with some photos."

Joe waited for her to look at the report. Paying no attention to it, she slid back in her chair and spat her reaction out in a venomous streak. "That Jewish bitch. I should have known. Wait 'til I get my hands on her and Richard. They'll rue the day."

Joe, sure her reaction was more theater than sincerity, figured this whole routine had been staged by Mrs. Browning for his benefit. The thought crossed his mind that it might also be a game that she and Richard played to amuse themselves.

She wiped her eyes as if she had been crying, but Joe saw no tears. "Oh, excuse my outburst, Joe. I'm so embarrassed and devastated. What'll I do?"

"I think your options are to do nothing, tell your husband you know, get a lawyer, or get your hands on them as you suggested. I recommend you see a lawyer."

"Please help me, Joe. Let's go out for a drink and lunch and talk it over."

"Mrs. Browning, you hired my firm to follow your husband and determine if he was having an affair. Per our agreement, we have accomplished both. While we didn't witness your husband and Rebecca Koch having sex, the circumstantial evidence is compelling. Since your husband didn't follow the Ten Commandments, the next step is your decision. We will stop following Mr. Browning around."

She jumped up, straightened her skirt out, and glared at Joe as if she hated him. "You can't speak to me that way. My husband's cheating on me." In a few short minutes, Joe had observed her demeanor swing from flirtatiousness to vindictiveness to embarrassment to outrage. "You're treating me like a—"

There was a knock on the door. Sam stuck his head in and said, "Excuse me, Joe. Sorry for the interruption. I've got an appointment to see our friend later this afternoon. I'm going over to my office to check a couple of things before I go see him."

"Come in, Sam. I'd like you to meet Mrs. Browning. We just finished. I told her what we learned from our surveillance of her husband's activities. Mrs. Browning, meet Sam Rucker. He has his own private investigation firm in the colored district. Sometimes we work together when we have mutual interest in a case."

"Hello, Mrs. Browning," Sam said. "Pleasure to meet you."

Joe had watched her carefully since Sam entered the room. Her demeanor had changed again. She smiled benignly and didn't look at Sam with surprise or fear as most people did when they first met him.

"Pleasure is all mine, Sam," she said, admiring this tall, handsome black man. "Did you help with my investigation?"

"No, ma'am. Brendan did the hard work."

"My, my. What a good-looking team you have, Joe. Maybe you can help me next time, Sam?"

"Yes, ma'am. I'll be happy to do whatever is necessary."

"Well," she said, "I must be on my way. I have another very important appointment shortly."

Mrs. Browning walked out of the office in an imperious manner as if nothing of consequence had happened. She didn't take her copy of the report.

CHAPTER 33

MARCUS GILBERT

MONDAY—FEBRUARY 23, 1948

Sam sat in an eighteenth-century Louis XV chair, facing Marcus across an even more ornate Louis XV writing desk. His office occupied the entire top floor of the building housing his bank, giving him an expansive view of his legitimate and illegitimate fiefdom in Scratch Ankle.

"What's do I owes this pleasure, Sam? Ain't seen ya 'cept at church for months."

Sam had always marveled at Marcus's appearance and dress: medium height; significantly overweight; round, benign face unless challenged; and large eyes capable of an icy, cruel stare on demand. He dressed well in the best men's suits available. He demonstrated his wealth and power by wearing a gold tiepin featuring a large diamond, matching diamond cufflinks, and a large diamond ring.

"Yep, since last October," Sam said. "Been keepin' my nose to the grindstone. Say, you've made some changes to the office." Sam thought the office décor was an awful mishmash of expensive, beautiful, ill-matched furniture, carpets, Italian tiles, famous paintings, and a variety of antique objects of different periods, all arranged in a haphazard fashion with no attention to symmetry or continuity.

"Yeah, it's bettah. Yolanda come up here in December from New Orleans. I don't know how she done it, but she talked my wife, Hattie Mae, into doin' away with them goddamn statues and columns. Hated the fuckers. I's always bumpin' into 'em, especially if'n I had too much to drink." Marcus laughed at his joke on himself.

"Yolanda did a good job," Sam said, laughing along to please Marcus. He was unsure if Marcus knew that he and Yolanda were involved. He hoped not. If so, Marcus might be more wary of him.

"Whatcha wanna see me 'bout? I knows this ain't no social call."

"No, it's serious," Sam said. He had carefully planned how best to start the conversation. He figured success or failure would depend on Marcus's initial reaction. "I want to tell you about some talk I've been hearing lately on the streets and from other sources around town. You and I don't agree on a lot of things. But we've always talked straight to each other and helped each other out."

"Yeah, that's so," Marcus said, nodding. "What's this here talk 'bout?"

"The fire last July that destroyed your warehouse on the Southside."

"Weren't my warehouse. Belonged to Stanford Ramsey. I rented it. Stanford and me got insurance checks for our losses. No big fuckin' deal."

Sam was pleased Marcus was serving up perfect segues. "Yeah, that's part of the talk."

"Cmon, Sam. Spit it out."

"The word on the street is the fire was arson."

"A fuckin' lie." Marcus said, getting agitated. "The cops' report said no arson. The insurance company guys said no arson. Who's makin' this shit up?"

Sam smiled in hopes of calming him down. "Marcus, I'm no snitch. In my work, I can't reveal my sources or I'd be out of business. I think you operate the same way. As I told you, it's talk on the street and around town. I don't know if it's true or not. I'm just tellin' you what I hear."

"Okay. But did ya talk to Black Bronco?"

"Hell, I talk to him often," Sam said, glad Marcus had put Black Bronco's name on the table. "Every time I see him in the Ankle, we shoot the breeze about who's the good guys and bad guys."

Marcus snapped back. "I knows who they are. And I take care of 'em in the 'propriate way." He smiled condescendingly.

"I know you do, Marcus. You're a fair man, always have been. Don't put up with any bullshit but treat folks right."

"Yeah, so what? Why ya tellin' me all this? Whatcha want this fair man to do 'bout it?" Marcus asked.

"It's not what I want. It's gotta be what you wanna do about it. You know if the wrong folks hear this talk, it could mean trouble for you."

Marcus paused, then said, quietly and icily, "Sam, ya tryin' to blackmail me?"

Sam replied, feeling Marcus was right on schedule. "I ain't never blackmailed you or taken a dime from you. And I ain't starting now. Use what I heard any way you want."

"So you heard things. Whaddaya think I oughta do with it?"

"Shit, I don't know. Your call. What's the risk of doin' nothin'? Maybe it'll blow over. Or maybe it blows up. Or maybe you pay the insurance money back. Maybe that'll put a lid on it."

"Lot's of fuckin' maybes. And maybe this is how ya get your hand in my pocket."

Sam decided to ramp it up. "Goddamn it, Marcus, you're not listenin' to me. I never accepted a dime of your money. And I don't want any fuckin' insurance money. At this point, I don't give a shit what you decide to do."

Marcus cooled down. "Ya still workin' with the cracker, Joe McGrath?"

"We work an occasional case together. You know he's got his own detective agency, right?"

"So I hear. Well, I 'preciate ya worryin' about me. Lemme think on it."

"Fine," Sam said, not sure if Marcus was being sincere or just putting him off. "I don't need to know what you decide to do. Told you what I heard. Ain't none of my business now."

"That bettah be right. Ya come back and see me sometime."

"I'll do it." Sam walked slowly toward the office door but turned before he opened it. "One other thing. There's also talk on the street that someone killed Willie Thompson, the warehouse night guard."

Sam walked out of the office, shutting the door behind him.

CHAPTER 34

WAIT AND SEE

TUESDAY—FEBRUARY 24, 1948

O N HIS WAY TO THE OFFICE ON TUESDAY MORNING, Joe stopped at the cops' diner for breakfast. He hadn't been there in a while, and he wished Sam and Brendan could join him. But he knew only too well they would create chaos and end up in the clinker for violating Birmingham's segregation law that prohibited coloreds and whites from eating in the same facility unless separated by a wall. Besides, since cops mostly frequented the diner, Joe would find himself even more persona non grata with the police department.

Joe nodded and said hello to a few officers he knew and sat at the counter. Helen was at the other end of the counter and in her loud, brassy voice announced to the whole café, "Well, if it ain't Big Dick. Where you been? You avoiding me?"

Laughter rippled through the café, and a cop shouted out, "Ya bettah take care of Helen, Joe. She's apinin' for ya."

Joe laughed with them and motioned to Helen to tone it down. "Hi, Helen. Been busy as hell getting the agency up and runnin'. You're lookin' mighty fine."

"Thanks." She walked over and faced him. "I'm still waiting for your phone call. Whatcha have?"

Joe ordered two eggs over-easy, grits, bacon, and toast. She brought his order and poured him a cup of coffee, spilling some on the morning paper he was reading.

"Oh, I am so sorry," Helen said.

Joe nodded, knowing full well it was intentional.

As he paid the cashier, Helen called from the back of the café, "Call me, Big Dick. I'm lonely."

Three cops sang out together in their best falsetto, "Call me, Big Dick. I'm lonely."

Joe smiled, doffed his hat, waved to all the cops, bowed to Helen, and left.

SAM WAS AT HIS DESK WHEN JOE ARRIVED.

"Hey Joe. Had an interesting conversation with Marcus."

"Mornin', Sam. I'm all ears."

Sam described the conversation in detail. Joe listened, nodding now and then.

"Sounds like it went well," Joe said. "Marcus even put Black Bronco's name in play when he asked you if you had talked to him."

Sam smiled knowingly. "Exactly. Couldn't have written the script better myself."

"You did write the script. Do you think he bought it?" Joe asked.

"Hard to say. It's wait and see time."

The two looked at each other quietly, absorbed in thought about the likelihood of success, when Brendan walked in.

"Mornin', guys. Sounds like the Mrs. Browning caper is over, right?" Brendan asked, sounding eager and ready to go.

Joe smiled at Brendan's enthusiasm and use of crime novel language. "Yep, as I told you yesterday, it's all over. The ball's in her court to deal with her husband."

"Well," Sam intoned, "I've got one regret."

Brendan looked confused and concerned as if he had done something wrong. "What?"

"I never got the same view of Mrs. Browning that you and Joe got," Sam said. "Ain't fair."

Brendan, still unsure how to react, looked at Joe for help. Joe and Sam laughed.

"Gents, I think we should table for good the Mrs. Browning story," Joe said. "Some folks might not appreciate our humor. Besides, I need to call Forrester and put him on notice he may hear from Marcus or Stanford or both."

"C'mon, Brendan. Let's get a cup of coffee," Sam said.

"Hi Joe," Kendall Forrester said. "Got any news for me?"

"Morning, Kendall. Yes, but a big maybe in what I've called about. You may get a phone call from Marcus Gilbert or Stanford Ramsey or both. They may offer to withdraw their insurance claims on the warehouse fire and return the money. I suspect they'll also stipulate that the offer is contingent on your asking no questions."

"Are you kidding?"

"Nope. As I said, it's a big maybe. We've taken some steps to make them consider this action. They're unpredictable people. We don't know which way they'll turn."

"So if I agree to accept the money with no questions asked," Kendall said, sounding decidedly unconvinced, "I have to sit back and wait for them to light another fire and make another claim?"

"We put a bug in their ear that someone, not by name, knows the warehouse fire was arson. If this move settles things down, I don't think they'd be stupid enough to set another fire. If you're concerned about that, wait several months and cancel their outstanding policies with your company."

"I need to know what you told them and how else it might affect my business."

"Kendall, this is important. Sam and I have put in motion something that may get your money back. We're the ones at risk if this thing blows up, not you. The less you know about it, the better to shield you from repercussions."

"So I just wait and see?"

Joe smiled at Kendall's use of the phrase. "That's what we're doing. Let it percolate for a week or two. The scales of justice balance slowly."

"Lovely thought," Kendall said, clearly irritated. "Don't worry, you'll hear from me one way or the other."

Joe heard a click, then a dial tone. He walked into the pantry where Sam and Brendan stood drinking coffee.

"Well?" asked Sam.

"This better work or we'll probably lose a good client."

CHAPTER 35

FORRESTER'S DELIGHT

TUESDAY—MARCH 2, 1948

As JOE DROVE TOWARD DOWNTOWN early Tuesday morning, the steel mills still cast an eerie orange glow over the city even as darkness faded. He wanted to be in the office before Sam arrived. Sam planned to bring Dave Williams, the Miles College student working part-time for him, into the office for the first time to meet everyone.

There had been no word the past week on The Marcus Caper, a tag Joe and Sam had put on Forrester's case to match Brendan's youthful enthusiasm with crime fiction lingo. Sam had been monitoring the buzz in Scratch Ankle, but all was quiet. He had noticed that since last Friday he had not seen Black Bronco in the Ankle, which was unusual.

When Joe got to the office, Sally and Brendan were already there, with a pot of coffee brewing and donuts for the occasion. The walk-in trade had been good the past week. Three new clients with different problems had been added to the caseload: a missing teenage son, a suspected embezzler, and another suspected adulterer, although the wife lacked the zest of Mrs. Browning.

Joe was working on the assignments for the cases when Sam and Dave arrived.

"Sam, would you like a kiss this morning?" Sally asked.

"Why, Sally, I'd love a kiss," Sam said, selecting a Hershey's Kiss from the bowl on her desk.

"Would you like a kiss, young man?" Sally asked.

Flustered about what was going on, Dave said, "Uh, yes, ma'am," and he took a Kiss.

"Sally," Sam said, "let me introduce Dave Williams. He's been working in my Scratch Ankle office for a while. He's going to spend time here helping us out. Dave, this is Sally Bowers, the best office administrator in Birmingham."

"It's pleasure to meet you, Dave," Sally said, extending her hand. "We play a silly kiss game here."

"Yes, ma'am." Dave took her hand cautiously. "It's pleasure to meet you too."

Joe and Brendan, who overheard the kiss exchanges, came into the reception area. Sam made the introductions. Joe had met Dave once when he was investigating the first prostitute's murder last September. Dave looked as Joe remembered him: early twenties, six feet tall, slim, light brown in color, always determined but with a pleasant face.

After all the formalities were complete, Sam said, "Dave, when we're the only ones in the office," he paused, and waved his hand at the others, "we use first names. But when someone else is here or in public, colored or white, it's back to Mr. McGrath, Mr. O'Connor, and Miss Bowers or Miss Sally.

"Yes," Dave said.

"You'll use the desk in the conference room. If we can make space, we'll put Brendan's desk in there too, so you've got company. Occasionally, you two will have to step out if we need the conference table for a client meeting. Brendan will show you around. Sally will give you a key. As I told you earlier, you're still on my payroll. If anybody asks, we work part-time for the McGrath Detective Agency."

Since Dave still appeared uncomfortable, Joe spoke up, hoping to break the ice. "Dave, do you remember when we met? I interviewed you at the New Home Hotel last September the morning a woman was murdered in the alley behind the hotel. You were the hotel night clerk."

"Yes, sir, Mr. McGrath, I—"

Sam nudged Dave.

"Yes, Joe, I sure do. You were very polite to me and the older colored gentleman you interviewed. Of course, I followed the case in the newspapers. It sounded like a tough case."

"It was, but Sam and Brendan helped me a lot, especially Sam. Now I'm looking forward to working with you. PI work is different from being a cop. And as Sam likes to say, I now work in the shadows."

Dave finally grinned, "Yes, the Shadow knows!"

All five laughed, and Joe realized the ice had broken. "Let's go in the conference room and have the coffee and donuts Sally's set up."

They were talking about Dave's college work when the phone rang. Sally went to her desk and answered.

"It was Kendall Forrester, Joe. He's coming over right now to see you."

Joe tilted his head. "How did he sound, Sally?"

"Other than the urgency in his voice," she said, "I couldn't tell."

"Well, we'll know soon enough. Sam and I'll meet with Forrester in here."

"Maybe we should clean up the conference room," Sam said.

"Just the donut crumbs," Joe said. "We'll probably either continue the celebration or turn it into a wake. Brendan, you and Dave go in my office. Show him his desk. And Dave, welcome to 'we few, we happy few, we band of brothers.' "

Dave turned to Sam with a questioning look.

Sam smiled, shrugging his shoulders. "Joe talks like that all the time. He thinks he's Shakespeare."

Twenty minutes later Forrester arrived. Sally showed him into the conference room and shut the door.

He stood quietly for a moment, staring grimly at Joe and Sam, then laughed and said, "Goddamn, it worked."

'Have a seat, Kendall," Joe said. He decided to play him along. "What worked?"

"For Christ's sake, what do you think?" Kendall asked, and he proceeded to answer his own question. "Stanford Ramsey called me late yesterday afternoon. And he said damn near verbatim what you told me last week. He and Marcus are going to withdraw their claims and repay all the payments associated with the warehouse fire."

"Terrific news."

Kendall looked disappointed. "Aren't you excited about it?"

"Excitement's not our stock-in-trade, Kendall. We specialize in being low-key and levelheaded."

Kendall smiled, "It works. I sure as hell can't complain about the results."

"Aim to please. Did Stanford explain why they decided to return the money?" Joe asked.

"He said he had become aware of recent information indicating the warehouse fire might have been arson. He added that even though it wasn't conclusive it was arson, he and Marcus had discussed it and agreed the correct thing to do was to return the money."

"Any conditions?"

"Oh yeah, Stanford never deals without some conditions. We can't ask any questions. We, my company, have to take no subsequent legal actions against him or Marcus if the fire is definitely proved to be arson. I agreed. He said the checks would be delivered this morning, and they were."

"Well, mighty fine news, Mr. Forrester," Sam said, trying to offset Joe's rather brusque style. "I'm just curious. Did Mr. Ramsey sound upset?"

"Nope, Sam, he was all business. Joe, I got to tell you, I'm very pleased with how you made this happen. You scripted things perfectly."

"I didn't script anything, Kendall," Joe said, his voice sharp. He pointed at Sam. "We wouldn't be talking this way today but for Sam. He wrote the script. He sold the script. And the edited version of the film came out just as he predicted it would."

Kendall tilted forward in his chair. "Sam, I offered you a feeble apology for my behavior last time we talked. I humbly offer it again and thank you. I don't know how you did this, but it was brilliant."

Sam nodded and said simply, "Thank you."

Joe, now more conciliatory, said, "We have one condition, Kendall. Don't tell anyone—your employees, your family, your friends, not anyone—how all this came to be. Sam and I and our businesses are the ones at risk, not you, if things unravel. We don't think they will, but silence is golden."

"You have my word. You two got my money back and," Kendall said with a devilish grin, "I can't wait to cancel their remaining policies in a few months." He pulled two checks out of his coat pocket and handed them to Joe. "Here's a check for your last invoice, and here's one for three hundred dollars for this month's retainer. Can you get me a copy of the invoice?"

"Do you have an issue with it?" Joe asked.

"Yes, just get a copy."

Joe went to Sally's desk. She found a copy, and Joe gave it to Kendall.

Kendall reviewed the invoice, pulled out his checkbook, and wrote a check made out to Sam Rucker. Handing it to Sam, he smiled and said, "Here, you earned every penny."

Joe looked over Sam's shoulder at the check. The check amount corrected Sam's billing rate to five dollars per hour, the same as Joe's.

Joe stood up. "Well, this deserves a celebration worthy of more than coffee and donuts. I have a bottle of fine Kentucky bourbon in my office just perfect for this moment. Anyone object to a little snort this early in the day?"

AFTER JOE WALKED KENDALL to the office front door, he came back to the conference room to discuss the outcome and saw Sam endorsing the check Kendall had given him.

"Here, this goes in the general account," Sam said, handing the check to Joe. "Good work does pay off."

"So it does, as you said it would. I thought things went well."

"Couldn't have gone better. But weren't you a bit harsh on him at first?" Sam asked.

"I suppose. Even though I made those comments about being low-key and levelheaded, I was still mad at him for the way he treated you earlier."

"Joe, I appreciate your concern, but as I've told you before I'm fully capable of handling situations like that myself."

"Yeah, I know. Sorry," Joe said feeling a little deflated.

"Hey, Boss Man. Perk up. I really do appreciate the remarks you made about the script."

"Right," Joe said smiling. "Back to business. Before you got in this morning, I thought about how to make assignments on our new cases. We put Brendan on the adultery case. He handled Mrs. Browning well. I take the missing kid case and have Dave tag along with me. It'll give him a feel for how I work and exposure to the white folks we have to contact. I'd like to see how he handles the situation. Sound okay?"

"Sure. How about the embezzlement case?"

"You have any problems getting started on it? We need to know more about the client and his business, and more about the suspected embezzler."

"Say what you mean, Joe. Can I find out anything useful about some white men and their business? Absolutely. Don't ask me how. As we told Marcus and Kendall, our contacts are confidential. Seriously, I've got my ways."

"That's good, and I'm trying, Sam. We'll talk to Brendan and Dave after lunch and get rolling. Next week, I'd like to go to Montevallo and take Brendan with me. It'll be good training for him. Can you handle the office?"

"Yeah. It's good you're taking Brendan. Besides the training, it'll build his confidence in what we do, and youngsters always enjoy time away from the office."

CHAPTER 36

BRENDAN IN MONTEVALLO

MONDAY—MARCH 8, 1948

J OE AND BRENDAN WORKED IN THE BIRMINGHAM office Monday until midafternoon. Everyone in the office had started investigative work on the three new cases: lost teenager, purported adulterer, suspected embezzler. Joe had to spend time with Sam and Dave to discuss what could be done while he and Brendan were gone. He also called Adam and arranged a meeting so he could meet Brendan.

The night before Joe had called his mother to let her know they were coming. He had asked if he could invite Archie to join them for dinner on Monday evening since he hoped Archie would agree to show Brendan around the area on Tuesday while he was in Montgomery. It had amused Joe when she had hesitated but then said, "Of course, it'll be wonderful to see Archie."

To close the loop, he called Archie.

"Shoal Creek Farms and Stables. Archie Hamilton, speakin'."

"Archie, it's Joe. How's it goin'?"

"Can't complain. Horses and farmin' as usual."

"I'm leavin' for Montevallo in a few hours. This time I'm bringin' Brendan O'Connor with me. He was my sidekick at the police department the last four months I was there. He's a bright kid. I've gotta go to Montgomery on Tuesday to talk to Jason Partlow. Can you—"

"Goodness gracious, so that asshole's still alive. I hope you can get somethin' useful outta him."

"I'll sure try. Can you show Brendan around the area tomorrow while I'm gone?"

"Sure. Anythin' special you want him to see?"

"Yeah. Show him where the Pidds live. And one of their stills if possible."

"The dump they live in is easy. Stills are tougher. Most of 'em are in the backwoods, hard to find."

"Do you know where they are?" Joe asked.

"Not many of 'em. But I can find out anythin' about those two dimwits in a day or two."

"Don't worry about it now. Maybe later. I should be back from Montgomery around three o'clock unless somethin' good comes up with Partlow."

"Okay."

"One more thing. Please join us tonight at my mother's house for dinner. It'll give you and Brendan a chance to get acquainted."

"Sure, so you can convince him I'm only half a redneck." Archie laughed, paused, and added, "Have you talked to Elizabeth about this?"

"Of course. She's fine with it. Can you come?"

"What time?"

"Six."

"I'll be there."

Joe leaned back in his chair and smiled. Yep, they were up to something.

AT THREE O'CLOCK, Joe and Brendan left for the short drive to Montevallo. The cold, rainy weather had finally been broken by a warmer, dry spell the last four days.

"Ever been to my hometown?" Joe asked.

"Nope. I did date a girl who used to live there right after I started with the police department last year."

"Are you still seeing her?"

"No. She had broken up with another guy. I was a short term fling for her until she went back to him."

"Women! We should look for other employment."

"Things are better now," Brendan said, grinning. "Met a girl who's going to Birmingham-Southern College. We had our first date last week. We're going out again this weekend. Hey, you'll like this. She's an English major and studies Shakespeare."

"Aha, I stand corrected. She sounds wonderful. But we won't have women issues in Montevallo. It'll be all business."

"What'll we be doing? I mean, I know we're working to find your father's murderers. But what will I do?"

"Today, you're gonna meet Adam Paige and Archie Hamilton. Adam's a childhood friend of mine. Now he's a successful lawyer and is giving us a hand. Archie is an older man. He initially comes across as a hick and redneck, but let me tell you, he's one smart guy. Because he's older, he knows more about the people who could've been involved in Dad's murder than I do. Archie will show you around Montevallo and Columbiana tomorrow while I'm in Montgomery."

"What are you going there for, Joe?"

"To interview Jason Partlow. He's the lawyer who handled the defense of the colored guy my father represented until he was killed. Partlow did a terrible job, almost like he wanted the defendant found guilty. Maybe he was ordered to botch the defense."

"Will he cooperate?"

"I'll find out. After we see Adam, we'll go to my mother's house. She's looking forward to meeting you and has a room for you. And, if I know her at all, she's been planning supper for days. Archie's going to join us too."

They went straight to Adam's office. Brendan and Adam seemed to hit it off well. He gave Brendan his office and home phone numbers and told him to call any time.

Joe finally had to break up the conversation. "Sorry, Adam, we've got to get going."

"Let me know what I can do, Joe. Nice to have met you, Brendan."

As they walked to the car, Joe said, "C'mon, I'll drive up Main Street on the way to Mom's house and show you the sights. Joe pointed out the library, city hall, the movie house, and Julie's Café. "Damned good place to eat from early morning to late afternoon."

As they went in the front door, Joe called out, "Mom, are you home?"

"Hi, honey, I'll be right there," Elizabeth said, coming out of the kitchen, her apron tied around her waist. "Hello, you must be Brendan, I'm Elizabeth. I've heard so much about you."

"Hello, Mrs. McGrath. It's nice to meet you. Joe talks about you a lot. And thanks for letting me stay in your house."

"I'd have it no other way. Joe, your room is ready. Please show Brendan to the guest room. I'm sure you two want to freshen up. Dinner is about ready. I came home right after my three o'clock class to get it started." She looked at her watch: 5:24. "Oh goodness, I have to go upstairs and change."

"C'mon, Brendan. I'll show you your room," Joe said leading the way. He paused to look into the dining room. The table was elegantly set, more so than for the usual guests. He smiled knowingly, and said, "When I come home, Mom always says to me, 'Your room is ready.'"

"Yep, my mother says the same thing. It's as if we never left home."

CHAPTER 37

ELIZABETH'S DINNER PARTY

MONDAY—MARCH 8, 1948

J OE AND BRENDAN WERE IN THE LIVING ROOM chatting when the doorbell rang. Joe greeted Archie, and saw a late model Oldsmobile parked at the curb. Archie was dressed in dark brown wool slacks, a tan dress shirt, and a tweed jacket. There was no bulge in his jaw. He wasn't chewing tobacco.

"Wow, look at you, Archie. And a nice car to boot."

He smiled, "Special occasion."

"Any problems finding us?"

"A little. I had to ask two people for directions."

"Really?"

Archie laughed, "Just a little joke. I know the way well. Here, I thought we might enjoy a drink." He handed Joe a bottle of the same Kentucky bourbon they had reverently shared.

"Thanks, I will," Joe said. "Archie, this is Brendan O'Connor. Brendan, Archie Hamilton."

The two shook hands. "Glad to meet you, Brendan. So you worked with Joe as a cop in Birmingham."

"Yes sir, Mr. Hamilton. His trusted sidekick. Actually, I guess I still am."

"You sure are, partner," Joe said.

"I'm sure you are too." Archie said, "But no more 'sirs' or 'misters.' I'm Archie."

Elizabeth came down the stairs. The three men looked at her as she descended wearing a dark blue dress, belted at the waist and flowing down and out a bit to her mid-calf. A pair of black shoes with medium heels and a tasteful buckle, and a string of pearls provided perfect accents. Her hair was fixed differently, although Joe couldn't describe it. She looked stunning.

"Hello, Archie. It's nice to see you," she said, offering her hand.

Archie took it gently and said, "It's been too long, Elizabeth."

They stood quietly holding hands, their eyes locked in an affectionate embrace, until Joe broke the spell. "C'mon in. Let's have a drink of fine bourbon."

As they walked into the living room, Brendan whispered in Joe's ear, "Archie's nothing like you described."

"You're right," Joe whispered back, "he's on his best behavior tonight for my mother. You'll get a chance to see what I meant later."

Joe fixed bourbon and water for everyone, keeping his mother's light as she requested, knowing she preferred Scotch. The conversation drifted around work, weather, and the emergence of the Dixiecrat Party as a viable, segregationist force in Southern politics.

"Enough of the Dixiecrat's racist comments, gentlemen," Elizabeth said. "Joe, please come help me serve dinner."

The dinner was equal to the table: lettuce salad with oil and vinegar, pork loin roast, mashed potatoes, and asparagus.

"Oh, delicious, Elizabeth," Archie said. "Where did you get such good lettuce and asparagus so early in the year?"

Elizabeth beamed and said, "The chef at the college Faculty Club has contracts with a few growers who specialize in late winter and early spring crops. He graciously sold these to me. I had hoped to get some tomatoes. No luck."

Joe looked on, enjoying their interplay.

Brendan, realizing he had been quiet, said, "Archie's right, this dinner is delicious."

"Thank you, Brendan." She got up from the table. "Excuse me, I'll get the dessert."

After serving bread pudding with rum sauce and coffee, she smiled. "Brendan, tell me about yourself. I know you're from Mobile. And based on your name, I'm sure you're Catholic."

"Yes, ma'am. Did you know that Mobile has more Catholics than any other Alabama city?"

"No, I didn't. There aren't many Catholics in Montevallo. The closest church is St. Paul's in Birmingham. Do you attend Mass there?"

Brendan blushed. "Sometimes, but not as often as I should. The priest gives me a hard time when I go to confession."

"Don't worry. We're Catholic and seldom go to Mass. What is your education?"

"I went to parochial elementary and high school. My parents insisted I go to Spring Hill College in Mobile, a school run by Jesuits."

"I know of Spring Hill. It has a good reputation. How did you become a policeman?" Elizabeth asked.

"Almost by accident," Brendan said. "After my junior year at Spring Hill, I went into the Army for two years and finished college right after the war ended. I couldn't find work that interested me with my liberal arts degree. I saw a newspaper ad for police openings in Birmingham. I applied and was accepted."

"Joe's good luck," Elizabeth said, reaching out to touch Brendan's arm. "Joe speaks highly of you. You're a fine young man. What are you doing tomorrow?"

"Archie's agreed to show Brendan around the county," Joe said, "while I'm in Montgomery.

"Speaking of tomorrow, Brendan, can you meet me at Julie's Café at ten? I have to do farm chores earlier in the day," Archie said. "I can pick you up here if that helps."

"Joe, how far is it to the café?" Brendan asked.

"Four or five blocks."

"I'll walk. The weather's fine. I'll meet you there, Archie."

"We've got a deal. Well, farm boys get up early, so I reckon I'll head on home," Archie said as he stood. "Elizabeth, thank you for the wonderful dinner and for sharing these two fine young men with me. Nice seeing you again. I hope it's not too long until the next time."

AFTER ARCHIE LEFT, Joe and Brendan helped Elizabeth clear the table and wash dishes.

"You boys are going to be busy tomorrow," Elizabeth said, turning out the kitchen lights. "Will you be back in time for dinner?"

"You bet we will. What are we having?" Joe asked.

Elizabeth giggled. "Surprise pie."

They went upstairs to their bedrooms. As Joe lay in bed, he wondered if he had made a mistake introducing Adam and Brendan.

CHAPTER 38

JASON PARTLOW

TUESDAY—MARCH 9, 1948

Tuesday morning Brendan cleared the breakfast table while Joe washed dishes. Elizabeth sat finishing her coffee, preparing to leave for work.

"I'm off, boys," she said, "Thanks for cleaning up. Don't be late tonight for surprise pie."

After she left the house, Brendan asked, "What's surprise pie?"

Joe laughed. "Mom's expression for a nice casserole or pot pie dish. It'll be made out of whatever's left in the fridge."

"Oh?"

"Don't worry. It'll be better than good. I've got to call Sally. I want to leave for Montgomery soon. I'll be in Mom's study."

"McGrath Detective Agency. Sally Bowers speaking."

"Hi, Sally. Things okay?" Joe asked.

"Fine. Sam's at his office. I talked with Jason Partlow."

"That's why I called. Have I got an appointment to see him today? I'm getting ready to drive to Montgomery."

"Yes. Eleven thirty. Called him several times yesterday and finally got him at five o'clock. Don't think there's a secretary or anyone else in his office. Anyway, I said I was Sandra Taylor calling for Jack Martin, a Birmingham businessman who needs legal help."

"Did he ask any questions"?

"Only one. Wanted to know what kind of legal help you needed. I told him it involved financial shenanigans."

"He didn't even ask for our phone number?"

"Nope. I think the words 'financial shenanigans' got him. After I said that, he sounded eager to meet with you."

"Excellent, Sally. I'll try to call you later today."

Back in the kitchen, Joe said, "Sally set things up with Partlow. I'm takin' off now. Want a ride downtown?"

"No thanks, I'll walk," Brendan said. "I'll look around town before meeting Archie."

"Don't let him intimidate you. He was on his best behavior last night. But in public, he loves to play the hick. He knows everyone in the area—rich, poor, colored, white. See you later."

PARTLOW'S OFFICE WAS IN A RUNDOWN BUILDING on the edge of downtown Montgomery. With time to kill before the appointment, Joe found a nearby café and had a cup of coffee and a chocolate-covered donut.

Joe found Partlow's office on the second floor of the building and knocked on the door.

"C'mon in. It's not locked," a weak, high-pitched voice said.

Opening the door, Joe saw a man in his fifties sitting behind the single desk in the small office. "You Jason Partlow?"

Partlow stood. "One and the same. You must be Jack Martin. Right on time."

Partlow's appearance pretty much matched Joe's expectations. Short and paunchy, a wrinkled suit too large for him, thinning unkempt hair, jowls drooping loosely from this jaw, and a face covered with red blotches. *Yep*, Joe thought, *he's a drinker.*

"Wouldn't want to keep you waiting," Joe said.

"Mr. Martin, so you need legal help with some . . . ," Partlow paused and grinned knowingly, "uh, financial shenanigans."

"Yeah. But first a few questions."

"Shoot."

"In 1942, did you represent a colored guy, Jackie Simmons, on a murder charge in Columbiana? He was found guilty. Electrocuted."

Partlow sat up and stared hard at Joe. "Why the hell you askin' me that? You didn't come here lookin' for no legal help, did you?"

"Very astute, Partlow. I'm Joe McGrath, son of Peter McGrath, the lawyer who represented Jackie Simmons. My father was murdered midway through the trial. You were brought in to handle it."

Partlow looked as if he wanted to run. "You got no right to barge in here under false pretenses. You git outta here."

"I'll git outta here after you answer my questions. Did you handle Jackie's defense?"

Partlow said nothing.

Joe reached over the desk and grabbed Partlow's jacket by the lapels and abruptly yanked him up to his face. Joe smelled alcohol on his breath. "Listen carefully. I was a homicide detective with the Birmingham Police Department. I now own a private detective agency. I know enough about your practice to put you out of business, maybe even behind bars."

Joe shoved Partlow back into his chair. "Did you handle the case?"

Partlow, wide-eyed and mouth agape, barely muttered, "Yes."

"Who hired you?"

"Whaddaya mean? The court hired me."

"You know what I mean." Joe reached over and threatened to hit Partlow. "I wanna know who pulled the strings. As crummy a lawyer as you are, you couldn't have represented Jackie any worse unless someone gave you orders, even paid you off. Who was it?"

Partlow, his eyes blinking like semaphores, said, "Chuck Holder and Geoffrey Wallace."

"What did they ask you to do?" Joe asked.

"Make sure Jackie got the chair."

"Did they say why?"

"No." Partlow said, more relaxed since Joe had stepped back and wasn't hovering over him. "They didn't tell me nothin' except to make sure Jackie was found guilty and got the chair."

"You did a damn good job of that. Did you ever hear anyone mention 'the operation'?" Joe asked.

"What operation?" Partlow looked confused. "I never heard nothin' like that. Once, I did overhear Holder say to somebody on the phone that there's a meeting of ark tonight. Didn't make no damn sense to me. 'Cept maybe Noah was gonna be there too."

Joe faked a grimace. "Well, you are consistent. Your joke smells as bad as your law practice." Joe wrote the word 'ark' in his notepad. "What did they pay you?"

"The court paid me two hundred bucks."

Joe leaned into him. "Look, you piece of shit, what did Holder and Wallace pay you?"

When Partlow paused, Joe grabbed his throat. "What did they pay you, asshole?"

Partlow gasped. "Five hundred."

Joe released him and sat down. "Not a bad payday for two weeks. Especially, since you only went through the paces of being a lawyer. Where did you stay in Columbiana?"

"They paid for a fleabag duplex near town."

"What did you do when the court wasn't in session?"

"Went to a jook joint south of town. They sold bootleg in the back room if they trusted you. Messed around with a couple of babes working the place. A joint where coloreds and whites mixed, no problem. You know what I mean?"

"Yeah. What were their names?"

"I don't rightly remember. Something like Flo and, uh, maybe Bessie. Shit, I just bought them drinks and paid to fuck 'em."

"Did you hear any talk about my father's murder?"

"No, only heard he was murdered, and that's the honest to God truth."

"It sure as hell better be," Joe said. "Have you been back to Shelby County since the trial?"

"No. When the trial was over, I went back to Selma and later moved to Montgomery."

"Well, matches up well with the trace we put out on you. Before I go, here's the deal. You won't hear from me again unless I find out you've lied to me or talked to someone else about this conversation." Joe's grimace morphed into a wicked smile. "Heaven help you if you have. I'll be here in a flash with a couple of buddies and before we're through, you'll be begging us to kill you. Got it?"

"Yeah."

"What?" Joe said, louder.

"Yes."

"What?" Joe screamed.

"Yes, sir."

"Better. It's been nice talking to you, Mr. Partlow."

Joe slammed the door hard as he left. *What a creep*, he thought. *Partlow would probably sell his mother for a buck.*

CHAPTER 39

OMINOUS CLOUDS GATHER

TUESDAY—MARCH 9, 1948

J OE STOPPED AT A SEAFOOD RESTAURANT in downtown Montgomery and had boiled shrimp washed down with beer for lunch. When he arrived back in Montevallo at two forty, he went straight to his mother's and called out to see if anyone was home. Quiet, which didn't surprise him since it was early afternoon.

Joe called his office and talked to Sally and Sam. Sally was pleased things had gone well, since she thought Partlow might not show up.

When Joe told Sam about the meeting, he listened carefully and said, "Well, the noose tightens around Holder and Wallace."

Joe lay down on the sofa in the living room and had nodded off when the phone rang. He thought it might be Sam or Sally calling back or maybe even Susan Kelly with something about Carlton Teague.

"Joe McGrath here."

"It's Archie."

"Hi, Archie. You and Brendan have a good day?"

"No. He didn't show. I waited for him at Julie's Café until about ten thirty, and then drove around downtown looking for him. I even went to Elizabeth's house, but nobody was home. Have you seen him?"

A dark dread swept over Joe. "No. Damn, that's not like Brendan. He's very reliable. Did you ask anybody if they had seen him?"

"Yes. I described him to the folks in the café. No one there had seen him. One guy I asked on the street said he saw someone who looked like that walk past him at around quarter to nine. I think we should talk to Raymond Chapman. He can put his officers and the sheriff on alert."

Joe rubbed his forehead, trying to fight off the inner turmoil gripping him. He didn't like the idea of turning to the local cops, not knowing where their real allegiances lay. But he realized it was the best way to get a coordinated effort under way. "Yeah, we better do that. Can you meet me at Raymond's office?"

"Be there in fifteen minutes," Archie said.

Joe called his office and got Sam on the phone. "Sam, Brendan's missing. I'm concerned." He told Sam about his conversation with Archie and asked, "Can you come down here now?"

"Yeah. Right away," Sam said. "I'll call Hank and Mattie Ruth. I'm sure they'll let me stay with them."

"Thanks. I'll call you at Hank's in the next hour or two."

Joe got out of his car at the police department when Archie drove up in his pickup truck, an older model Chevy, paint fading and body covered with dents. It was almost five o'clock. As they entered the building, Raymond was talking to one of his officers in the lobby.

Raymond looked up and saw the two. "Well, I'll be damned. What an honor. What can we do for Birmingham's private detective and our own redneck liberal?"

"Can we talk in your office, Raymond?" Joe asked.

"Sure, c'mon in."

"I arrived in town late yesterday with Brendan O'Connor. He works for me. He was supposed to meet Archie this morning at ten o'clock at Julie's Café. He didn't show. He's missing."

"Is he white or colored?"

"White."

"An improvement," Raymond said.

"Don't give me that shit, Raymond," Joe said, getting heated. "He's twenty-six years old. Good kid. Ex-cop."

"Cool off, Joe. Where were you when this happened?"

"I drove to Montgomery on business this morning. I left him at Mom's house. He wanted to walk around town before meeting Archie."

"Does he have a car?" Raymond asked.

"No."

"Archie, what were you and Brendan meetin' for?"

"He'd never been to Montevallo," Archie said, reverting to his redneck voice. "I was s'posed to show him 'round while Joe goed to Montgumry."

"Does Brendan know anybody else in town?"

Joe spoke up. "Only Adam Paige. I introduced them yesterday."

Joe and Archie exchanged glances.

Raymond, noticing the glance, said, "Do you think Adam had something to do with Brendan's disappearance?"

Joe realized Raymond was sharper than he thought and regained his footing. "No, certainly not. Adam told Brendan to call or come see him any time. We'll check with Adam to see if he saw Brendan today."

Raymond tilted his head, looking unconvinced, but asked, "Any idea where to start?"

"No," Joe said. Archie shook his head.

Raymond shoved a piece of paper in front of Joe. "Write me a detailed description. You were a cop. You know what I need. I'll notify all my officers, send it to Sheriff Cate, and to a few police departments nearby. We need a photo."

"Brendan worked as my sidekick in homicide. He's one of ours, Raymond. Call BPD. They should be able to get you a photo," Joe said. He started filling out the form.

"Okay. I'll post copies of the Missing Persons report around town and add one with the photo after we get it. We'll wait and see. Occasionally someone comes to us with a lead pretty quickly." Raymond smiled. "Maybe Brendan's holed up in the cat house over in Columbiana."

Joe smiled tiredly. "I hope he's in a cat house. But not likely. He's a straight shooter."

Raymond, lips fading to a thin tight line, said, "I assume I can reach you at your mother's."

Joe nodded and handed the completed form back to Raymond.

"Here's my home number. Call me any time. How about you, Archie, your sanctuary?"

"It's a farm, Raymond, and you know the number. Let's go, Joe."

They stood in the parking lot and Joe asked, "Archie, do you think Raymond will do what he said?"

"He'll do it. He likes to act like an asshole. He's a good cop."

Joe smiled. "We'll get along. I've worked with both. Sam Rucker should be here soon. I asked him to come help. He'll be staying at Hank's house. Can you join us tonight at Mom's at six thirty?"

"Sure. I'm going back to the farm to check on some work that has to be completed. I'll pick up Sam at about six fifteen. It's on my way."

"Thanks. I'll tell Sam and Hank you'll be coming by. Do you know where Hank lives?" Joe asked.

"Of course I know where he lives. Hank's construction company built a number of the homes and structures on the farm. See you later."

Joe stood in the parking lot alone, knowing his decision to bring Brendan to Montevallo created this situation. And Adam's role in all this still gnawed at him.

CHAPTER 40

A SOMBER MEETING

TUESDAY—MARCH 9, 1948

WHEN JOE GOT TO HIS MOTHER'S, she was preparing dinner. She smiled, looking contented as she peeled potatoes. "Hi, honey. We'll have a nice dinner tonight. Oh, sad news, Judge Wilberforce passed away."

"Sorry to hear that. He tried hard to do the right thing at the end. Mom, sit down, please."

Joe watched as Elizabeth's contentment faded to concern. "Is something wrong?" she asked.

As he explained to her what had happened, a look of knowing fear came over her face. "Oh, Joe, that delightful young man. Do you think he'll be all right?"

"I don't know." Joe said, putting his arms around her and hugging tightly. Finally letting go, he added, "Sam's over at Hank's. I need to call him. I'll be right back."

Joe went to Elizabeth's study to make the call.

In a few minutes, he returned. "Got him. Sam and Archie are coming over at six thirty. Is that okay?"

"Of course," Elizabeth said, trying to act nonchalant. "I'll make something simple. Finger sandwiches and coffee. I also have a pecan pie I made for tonight."

"Thanks, but don't worry about it, Mom. We'll be all right."

Looking at her watch, she ignored Joe's comment. "I'll make the sandwiches and coffee, then freshen up."

Joe tried to read an early edition of the *Birmingham News* to no avail; the newspaper was sent to Montevallo each day on a Greyhound bus for local delivery. He was still aimlessly turning pages when the front door bell rang.

"Hi, Archie, Sam. C'mon in," Joe said, noticing that Archie wore his usual coveralls but wasn't chewing tobacco. "Let's sit at the kitchen table and talk. Any problems driving down, Sam?"

"Nope. Guess the Klan took the night off."

"Have a seat. There's coffee too," Joe said, placing a plate of sandwiches on the table. "I've never felt so impotent," Joe said, after a few bites of his sandwich, looking ashen and dour. "When I was a homicide cop, I just did my job. Now I don't know which way to turn."

"Joe, bring me up to date on what's happened since yesterday?" Sam asked.

Okay," Joe said in a flat voice. "I introduced Brendan to Adam. Mom prepared us a nice dinner last night, including Archie. I went to Montgomery and talked with Jason Partlow. Brendan walked downtown to meet Archie. They never met. Brendan hasn't been seen since. Archie and I saw Police Chief Raymond. He's going to put Missing Persons bulletins around the area and notify the sheriff and other law enforcement agencies in the county." Joe paused, his rote recitation complete.

Elizabeth came into the kitchen. She looked unsettled and wore a simple, light brown woolen dress. She had done nothing special with her hair and wore no jewelry. "Hello, Sam. Thanks for coming so quickly to help with what I hope is not a tragedy," she said, shaking his hand.

"Hello, Miss Elizabeth. I'm sure we'll find Brendan."

"Hello, Archie. It's nice to see you again so soon," she said, offering her hand.

Archie took it. "I had hoped it would be under different circumstances, Elizabeth."

"Join us, Mom."

She sat between Archie and Sam, facing Joe. "Let me know if you want more to eat."

Sam, sensing the tension in the room, said, "I have a theory. This is the second warning. The brick and note were the first one. Brendan will be returned alive, likely beaten, as the second warning. Either we drop the investigation and get out of town, or else."

"I hope you're right, Sam," Elizabeth said, unable to hide her doubt.

"I want to add something," Archie said. "Adam is becoming the common denominator in these warnings. It seems you come to town, see Adam and tell him what you're doing, and soon thereafter, we have a brick and a missing person."

Joe nodded and glanced at Sam.

Elizabeth, startled, said, "You mean Adam's involved?"

"Mom, we don't know for sure. It's circumstantial, not definitive evidence. But there might be a connection," Joe said, starting to sound more like his normal self. "The question is what to do—"

The phone rang, startling everyone.

"I'll get it," Joe said.

He picked up the phone in the study. "Joe McGrath here."

"Hi Joe, it's Raymond. Notices have been posted. The sheriff and police departments have been notified. I called BPD. My guy will be back with Brendan's photo soon."

"Good. Anything else?"

"Nope."

"Thanks, Raymond."

Joe returned to the kitchen. "You were right, Archie, Raymond's doing his job. And I got a few things out of Partlow."

Archie laughed. "I'm surprised you got anything out of that creep."

"Had to use a little friendly persuasion on him," Joe said, grinning as his ashen color faded. "Chuck Holder and Geoffrey Wallace hired him and told him to be sure Simmons got the chair. Said—"

"Geoffrey Wallace?" Elizabeth blurted out. "The history professor?"

"Yes, Mom," Joe said. "But we have to check out what Partlow told me."

Joe paused, watching his mother shake her head in disbelief, and then said, "Partlow said he never heard of 'the operation,' but did overhear Holder tell someone on the phone that there was a meeting of ark. Don't get it."

Archie, who was slouched down in his chair, sat up straight, look-ing surprised. "Well, well. It wasn't a – r – k. Partlow heard a – r – c."

"Like the arc in a circle?" Joe asked.

Archie's expression changed to one of concern. "I wish that's what it meant. It stands for *Aeternum Racialis Candoris*."

"Forever Racial Purity," Joe said, putting his high school Latin to good use. "Jesus, does it have anything to do with the Klan?"

"Indirectly. It was, maybe still is, a group of wealthy businessmen, lawyers, doctors, and college professors like Wallace. They met in secret. There wasn't a shred of evidence or even rumors tying them to any of the racial atrocities happening around here years ago, includ-ing your father's murder."

Joe, lips parted, looked at Archie suspiciously. "How the hell do you know so much if it was so secret?"

"Fair question," Archie said, unfazed by Joe's tone. "A few months after Peter's death, I was discreetly approached by the town's most prominent banker, a man I had known and respected for years. He said a group of his friends wanted to invite me to become a member of their secret fraternal society. That's when I learned the name of the group. He described the type of individuals in the group, but didn't mention names. Said its purpose was to preserve the southern way of life and maintain white racial purity. He quickly added they had nothing to do with the Klan and didn't condone their activities. He claimed everything they did was legal. I thanked him but declined the invitation. He asked me to keep our conversation quiet."

"Why would they have asked you to join their group knowing your beliefs and the way you operate your farm?"

"Another good question. I think they wanted to co-opt me in hopes of neutralizing any impact I may have had on the community. They never approached me again. I've heard nothing of them until you brought it up. Remember, Joe, live and let live."

Joe put his hands on the table and rhythmically tapped his fingers.

"You oughtta know," Archie continued, "there is a connection between your buddy Stanford Ramsey and Chuck Holder, and it's not a good one. On one of his horse buying trips to the farm about ten years ago, Stanford asked me how Chuck was doing. I said he was doin' fine. Stanford got real heated and said somethin' like, 'That son of a bitch cheated me out of a lot of money in a business deal we had in the twenties.' Then he calmed down. May have nothing to do with what we're talkin' about."

Joe stopped tapping his fingers, while listening to Archie bring Stanford Ramsey into the picture. He clasped his hands in his lap and said, "Interesting. Let's pigeonhole it for now." He looked around at the others. "Have to keep this to ourselves. Don't want people like Raymond, Adam, or the Holders finding out we know of A – R – C. Everyone agree?"

All three nodded.

"I'll serve the pie and more coffee," Elizabeth said.

While they ate dessert, the mood remained somber and the conversation subdued.

Joe slapped the table and stood. "Goddammit, I can't sit here and do nothing. We've at least gotta go out and look around."

"Which direction?" Archie asked.

Joe walked around the kitchen, rubbing his temple. "I know. We'll go out to the spot west of town where Dad's body was found. Probably a waste of time. I'm open to other ideas."

"Glad to see the old spark returning," Sam said. "But can you find the spot after all these years?"

"Some things you never forget, Sam. I remember the day my Uncle Andrew showed me the spot a couple of months after Dad's murder as if it were yesterday. I bugged him daily to show me. I think he agreed only after he had gotten your approval, Mom." He looked at her.

Elizabeth nodded, looking distraught.

"It's okay," he said quietly to her. Looking back at Sam, he spoke more forcefully. "Yes, I know how to get there. We'll need flashlights or better yet, bigger portable lamps. Do we have any?"

"I have two flashlights. They're in one of the kitchen drawers." She rummaged around in the kitchen cupboards and handed them to Joe.

"I'll bet Hank has lamps," Archie said. "He needs stuff like that for his work. Want me to call him?"

"Sure. Use the phone in the study."

Archie made the call and returned in a couple of minutes. "Hank's got several. I told him we'd be over soon. He asked if he could go with us. I said yes. You okay with it, Joe?"

"Of course, the more manpower we have, the better. Speaking of power. Sam, do you have your gun?"

Sam patted his jacket. "Right here."

"Archie?" Joe asked.

"No, but next time I will."

"Mine's upstairs. I'll get it and we'll get moving."

As Joe prepared to get in the driver's side of his car, he looked back at the house. Elizabeth stood on the porch, arms crossed, clutching herself. Joe couldn't see her face clearly but knew the anguish and terrible memories the evening had evoked.

CHAPTER 41

BALD ROCK

TUESDAY—MARCH 9, 1948

Aᴇᴛᴇʀ ᴀ ǫᴜɪᴄᴋ sᴛᴏᴘ ᴀᴛ Hᴀɴᴋ's to get four handheld, battery-powered lamps, the men prepared to get in Joe's Plymouth sedan.

"Where are we going, Joe?" Hank asked.

"We'll drive north on Highway 17 for three or four miles. After we cross a small bridge over a slough, off to the left should be a dirt road. It was in pretty good shape years ago. I don't remember how far Uncle Andrew drove on the dirt road. I do remember he parked off the road near a huge rock on the right. Do you know the road?"

Hank smiled. "You got a good memory. Yep, it's still there. The rock is called Bald Rock."

"Yeah, I know the road too," Archie said. "Has a few farms on it worked by the owners or sharecroppers."

"Well, I don't think we'll get lost," Joe said, "Let's get goin'. Hank, you sit up front and be the navigator."

As he got in the front seat, passenger's side, Hank said, "Well, I hope no one sees us with a white man chauffeuring a colored around."

The men laughed, lightening up the mood as Joe pulled from the curb.

There was little talk on the drive north on 17. Joe slowed when he came to the small bridge. "The dirt road should be on the left about now." He put the headlights on high beam.

"It's comin' up now," Hank said. "Turn left. The rock's two miles from here on the right."

Joe drove slowly, eyes darting back and forth between the side of the road and the odometer, when the rock loomed ahead in the car's headlights, it's top rounded like a man's head. "Goddamn, right on target, Hank. Just like I remember it." He parked the car off to the side of the road near the rock.

"Now we'll walk north from the rock through the brush and trees until we come to the spot."

"How far?" Sam asked.

"Don't know. It seems like we went straight for ten or fifteen minutes. We should go over a small hill and then hit a clearing," Joe said, leading the way.

After a couple of minutes, they decided to have two guys in front push the brush and limbs aside as the two behind held up the lamps to show the way. They alternated the pattern every few minutes. The terrain rose slowly for several minutes, then descended slightly and opened into a clearing.

"I think this is the place," Joe said. "Hand me a lamp?" he asked, as he had been the lead man when they entered the clearing.

Joe moved around, lamp in hand, examining the clearing. After a couple of minutes, he thought this wasn't the place. On the side of the clearing where he thought the tree should be, stood a number of varying height silver maples. Then he realized that the tree his father had been tied to would now be much taller. He scanned the maples with his lamp and saw it. He moved the beam up and down the tree and around its immediate periphery, his mind erupting with memories and emotions. He walked closer to the tree and heard running water, one sound he had forgotten. "This is the spot. This is the tree where Dad died," Joe said quietly, as if talking to himself.

The others walked over near the tree, stopping several paces behind where Joe stood. They remained silent, letting him handle the moment.

Joe said nothing for several minutes and then spoke in a slow monotone voice. "They tied him to the tree. He was beaten badly. He was killed with a single shot between the eyes. It was as if the killer wanted to be sure he could see it coming. He remained tied to the tree for almost three days before he was found. That's exactly the way my Uncle Andrew described the scene to me."

Joe started toward the men, but then looked back at the tree and said, his voice low, trembling with emotion, "I miss you. I love you."

He paused a few moments, and turned, facing the men. His lamp cast an eerie glow on his face, accentuating the tears streaming down his cheeks. "We can go back now. Brendan's not here."

They struggled though the brush and trees, hoping they were headed in the right direction. They came out on the dirt road about fifty yards to the east of the car and the rock.

When they got to the car, Sam asked Joe, "Want me to drive?"

"Of course not, I'll still be your chauffeur."

The ride back to Hank's was uneventful. At one point Sam said, "I looked at the brush and trees as we went in and out of the clearing. I also looked carefully around the clearing. I don't think anyone's been there for some time."

"You're right, Sam," Joe said. "It was a waste of time. Let's sleep on it and meet at Hank's at seven in the morning and decide where to look next. Okay, Hank?"

"Sure. I'll ask Mattie Ruth to fix breakfast," Hank said.

"Thanks. But ask her to keep it simple, please. I want to get going early."

At Hank's house, Joe helped him take the lamps into his garage. Walking back to the car, he overheard Sam and Archie talking.

"I guess this was really about Joe and his Dad," Archie said, quietly. "Sort of like a pilgrimage."

"Yeah, it was," Sam replied. "But if the worst comes to pass, it'll be about Peter and Brendan, and I don't know what we'll call it. But I'm sure the two are tied together somehow."

ARCHIE SAID GOOD NIGHT and got in his pickup truck to drive home. Joe smiled as he left. *Well, he's back to the old Archie except for the chewing tobacco.*

When Joe arrived home, he went upstairs, hoping not to wake his mother. She stepped out of her bedroom, wearing a bathrobe. He knew she had been waiting for him.

"Everything okay, honey? Did you find anything?" she asked.

"I'm fine. No. Wild goose chase. No one's been near the spot in a while."

"I'm worried about Brendan," Elizabeth said, holding up her hands for emphasis. They were shaking. Joe had never seen his mother like this. She had always been strong.

Although he was leery of Sam's assessment, in hopes of placating her concern, he said, "I think Sam has it right. He'll come back after being roughed up a bit as a second warning about what we're doing. Tomorrow we're meeting at Hank's at seven o'clock. Try to sleep."

"Okay," she said, looking unconvinced.

"Mom, one more thing. Did you ever hear about the group *Aeternum Racialis Candoris*?"

"I was pleased you got the Latin translation correct. The last time I remember hearing the name was well before your father's murder. But I never heard the sort of things about the group that Archie told us last night."

"Do you think we can believe what Archie said?"

Elizabeth stared hard at Joe. "He's an honest and trustworthy man."

Joe, a bit startled, said, "I have to be sure. Things are getting tough."

"I hope Archie is able to help you. He's an old friend."

"He's been very helpful," Joe said, hoping she would say more. When she didn't, he decided to let it go.

CHAPTER 42

THE STORM

WEDNESDAY—MARCH 10, 1948

J OE TOSSED AND TURNED IN BED, unable to sleep, his mind roiling with thoughts of Brendan. He had fallen into an early morning slumber, when he was startled awake by the alarm at six o'clock. He showered, shaved, and dressed, checked his gun, made sure it was loaded, and put a box of bullets in his pocket.

Elizabeth was in the kitchen. "Mornin', Mom. Did you sleep well?"

"No. . . . Cup of coffee? It's fresh."

"Sure. I have a few minutes before I have to go over to Hank's."

They were sipping coffee and chatting when the phone rang. Looking at each other, they hoped it would go away. "I'll get it in the study," Joe said.

"JOE MCGRATH SPEAKING."

"It's Raymond. Got a report on a body. My night officer got a call at six forty-one this morning from a sharecropper. White guy named Shorty Cummins. Lives just out of town. He's got a twenty-year-old son, Shortstuff. I know, it sounds weird, but Shortstuff's a bit tetched in the head. He was on his way to one of his favorite fishing holes on Shoal Creek this morning before daybreak. Not too far from the shack they live in. When he got there he saw a body, a man's body, and ske-daddled home like a jack rabbit and told his daddy."

"Shorty called it in?" Joe asked.

" Yeah. No phone. He had to drive to his neighbor's house. I called Sheriff Cate's office and told them what was reported. It's county, not city, so it's Cate's responsibility. I'm headed to Shorty's in a few minutes with Officer Davis. Cate's office will call the coroner."

"Did he say anything about the body?"

"Only that Shortstuff said it looked like a bird."

"Did Shorty look at the body?"

"No. I asked him. He got testy. Can't blame him. Most people treat him and Shortstuff like shit. He said something like, 'Goddammit, I knows you think Shortstuff's ain't got no sense. But he know the dif'ence 'tween a dead man and a live man. You gonna come out here or not?' We gotta check it out, Joe. Wanna go?"

"Yeah," Joe said, fearing the worst. "Will you call Archie Hamilton? He'll want to join us."

"Okay. He probably knows where Shorty lives. He won't have to drive far."

"Thanks. And Raymond, I'm bring Sam Rucker. The colored guy who works for me."

Raymond paused. "Well, okay. I hope it doesn't bother Shorty."

"Wait for me. I'll be there soon."

He called Hank, who answered on the first ring.

"It's Joe, Hank. Change of plans. Chief Chapman called. Body's been found near Shoal Creek. I'll pick up Sam in a few minutes."

"What happened—"

"Sorry, Hank. Can't talk now."

JOE AND SAM FOLLOWED CHAPMAN'S POLICE CAR to Shorty's shack. It was small, no more than three rooms, tin roof in bad shape, tar paper siding. When they got out of the car, a noxious stench hung in the air. Sam motioned toward the outhouse. Archie stood, holding his nose, in front of the shack with two men.

"Mornin' Shorty, Shortstuff, Archie," Raymond said. "This here's Joe McGrath and Officer Jeff Davis," and pointing at Sam, he added, "and Sam. Shorty, how's the missus?"

Shorty looked hard at Raymond. "She done passed away couple months ago."

"Oh, goddamn it. I'm so sorry. I didn't know."

"Most folks don't," Shorty said. Nodding at Sam, he added, "What's he doin' here?"

"Sam works for Joe. He'll tag along and see what we got. Sheriff Cate and the coroner are on the way. Shortstuff, can you lead us to the body?"

Shortstuff stepped forward, grinning broadly like a star pupil. It saddened Joe to look at the father and son. A number of Shortstuff's teeth were missing, and the ones left were dark and rotten. Shorty's mouth was clinched so tightly that Joe couldn't see his teeth. Both wore patched and frayed coveralls. Despite their age difference, they looked alike: rail thin with matted graying hair. Shorty appeared to be a beaten man. Shortstuff smiled constantly.

"Sho, Mistah Po-lice Man. Y'all follows me. I knows the way," Shortstuff said, sounding like a child.

The men followed Shortstuff, who was grinning and rambling on constantly. The others listened, saying little.

After ten minutes, Shortstuff stopped. "It be after them bushes and trees. This here fishing hole hard to find. It's my hole."

Shortstuff pushed the bushes and tree limbs covered in kudzu out of the way as they struggled through the foliage. He stepped aside when it cleared. The creek flowed languidly by as the early morning sun cast a golden hue on the treetops.

The six men and man-child looked at a scene they would never forget.

A tall water oak tree stood next to the creek. Inexplicably, it had been spared the kudzu vine. A man's body hung from one of the tree's upper limbs. The man's arms had been draped over and tied to a wooden rod, and his feet were tied together: a grotesque depiction of Christ's crucifixion.

Joe and Sam stared at Brendan, as a soft breeze blew his body back and forth ever so gently in the morning light.

CHAPTER 43

THE SADDEST DAY

WEDNESDAY—MARCH 10, 1948

T HE MEN STOOD FROZEN, staring at the awful tableau. Shortstuff, still grinning, blurted out, "See, don't he look like a bird? It's what I tell my Papa."

When Archie took a step toward the body, Raymond said, "Stop, Archie. Whaddaya think you're doin'?"

"I wanna get the body down. Can't let him dangle up there. The rope is tied to a low branch I can reach. I'll untie it and lower him to the ground."

"Get back. Everyone stay put. This is a crime scene."

Archie, looking hard at Raymond, stepped back.

"We've got work to do before we lower him," Raymond said. "Gotta wait for the coroner. Jeff, did you bring enough tape to enclose the perimeter?"

"Yes, sir. Looks like an ellipse. Maybe one hundred feet around. Did y'all know it's tough to calculate the exact circumference of an ellipse?"

Raymond looked at Jeff as if he were an idiot. "For Christ's sake, Jeff, tape the fuckin' place. Everybody stay behind the tape."

Raymond inhaled deeply, attempting to calm down. He knew he had to take control of the situation. As Jeff taped off the area, Raymond said to the others, "Watch your step. Somebody walked in and outta here. Might be footprints in the clearing or in the brush or along the path."

"Chief Chandler," Sam said. "As we walked here from Mr. Shorty's house, I looked for footprints. I didn't see any except for the ones Mr. Shortstuff made earlier."

Raymond glared at Sam. "How the hell you know the earlier prints were Shortstuff's?"

"When Mr. Shortstuff led us, I looked at one of his fresh footprints. As we continued, I looked ahead and the only footprints I saw matched his."

"So Shortstuff's the murderer?" Raymond said derisively.

"No, sir," Sam answered, ignoring Raymond's sarcasm. "From what I can see, the only footprints in the taped off area are the ones Mr. Archie made."

Jeff, who had nearly finished taping the perimeter, called out, "I heard what Sam said. He's right. Haven't seen any footprints."

"Well, now I got a footprint expert to go with my math expert," Raymond said. He started to say something else to Sam when he saw that Jeff had finished. "Jeff, go back to the car and call headquarters and make sure the sheriff and the coroner are comin'. If you can't get through on the car radio, find a house close by with a phone and make the call." Looking at Shorty, he asked, "Anyway to drive a vehicle in here?"

"Sho. Back up yonder at the house, look for a dirt road 'bout, oh I reckon twenty foot to the left of where y'all parked. It ain't a good road, covered with weeds and shit, but it oughta get you down to the creek not too fer from here. What the hell, Shortstuff, you go with the po-liceman and show him."

Shortstuff looked pleased to help. "Yes, Papa."

JOE WAS HAVING A HARD TIME thinking straight. He had recognized Brendan as soon as he saw the body. He had choked back vomit, something he hadn't experienced as a cop. His head felt like a time bomb about ready to explode. Even so, he had filtered out some of what Raymond said and was glad to hear he was taking charge.

His self-imposed stupor continued until his mind focused on one question: *Who the fuck did this? I'll kill bastard.* At the same moment both Jeff and Shortstuff inadvertently bumped into him as they turned to go back to Shorty's house.

"Sorry," Jeff said, following Shortstuff.

Joe stepped closer to the others and said, "Raymond, you're doing a good job."

"What I'm paid to do. I'm sorry about Brendan." Motioning at the tree, Raymond asked, "It is Brendan, isn't it?"

"Yes."

"Don't worry, we'll find the assholes who did this."

Joe wanted to say he was worried, but said, "Thanks, Raymond. Any idea how many might be involved?"

"Not sure. Probably more than a couple. It would've taken several guys to handle him the way they did, but there aren't any footprints visible from here."

Joe had failed to do his usual quick visual inspection of a crime scene. He scanned the area. "You're right."

"Yep. I know it ain't easy," Raymond said and then called out to the group, "Y'all try to relax. We're on hold until the sheriff and the coroner get here."

THE MEN TALKED IN HUSHED TONES AS IF AFRAID they'd disturb Brendan. After twenty minutes that seemed interminable, they heard voices and brush being pushed back. "This here way y'all."

They recognized Shortstuff's voice.

CHAPTER 44

THE CORONER

WEDNESDAY—MARCH 10, 1948

Shortstuff came out of the brush followed by Jeff, Sheriff Cate, and the coroner. His two assistants carried a body bag and two satchels.

"Hey, Harold. Hi, Merlin," Raymond said, sounding relieved. "Glad y'all got here. We need your help."

"So I see," Sheriff Harold Cate said, staring at Brendan's body swinging gently back and forth. "Whaddaya know so far?"

Raymond explained what had happened and how they found the body.

"Mornin', Joe. Well, Archie, didn't think you'd be here," Cate said, ignoring Shorty.

"I'm a friend of Joe and Brendan's," Archie said, pointing at Brendan's body.

"Who's the colored boy?" Cate asked.

"My name's Sam Rucker, Sheriff."

Cate snapped. "I wasn't talkin' to you, boy."

Sam stiffened but said nothing. Joe spoke up, "Sam works for me, Harold."

"How nice. You know our coroner?"

"No."

"This is Merlin Ansley. Merlin, Joe's a private investigator in Birmingham. Before that he was a homicide detective with BPD."

The men nodded. Joe had finally met a coroner who looked like one. Unlike his buddy, Frank Cutler, Ansley was tall and thin, his face smooth and white as an autopsy body. Joe put him at fiftyish.

"Work to do, gentlemen," Ansley said. He looked carefully at the crime scene and added, "Damn, Raymond, it doesn't look like anyone's been here. Just a few footprints right in front of us."

"That's right, Merlin. Ground's smooth as a billiard table. Whoever hung him musta swept the area."

"Maybe we'll find clues on the body or the clothing," Merlin said. "Harold, you and Raymond follow me. We'll take a few photos, then lower him. Have a couple of guys look around the area carefully. Maybe they'll spot a footprint we can't see or something else. Joe'll know what to do."

"Yeah, and Archie can help," Raymond said, adding as an afterthought, "Oh, Sam can help too. He's good at spotting footprints. You three fan out and take a look."

"Sam, you take the left side," Joe said, glad to be busy. "Archie, the middle. I'll do the right."

Joe studied the ground well to the right of the others and noticed a small, shiny object in the dirt. Everyone was preoccupied. He picked it up. It was a silver-colored necklace holding a small medallion. He put it in his pocket.

"Billy, untie the rope and lower the body," Ansley said. "When his feet hit the ground, we'll grab both ends of the stick holding his arms and lay him down."

Joe called Sam and Archie back together. "Find anything? Any footprints? I didn't."

They shook their heads. "The guys who did this knew what they were doing," Sam said. "All of the ground's been raked with a broom or clumps of branches. You can see sweep marks in places."

Joe was standing well back from the body when he saw Ansley looking at a piece of paper pinned to Brendan's jacket.

"Raymond, Harold, take a look at this," Ansley said.

The men kneeled and studied the paper. Raymond turned, looking for Joe. "Hey Joe, c'mon over here and read this."

He got his first good look at Brendan's head, the only visible part of his body. It was bruised in several places. Dry blood and saliva were evident over parts of his face and near the mouth. He knelt down and read the piece of paper: *mcgrath this here you last warnin. you and that black basterd rucker git outta town or you gonna be next.*

He recognized the handwriting. It was identical to the note tied to the brick thrown through his mother's window.

"Heart-warming note," Joe said, writing the message in his notepad. "What else can I do to help?"

"Just move aside," Ansley said. "I got more work to do. Billy, before we untie the arms and feet, I'd like to try and get a few photos looking down on the body. What about climbing up the tree a little bit?"

Billy looked at the oak tree with trepidation when Sam said, "Mr. Coroner, I can lift your photographer up high enough to get photos."

"Might work. Billy?"

Billy looked at Sam and the tree and said, "Let's try it." He wasn't a huge man, but at 150 to 160 pounds, he was no bantamweight.

Sam moved within a few feet of the body. "Mr. Billy, you stand here." Sam pointed at a spot in front of him. "Stand straight and rigid. I'm gonna squat down, put my hands on your hips, and lift you up as high as I can. You ready?"

"I reckon."

Sam lifted Billy and held him motionless at arms' length above his head for well over a minute. The only movement was Billy operating the camera as he took several pictures.

"Got your pictures, Mr. Billy?" Sam asked.

"Yeah."

"Ready to come down?" Sam asked, his body showing no strain to the effort he had made.

"Yes," Billy said, adding, "Are you okay?"

"I'm doing fine, Mr. Billy." Sam lowered him slowly, squatting a bit as he put him gently on the ground.

The men stared at Sam, realizing they had witnessed a remarkable feat of strength.

Even Sheriff Cate was impressed. "Hey Sam, if Joe don't treat you right, come see me. I sure as hell can put you to work."

Sam nodded at the sheriff.

"Good work, Billy," Ansley said. "Let's take a look at the body."

Joe wanted to scream. *The body's not a body. That's Brendan O'Connor, a fine young man.*

Ansley removed the noose. His assistants untied the arms and feet, and bagged the ropes for further analysis. Ansley then motioned the two men to stand back. He unbuttoned the shirt and opened it to see the upper torso of the body. He examined the neck and felt down the back and spine as best he could from this position. He unbuckled the belt, lowered the pants, and inspected the lower torso and buttocks. He looked under the fingernails for evidence of a struggle. Finally, he measured the body's temperature.

Looking at his assistants, he said, "Okay boys, bag the body and carry it back to the van. It's a tough carry through the brush. Try not to mishandle it. I'll be right along." Turning to the others, he said, "Mr. O'Connor died of strangulation as a result of being hung by his neck. Based on his body temperature and the level of rigor mortis, he died early to midafternoon yesterday. The final examination and autopsy will give us a more precise time. Appears to be blood under the fingernails. Perhaps there was a struggle. Who can make a positive identification of the victim?"

"It's Brendan O'Connor," Joe said. "I knew him well. We worked together. Archie and Sam can also provide identification."

Archie and Sam spoke in near unison. "It's Brendan O'Connor."

"That's sufficient for now," Ansley said, "but I will need the next of kin to make the final identification before the body can be released from my custody. Who can contact the next of kin?"

"I can, sir," Joe said. "I've met his parents. They live in Mobile. I'd like to notify them. Okay?"

"Fine by me," Ansley said. "Sheriff?"

Cate nodded.

No one said anything. Most stood staring at their feet, harboring their own thoughts.

Ansley picked up his two satchels, preparing to leave, when he said, "Goddamn it, we haven't had a lynching in the county for years. Now look what someone has done to this white man. Neither his neck nor spine was broken. He dangled in the air for ten to twenty minutes until he could no longer breath." He left the scene without another word.

"Okay, we can go too," Cate said.

"Harold, I'm gonna leave Jeff here," Raymond said. "I'll send a couple guys out here with equipment to sift though the dirt. They might find something. Okay with you?"

"Yeah, good idea."

"Jeff, you guys also search the brush and trees leading in and out of here. Maybe you'll find something on the ground or a piece of fabric on a limb. When you're satisfied you've covered the area, remove the tape and come back to headquarters."

"Yes, sir. Can you have the guys bring water and something to eat?"

"Will do," Raymond said. "I'll call when I get back to the car."

Back at Shorty's, Joe said to Archie and Sam, "Can you come to Mom's house so we can talk privately?"

"I've got a few things to do at the farm," Archie said, getting into his pickup. "I'll be over in a couple of hours. Can Sam go with you?"

"Sure," Joe said. "Why don't you drive, Sam? I can't . . . I just can't."

As they drove toward town, Joe felt numb. Tears spilled from his eyes. He glanced at Sam, who stared straight ahead as if focused only on driving, yet Joe could see his moist eyes as he blinked.

Joe kept weeping, realizing how much he depended on his partner.

CHAPTER 45

THE CALL

WEDNESDAY—MARCH 10, 1948

JOE HELD HIS MOTHER, consoling her at the news of Brendan's death. She pushed free, took a deep breath, and said, "I couldn't go to school today waiting to hear what happened. I need to lie down." She went upstairs.

Sam was in the kitchen scrambling eggs and making coffee. Joe called to him, "Sam, I'll be in the study. I'm going to call Sally and then Brendan's parents."

"Okay."

Joe picked up the phone, paused to rub his eyes, and dialed the operator.

"McGrath Detective Agency. Sally Bowers speaking."

"Sally. Joe. I've got terrible news. Brendan was murdered."

"Oh, Joe . . . how awful . . . I . . ."

"It was my fault. But right now I have to call his parents. I hope you have their phone number in his file."

"Of course. Just a second," she said. "Here it is: AZalea 2131. Their first names are Patricia and Brian."

"Got it. I met them when they visited Brendan. This is going to be hard."

"I know."

"I'll call you later."

"Don't worry. The office is fine. Young Dave Williams is working out well."

"That's good. Sally?" He didn't want to hang up. "Never mind . . ."

"Joe, awful things happen every day. I know you don't want to make the call, but you'll find the words."

"Thanks."

He set the phone down and paused, hating this aspect of his work. He had made many calls like this as a cop, but he had never imagined having to make one quite like this. He slapped his head. *Do it, McGrath.* He called the operator again.

"Hello," a woman's voice said. "Joe?"

"Yes, Mrs. O'Connor. It's Joe McGrath."

"Nice to hear from you, Joe. Brendan called me a couple of days ago and told me he was happy to be back working with you. He admires you so. He said private detective work is much more exciting than police work," she said, laughing. "You know how young men are. Are you in Montevallo? He said you two were going there."

"Yes, ma'am. I'm calling you from Montevallo. It's my hometown." Joe paused, steeling himself to continue. "I'm sorry, but I have bad news."

"Is something wrong with Brendan?"

Joe heard the anxiety in her voice. "Yes, ma'am. He's . . . He's . . . dead."

"No, that can't be," she said, her voice unsteady.

"I'm sorry, Mrs. O'Connor."

Joe heard a muffled conversation, and then a man exclaimed, "What?"

"Joe. Brian O'Connor. This is a bad mistake, right?" he said, angrily.

"No, Mr. O'Connor, I wish it were. I'm so sorry," Joe said, realizing how weak and useless his apology sounded.

"Brendan told us several times," Mr. O'Connor said quietly, "we might get a call like this. But I can't . . ."

There was a long pause. "Mr. O'Connor?" Joe asked.

"When? How?"

"Yesterday. We were working on a case together. He was kidnapped and murdered," Joe said, hoping Mr. O'Connor wouldn't push him on how Brendan died.

"How did he die?"

Joe didn't want to tell him the gruesome details of Brendan's death, at least not right now. "We're waiting for the final autopsy report."

Joe heard a bang. "Are you all right, Mr. O'Connor?"

"Of course not," he said, almost screaming, and then a bit more subdued, he added, "I hit my head against the wall."

"I'm sorry, Mr. O'Connor. This is the hardest phone call I've ever had to make."

"Yes," he said quietly. "When can we see him?"

"He's with the coroner in Columbiana," Joe said. "An autopsy is required under state law in a murder. Before the coroner will release him to your custody, you will have to identify him. That's also required by law."

"I'll get our daughter to stay with Patricia. She's too fragile to make a trip like this. I'll leave for Montevallo soon. I think I can be there in about four hours," Mr. O'Connor said, sounding determined.

"Are you sure you can drive alone? Is there someone who could come with you? Or I can be there in four hours and bring you back here."

"I'll be there soon."

"Yes, sir. Let me give you my address and phone number in Montevallo. It's my mother's home."

After Joe gave him the information, Mr. O'Connor said in a stoic, mechanical monotone as if detached from the news, "I'll see you soon."

"Thank you, sir." Joe said, feeling empty. "Drive carefully."

JOE AND SAM ATE THE EGGS AND TOAST Sam had cooked. Joe was telling him about his conversation with the O'Connors when the front doorbell rang.

"I'll get it," Joe said as he went to answer the door. "Hey, Archie. We're in the dining room. Want some coffee?"

"Sure. Hey, Sam."

"Hi," Sam said.

Elizabeth called out from upstairs. "Joe, who's at the door?"

"It's Archie, Mom."

"Oh, I'll be right down."

Elizabeth came into the room and the men stood. She smiled weakly. "Sit down, please. No school for me today. I'll have coffee too."

Joe got the coffee and told them that Mr. O'Connor was on his way to Montevallo. He added, "I also called Harold and Raymond and told them. Harold said he'd call Mr. Ansley and find out when the viewing could be done."

"Christ, Joe, must have been a tough call." Archie said.

Joe felt completely exhausted, as if he hadn't slept for several days. "The hardest. I often made calls like this in homicide, but never . . . never anything like this."

Joe's head sagged. He rubbed his chin lost in thought, then raised his head and looked around the room as if possessed. He jumped to his feet. "Goddammit, if they want war, then war they'll get. We'll go for the Pidds, then Adam, then—" He stopped abruptly and stood quietly.

He had stunned the room, but Sam said evenly, "I'm ready, Joe. But first, we have to honor Brendan and his parents."

Joe slumped into his chair. "You're right, and we will. But I mean what I said. War! These fuckers deserve no less." Smiling wanly, he added, "Sorry, Mom."

She nodded and smiled at him.

"I'm ready, Joe," Archie said. "How should we handle Brendan's body when the coroner releases it?"

Joe said nothing.

Sam spoke up. "Mr. and Mrs. O'Connor need help. I can accompany the body on the train to Mobile. Archie will need to talk to the railroad folks to make sure a colored person can ride with a coffin. Joe, you drive Mr. O'Connor back to Mobile in his car. Both of us can help with the final arrangements and funeral in Mobile. Then we can ride the train back to Montevallo and get on with the business at hand."

"Sounds like a good plan," Archie said. "Joe?"

He noticed the concern on their faces. "I'm okay. I really am. And thanks, Sam, it's a good plan." A devious grin crossed Joe's face. "We can work on our war plans on the ride back. I've got some ideas."

The phone rang. "I'll get it in the study," Joe said.

"Joe McGrath here."

"It's Raymond. Harold asked me to call you. Ansley says he'll be through with the autopsy by one o'clock. Mr. O'Connor can view the body any time after that."

"Thanks, Raymond. When Mr. O'Connor gets here, we'll go to the morgue. Can we go late if necessary? I'm sure he'll want to see his son, whatever time he gets here."

"We've already put Ansley on notice. We'll find whoever did this. As you said, Joe, Brendan was one of us."

Joe hung up the phone quietly. *I sure as hell hope Raymond means what he says.*

CHAPTER 46

MOBILE

THURSDAY—MARCH 11, 1948

T HURSDAY MORNING'S BRIGHT, SUNNY SKY belied Sam and Archie's mood as they lifted Brendan's coffin onto the Montevallo station's loading platform. The Southern Railway 10:42 a.m. train was due any minute on its way to Mobile with stops in Selma and a few other towns. Archie had made the arrangements for Sam to accompany the coffin. The stationmaster had even written a letter authorizing Sam to be on the train with the coffin in case people questioned him. Elizabeth, who decided to cover her classes today, had fixed Sam a sack lunch for the trip.

"Brian, you doing okay?" Joe asked, honoring his request to call him by his first name.

"Yes."

When the train pulled into the station, they watched the coffin being loaded into the baggage car. Sam joined the coffin, and they said goodbye and wished him well.

Brian stepped forward and added, "Sam, thank you for doing this for my son and our family."

"Brendan was my good friend too," Sam said. "I'm proud to do this. See y'all in Mobile. Too bad I'm too late for Mardi Gras."

Even Brian smiled at Sam's Mardi Gras comment as they walked back to their cars. Brian had called a Mobile mortuary early that morning. The mortuary would take the body and complete the preparations for the funeral. Joe and Brian headed for Mobile, wanting to arrive before the train.

As Joe drove out of Montevallo, he gazed briefly at Brian, amazed at the similarity between father and son. Though about twenty-five years older, Brian had Brendan's youthful look with a few wrinkles, a ruddy complexion with faded freckles, and reddish, graying hair. They chatted briefly, but then quietly melded into the thumping rhythm of the tires and highway communicating with one another.

Joe couldn't help thinking about yesterday. Brian had arrived in Montevallo at four twenty in the afternoon. Joe immediately drove him to the morgue in Columbiana. Ansley and his assistant were ready for them, but nothing could prepare a parent for such a moment. Joe stood behind Brian when Ansley removed the sheet, revealing Brendan's face. Brian's knees buckled at the sight. Joe put his hands to Brian sides, but he righted himself. When Ansley asked him if he could identify the body, he could barely utter, "That's my son, Brendan." After the viewing, they went to Elizabeth's house for the night. She had put Brendan's belongings into a suitcase for Brian, and cleaned the guest room and changed the sheets. No one mentioned that Brendan had recently slept in the bed.

Joe and Brian stopped once to get gas, use the bathroom, and eat Elizabeth's sandwiches. They got to the Mobile train station before the train arrived and watched the mortuary load the coffin into the hearse. Sam joined them for the drive to Brian's house.

"Trip go okay?" Joe asked.

"Just fine. A couple of crackers in Thomasville gave me a hard time. But the letter and—what did you call it, Joe, oh yeah—friendly persuasion solved the problem. I couldn't use the whites-only toilet. I had to get off a couple of times at stops and take a leak, usually between the baggage car and the next car behind the coupling so I could get back on in a hurry. A normal day at the office," Sam said with a grimace.

"I called Patricia," Brian said, "The Vigil for the Deceased, our Irish wake, is at the funeral home at six. Then family and friends will gather at our house to continue the wake. We want you two to join us."

"You have too much to deal with besides us," Joe said.

"We insist. You and Sam have been so kind and helpful," Brian said softly but with determination. "Brendan thought highly of both of you. I know he'd want you there."

"Thank you," Joe said. "Has the funeral service been planned?"

"Yes. Requiem Mass is tomorrow at ten o'clock at the Cathedral-Basilica of the Immaculate Conception followed by the graveside service. It should be over around noon."

When they got to Brian's home, they met Patricia and Brendan's sister, Bronagh, who had been staying with her mother since Brian left. After a brief conversation, Joe and Sam excused themselves. They needed to discuss their return plans after the funeral services.

"Joe, after the services tomorrow," Sam said, "I'd like to take the train to New Orleans and see Yolanda. I'll ride the first train back to Birmingham on Monday."

"Sure. The creeps we're after won't run away. I'll take the train to Montevallo tomorrow, drive to Birmingham, and spend the weekend with Diane. I gotta spend time in the office on Monday and see how things are going. We'll go back to Montevallo on Tuesday. Let's call Southern Railway and check on schedules."

The schedules were fine. Sam could catch a train to New Orleans at 3:22 tomorrow afternoon, and Joe could get one to Montevallo at 4:34.

From Joe's perspective, the vigil service was an embarrassment. The family had to endure well intended, but often annoying and lengthy words of condolence from friends, and several boring and self-serving eulogies. Sam suffered the usual indignities of entering through a side door and sat in the back to one side.

Joe was incensed when the priest said, "My brothers and sisters, please join me in prayer as we celebrate this young sinner's passage to God's kingdom." Yet when he glanced at the family, they didn't appear offended, just distraught. Joe admitted to himself he wasn't the best judge of the priesthood or of Catholic services.

After the vigil service, friends and family joined the O'Conners for an Irish wake.

After the guests had several drinks, Patricia and Bronagh and their maid set out heaping platters of fried chicken, mashed potatoes and gravy, turnip greens, biscuits, and key lime pie. But not forgetting their heritage, they also added a heaping platter of corned beef and cabbage. A few eyebrows arose when Patricia took Sam by the arm and led him to the serving table. Everyone tried to keep the conversation light and off the subject on everyone's mind: Brendan's death.

Brendan's older brother, Colm, took control of the wake, which had gotten noisy and jovial. He called out, "Ladies and gentlemen, I hope you have a glass of Jameson Irish Whiskey in hand or any other libation of your choice. Please, join me in a toast to the greatest O'Connor of them all, Brendan."

Colm proved a godsend. "Now, I want to tell you some stories about Brendan and me when we were young lads," he said, in his best southern, Irish accent. "Year round, but especially in the summer, we spent hours in the fields and by the stream near our house. We sat in the shade of trees, fishing poles dangling in the water. It mattered not if we caught a fish. We sat talking about our young lives and aspirations, and the next prank we wanted to play on our parents or Bronagh. I don't know how the poor lass survived our childish misbehavior. I can't tell you all of them. It would shock dear Mom and Pop."

A shout came the back of the room. "Come on, Colm, share some."

"Okay. Here's one about Brendan and me when we were thirteen. It's not funny, but until today, I didn't realize how important it was. We were lying on the bank of the stream on a warm, sunny day. Dappled light filtered though the trees, lulling us to sleep. I don't know for how long. When we awoke, we stretched and yawned and kidded about our nap. Then Brendan said, 'I had a dream, Colm. I was a cop standing at attention in front of a large group of cops. A man walked forward in a well-decorated uniform. The others snapped to attention and saluted, but they were looking straight at me. The man, I suppose the chief, prepared to hang a medallion around my neck when a dark cloud appeared, and I woke up. What do you think the dream meant, Colm?' Brendan asked. I told him I reckoned he wanted to be a cop, but the dark cloud meant it wasn't to be."

Colm paused and added, "This story shall the oldest son tell his father and mother, for on this day, a young lad was raised to manhood and immortality."

The group stood silent, reflecting on the story. Joe looked around to see if anyone seemed to recognize Colm's allusion to the famous speech Shakespeare wrote for Henry V on the eve of the Battle of Agincourt. Some nodded, but he was unsure of their intent.

Colm continued to regale the room with childhood stories about his and Brendan's antics and misconduct.

Even the teariest broke into laughter.

The last guests left at eleven o'clock and the laughter ceased. Joe and Sam and the family drifted off to their bedrooms as the grief-laden shroud regained its grip over the household.

CHAPTER 47

THE MASS AND BURIAL

FRIDAY—MARCH 12, 1948

A S MUCH AS JOE WANTED TO SUPPORT Brendan's family, he had not been looking forward to the religious ceremonies required when a Catholic died. The vigil service had been hard, but at least, the wake at the family's home proved a welcome relief. He had not attended Mass in quite a while, and he remembered with distaste the few funeral services he had attended.

On Friday, there was a large crowd for the Requiem Mass, although it didn't begin to fill the huge church. It was difficult for the family to sit the entire service staring at Brendan's coffin positioned front and center in the church.

Joe experienced his usual level of discomfort in a church, although as the Mass progressed, the rituals offered him a sense of contentment and peace he hadn't felt since Brendan was missing. Sam continued playing the side door game. A young priest met him and escorted him to a seat on the last pew in the church. As the service ended, the priest led him out the door to the front of the church.

The final step in this arduous process was the funeral procession to the cemetery, the Rite of Commitment. Things went reasonably well until Brendan's coffin was lowered into the ground, and the priest intoned the final prayers. Patricia wailed. Other family members cried, along with many of the guests. Finally, Colm stepped forward, picked up a handful of dirt, and threw it on top of his brother's casket. Hesitantly, other family members and friends followed suit.

Sam and Joe stood well back of the crowd, watching these heart-rending moments. Joe looked at Sam and shook his head as if to ask: *Why do they put the family through such an ordeal?* After the service concluded and the crowd dispersed, they went to the mortuary car holding the O'Connor family and said their goodbyes. They begged off going back to the family home where most guests were now headed. Patricia, Brian, and Bronagh got out of the car and gave both men hugs and thanked them.

Joe hailed a taxi for the ride to the train station. The driver balked at taking Sam until Joe offered him an extra five dollars.

After Sam left for New Orleans, Joe boarded the train to Montevallo. He sat alone, still overwhelmed with sorrow and guilt. The only pastime that distracted him on the train was planning the actions necessary to find Brendan's murderers.

Joe arrived in Montevallo before nine, got his car, and drove to his mother's, knowing she'd want to hear about the funeral services. Seeing the house well lit, he was confident she was still up.

Not wanting to burst in and frighten her at night, he called out, "Mom. It's me." He opened the door slowly and repeated, "Mom. It's me."

He heard her voice before he saw her coming toward the door. "Oh, Joe. I'm so glad you're back."

She hugged him, not wanting to let go, as if their embrace might change things. Finally stepping back, she said, "Are you okay? How is Brendan's family? Where's Sam? Are you staying the night? Are you—" Stopping abruptly, looking ashamed, she added, "Listen to me rattling on. Come sit. Would you like a drink?"

"A Coke, please. Then I'll tell you everything."

They sat at the kitchen table. Joe drank the Coke and nibbled on potato chips. He unraveled the events of the last two days, omitting only two things; his negative thoughts and feelings about the services, and the indignities Sam had to endure.

Elizabeth, drooping over in sorrow, holding her head, said. "My goodness, . . . the poor family. How are they doing?"

"I suppose as well as can be expected. They're a close, loving family and have a number of good friends. Time will also be their other friend."

She looked at him somberly, "You're wrong and you know it. Time's only an illusion. It doesn't heal such wounds. It only dulls the senses, and any relief is but ephemeral."

Joe nodded, both obediently and knowingly. "It's not Shakespeare, but it should be. . . . I'm not staying tonight. I want to spend my ephemeral time with Diane, and I have to visit the office. Sam and I will be back next Tuesday. "

"I understand," she said, trying to hide her disappointment. "How will you keep the office going with all that's happened?"

"Not sure. I might ask John Stavos to work with us. He's retired from the police department. He was a patrol sergeant, and we got along well. . . . Excuse me, Mom. I need to call Diane. I haven't called her since Brendan disappeared."

In the study, Joe had decided to say nothing to Diane about Brendan's murder at this time to avoid prolonging the conversation and her anxiety.

"Joe, is that you?"

"Yes, honey. I'm getting ready to leave Mom's house."

"Where have you been? You haven't called for days."

"I know it's a weak excuse, but we've been so busy I just couldn't find time. Is it too late to stop by?"

"Joe McGrath, if you don't, I'll never speak to you again."

"Yes, ma'am. Can't wait to see you. I miss you."

As he drove to Birmingham mulling over the events of the last few days, he realized he hadn't thought about his father's murderers since Brendan's death, when the obvious finally hit him. *Of course, of course, why didn't you see it, McGrath? There has to be a connection.*

CHAPTER 48

THE GREEK

MONDAY—MARCH 15, 1948

T HE WEEKEND WITH DIANE had provided the therapy Joe needed, a relaxing mix of lovemaking, great food, and a movie.

Joe had told her how Brendan died, omitting the gorier details and things like his mistrust of Adam and the medallion. Even though Diane hadn't known Brendan well, she had a hard time understanding how anyone could have murdered him.

Over the years, Joe had learned it was best to keep his work to himself and not talk about cases even after they were closed. It seemed to him that most people did not appreciate the complexities of police work. They wanted the gory details to stimulate their imaginations, and considered everything in black and white terms, racially and otherwise.

JOE LEFT DIANE'S APARTMENT before eight on Monday. He needed to make a quick stop at his apartment to pick up clean clothes and another gun, a Colt Official Police 38. He had purchased it after he left the police department and enjoyed the feel of its heft.

He drove slowly toward the office, the windshield wipers trying to keep up with a heavy rain. The brief spell of good weather had been replaced by a cold, windy wet day. He struggled to see as he negotiated a left turn. After parking the car, he fought to keep the umbrella from collapsing and thought, *Goddamn, beware the Ides of March.*

Sally was sitting at her desk when he walked in, dripping wet.

"Hi, Sally," Joe said simply, shaking off his raincoat. "How are you?"

"Good morning, Joe. Not much better than you, I gather by your look."

"You gather correctly. At least, Diane and I had a nice weekend." Joe raked a hand through his wet hair and looked away. "I mean . . . I . . . I'm sorry, a stupid thing to say."

"I understand," she said, smiling knowingly. "I visited a good friend in Tuscaloosa this weekend. It does help."

"Yes it does. Do you remember John Stavos, a patrol sergeant at BPD who retired a few years ago?" Joe asked.

"Of course, I knew John well. A gentleman and a good policeman. He came on the force a few years after I started."

"He's coming in at eleven. I asked him if he'd like to work with us. He laughed and asked why we would want an old Greek. I told him basically what you said."

Sally looked please. "I think he'd work out well."

"I hope so," Joe said. Concerned, he pursed his lips. "Sam will be in today soon after one o'clock if his train is on time. I want John to meet Sam and Dave. Have to make sure he'd be comfortable working in our unique set-up."

"I'll be surprised if he's not. He's the son of Greek immigrants. Once he told me about the racial bigotry he and his family had to endure."

"Hmmm. Say, I need a cup of coffee. Want one?"

Sally nodded, and Joe went into the pantry and got coffees and two croissants. He put the coffee and pastries on Sally's desk, and sat in the chair beside Sally's desk.

"More about John, Miss Sally?" Joe asked.

"Of course, Mister Detective. He was six years old when he came to Birmingham. After he started school, kids teased him unmercifully about his given name, Yianni. When his parents learned of this, they had his name changed to John. But they refused to change the family name."

"How do you know this?"

"Just like a detective," Sally said, imperiously, "by asking questions. I worked in the patrol section years ago and got to know John well. He was assigned to work patrol in Ensley where many Greeks initially lived and worked his way up to sergeant before he retired. And, unlike so many of our officers, he always seemed to treat everyone fairly."

Joe grinned, enjoying the games Sally played with him. "Thank you, my local historian. Before John gets here, you need to do two things. Lock the Kendall Forrester files in the safe. I don't want John to know about the case. It's too sensitive. Mum's the word."

"I'll put them in the safe. What's the second thing?"

"This is tougher. Go through Brendan's desk and box up his personal belongings. If John joins us, he'll use that desk. Brendan's older brother, Colm, is coming to Birmingham to get his personal possessions. I gave Colm your name and the office number. He said he'd be here this week or next depending on his work schedule."

"I'll get right on it," Sally said.

JOE WAS WAITING FOR JOHN in the conference room when Sally walked in. She handed him a booklet, and said, "This is Brendan's appointment calendar. Read the entry on March thirteenth."

Joe read the entry: 'P/U Rachel at 5 pm, dinner & movie' followed by her address and phone number and a childish drawing of a heart with an arrow through it. He looked at Sally as if pleading for help. "Oh, my God." Joe put the calendar down. "This must be the young lady he told me about last Tuesday. He met her a few weeks ago and had a second date planned with her when we got back from Montevallo."

"Don't you think we should call her? She probably thinks Brendan stood her up."

"Of course, you're right. I'll call . . . I'll—" Joe's head fell in despair.

Sally put her hand on his shoulder. "I'll call her, Joe. You've made enough tough calls."

Joe raised his head, embarrassed and relieved. "Thanks, Sally. I've never felt this way about a murder victim, not even my father. Maybe I did and don't remember. Things have been a blur lately."

"I understand. In our work, murder is the norm. We've been inured to it. But this is different."

"Yeah. I gotta get a grip on myself. John will be here soon."

Joe's respite was short-lived. John entered the front door, and Sally hurried out of the conference room to occupy him and give Joe a little more time.

"Hi, John. Welcome to McGrath Detective Agency."

"Sally, you're part of this deal?" John said, delighted to see her. "If I had known, I'd have signed up immediately. Thought you were still with the department. Haven't seen you since I retired."

"I retired from the department a month ago and joined Joe. I was his secretary in homicide. How are you?" she asked, surprised at the weight he had put on. He was in his late fifties, five eight, with a solid and firm build but for his bulging stomach. His skin was light brown, full head of hair, once jet-black, now graying, and a round face with a pugnacious nose.

"I'm doing fine and even better now seein' you. Where's—"

Joe came into the reception area. "Hi, John. Thanks for coming in. Sally told me you two were friends."

"Friends!" he exclaimed. "Joe, we damn near grew up together in the department."

"You should be right at home here. She takes good care of us. Let's get coffee and go into the conference room. We've got lots to talk about."

JOE EXPLAINED HOW THE DETECTIVE AGENCY came into being and summarized the type of cases they were working on, leaving out the Forrester job. He briefly reviewed the work they were doing in Montevallo. Joe paused and asked, "Did you ever meet a young man named Brendan O'Connor who recently worked with me in the department?"

"Can't say that I have. What'd he do?"

"He was my sidekick our last four months with the department, and then joined me in this office. Young kid. Twenty-six years old. Smart, go-getter. Woulda been a great cop or detective."

"Whaddaya mean, woulda been?"

"He was kidnapped and murdered last week in Montevallo while working with me on my father's murder. Some fuckers didn't like what we were doing and lynched him."

"Jesus Christ! I thought private detective work was pretty straight-forward stuff."

"I guess we did too—cheating spouses, cheating business partners, cheating this and cheating that. I didn't ask you to come here to work with us in Montevallo. We need help in Birmingham with the usual stuff. Say, you want a Coke or more coffee?"

"Coke sounds good. But I need to pee somethin' bad," John said, grinning. "Older man's bladder, you know."

Joe, liking John even more than he remembered, said, "Well, we'll get you a pee pot to use when you're workin' stakeouts. Out the office door, to your right a few doors. It's on the left. I'll get the Cokes."

"WELL, WHADDAYA THINK SO FAR?" Joe asked, taking a sip of his Coke.

"I'm interested. I think I can handle the Birmingham jobs you've got goin'. Need to talk money and time. I may not be able to work around the clock like I did when I was a cop."

"Good. I'm sure we can work out money and time. Gotta ask you another question. Do you know Sam Rucker, the colored private eye with an office in the Ankle?"

John raised an eyebrow, surprised at the question. "Don't know him, but I heard he helped you solve the Yarbo case a few years ago. What's he got to do with this?"

"There's a good café next door. I'll explain over lunch."

CHAPTER 49

SAM AND THE GREEK

MONDAY—MARCH 15, 1948

THE CAFÉ, A POPULAR ONE with business types in this section of downtown, was nearly full. Joe got a table in the back corner.

"Nice joint. Never been here," John said. "Do you ever go to the cops' diner? I go now and then to rub elbows with the blue." Grinning he added, "You know Helen has the hots for you."

Joe played dumb. "Aw, shucks, she kids around with everybody."

A waitress walked over. Good-looking brunette. "Y'all want to order?"

"You bet, Sugar," John said.

She shook her head in disgust. "The sugar's on the table. Y'all gonna eat sugar or order?"

"We'll order," Joe said, suppressing a smile. "It's on me, John."

JOE FINISHED A CHICKEN SALAD SANDWICH and said, "Did you read about the prostitute murder cases I handled last year?"

"Yeah," John said, eating a last bite. "Three murders. The guy who did it killed himself. Rich, white guy named Abernathy."

"Right. Sam Rucker helped us identify the killer. He did stuff in the colored community we couldn't do. Abernathy might still be on the loose but for Sam."

"That's good," John said, sounding unsure of himself.

"Sam and I still work together," Joe said, knowing this is where things might get difficult. "In the private detective racket, you have to scratch for your clients. They don't line up on police rap sheets. Sam and one of his associates, a young man named Dave Williams, work for me part-time. They usually handle the colored cases. Brendan and I handle the white cases . . . shit, or did handle them. But all of us often work together." Joe paused to see what John might say.

Rubbing his neck and turning his head right and left, John said, "An interesting arrangement."

Joe waited to see if he would continue.

"Well, what the hell, coloreds and whites work side-by-side in a lot of places. I know it ain't always fair."

Joe wanted to say, *It's never fair,* but he let it go.

"Damn, what am I saying? It ain't fair," John said, his voice rising. "Joe, didya ever hear how the early Greek immigrants were treated in Birmingham? We—" He stopped, realizing several people in the café were staring at him.

"Sally told me a little bit," Joe said, pleased with the turn in John's comments. "Fill me in."

"Goddamn right I will," John said, lowering his voice. "Us Greeks got a good taste of what coloreds get everyday when we first came to the city. I get treated okay now. So I guess you're asking me if I can work with Sam and Dave."

"They're part of the deal. They work in my office a lot. You gotta be comfortable with them or it doesn't make sense to come on board."

John rubbed his lips, looking sanguine. "Yeah. I think I can work with them. Are they good guys?"

"Yeah. Sam was in New Orleans over the weekend. His train arrives at one fifteen this afternoon. He'll pick up Dave and come over to the office to meet you. There's an office rule you need to know. When Sally and us guys are in the office with no clients, it's first names for everybody. When a client's present, Sam and Dave go with mister, miss, and missus with whites including Sally, you, and me. You okay with everything so far?"

"You bet," John said, shifting in his chair excitedly, as if a little boy waiting for the recess bell. "Goddamn, this is gonna be different."

Joe smiled and then laughed. "Yep. Different it'll be."

Joe and John were talking in the reception area when Sam and Dave arrived at two o'clock. Joe greeted them, noticing John's mouth was agape at the sight of Sam.

Joe shook hands with Dave and said, "Good to see you, Dave."

Dave glanced at John, who looked uncomfortable, and said, "Hi, Joe. I couldn't believe what Sam told me about Brendan. I'm sorry."

Joe nodded and turned to Sam and shook his hand. "Everything go okay in New Orleans?"

Sam smiled impishly. "Couldn't have gone better."

"I want you guys to meet John Stavos. He's retired BPD and may start to work with us. Sam, I'd like you to meet John," Joe said, "John, Sam."

Sam offered John a handshake. There was a momentary hesitation before he took Sam's hand.

"Good to meet you, Officer Stavos," Sam said, "People always said good things about you when you worked the Ankle."

John relaxed. "Thank you. It's John, Sam. You did a good job on the Yarbo case."

"Did my best. John, this is Dave Williams. He graduated from Miles College and works for me now."

John took the initiative and shook hands with Dave. "Glad to meetcha."

"Likewise."

Joe, wondering how the meeting might go, said, "Sam, John and I have talked about our outstanding case load and how the office works. Why don't you three use the conference room to get better acquainted."

"Good idea," Sam said.

Sam led the discussion, telling John about his office in the Ankle and the type of work he did. He had Dave explain his college degree and his interest in detective work.

"What's your background with the BPD, John?" Sam asked.

"Beat cop. Mostly in the Ensley area," he said, smiling. "A lot of Greeks live there. I also worked the Ankle. I know you're a private eye, but have you had police training?"

"Degree in criminology from the University of Chicago. Ten years experience as a private eye."

John, surprised, said, "No shit. Joe's got that degree and a degree in English lit. Chief Watson called him 'The Professor,' but more as an insult than a compliment."

Sam grinned. "Well, I reckon it's better than what he called me."

"You're right about that. Goddamn, Sam, you're okay."

Sam was bemused. Maybe John would work out. "About the nicest thing a white man ever said to me. Whaddaya think? Can we work together?"

"Yeah . . . yeah . . . I think so," John said, nodding vigorously. "This'll be interesting."

"An understatement. Let's go tell the boss we're good to go."

"Okay. Say, did you guys hear what the pimp said to the cop when he was gonna arrest him, adding his record stunk?" John asked.

"Can't say that I have. Have you, Dave?"

He shook his head.

As Sam opened the conference room door, John said, "My record is as clean as my ladies."

JOE HEARD THE LAUGHTER, walked out of his office, and saw the three men grinning. *Goddamn, looks like we got a new detective.*

CHAPTER 50

BACK INTO THE FRAY

TUESDAY—MARCH 16, 1948

"Be good to get my car back. It's still at Hank's," Sam said, on the drive to Montevallo Tuesday morning. "Didn't realize how much I'd miss the damn thing."

"Don't worry. I talked to Archie last night. We're gonna meet him at Hank's at ten o'clock. You'll have your car. We'll talk about goin' after the Pidds. Archie's been doin' some spadework on where their stills are located. Then we'll pay them an unplanned visit."

"I'm gonna enjoy this," Sam said, grinning like a Cheshire cat.

Joe parked at Hank's house and saw Archie's pickup truck in the driveway. Archie greeted them at the door. "Ah, the two wanderers from the big city. What news from the north?"

Sam replied, "We bring tidings of great joy. The world's still fucked up."

"So it is," Archie said, laughing. "C'mon it. Hank's tendin' the kitchen."

Hank was drying a skillet when they walked in. "Hey Sam. Joe. How's it goin'?"

"Fine," Joe said, adding as he shook his head, "until these two would-be philosophers mentioned world affairs."

Hank, looking confused, ignored Joe's lament and asked, "I hope things weren't too tough in Mobile."

"It was. The family's doing as well as can be expected. . . . Let's get down to business. Can we talk in the kitchen?"

"Sure, sit down. I've got coffee," he said, filling the mugs on the table.

"Thanks, Hank. What did you learn about the Pidds and their stills, Archie?" Joe asked.

"They have several but the biggest one's not far from their house in the sticks east of Columbiana," he said. "They work the big one frequently. I've got instructions on how to get there. It's located on an old logging road."

"Christ, if they're so easy to find, why haven't they been busted?" Sam asked.

Archie laughed. "You don't understand south Shelby County yet, do you, Sam? Nobody gives a shit about the Pidds, but no one will fuck with them. Folks know 'the operation' protects them with their money and, if need be, their muscle."

"Goddammit, protection or not, I want to go after the sons of bitches," Joe said, his frustration building. "No matter what, it should smoke 'the operation' out of hiding."

"You can bet it will," Archie said, evenly. "Be prepared for a battle. Those folks protect their interests. That's what the brick and Brendan were about."

Joe felt gut punched by Archie's comment. "Anyone want out?"

No one spoke.

"Good," Joe said. "How soon can we visit the twins, Archie?"

"Tonight," he said, stomping his foot as if squashing a pest. "I'm sure the boys can't wait to see us. I'm told they usually work the big still midweek. We go to their house first. If they're not there, we head out to the still. If they're home, we take them with us. Dealing with them at their place of business seems appropriate."

"What time?"

"Meet here at nine. Guys work stills late into the night. Okay, Hank?"

"Sure."

Sam drummed his fingers on the table. Joe knew he was agitated.

"Got a suggestion," Sam said in a brooding tone. "No matter what, there's gonna be plenty of angry whites eager to string up the two darkies who were involved. After it's over, Joe and I will hustle back to Birmingham, and Archie will return to Valhalla." Sam smiled at Archie. "But Hank, you gotta continue living here. You should stay in the background."

Hank glowered at Sam. "I'm not big like you, but I can take care of myself."

"It has nothing to do with size," Sam said. "It's the Klan, 'the operation,' and other white lunatics out there. You got too much to lose."

"Sam's right, Hank," Joe said. "You're one of my best friends. We'd do anything for each other. But it's more than just you and me. You gotta think about your family and business and friends."

"They're right, Hank," Archie added.

Hank looked forlorn. "Okay," he said, despondently. "But I still wanna help."

"You bet you will." Joe said, feeling the conversation was getting out of hand.

"Just to be safe, we won't meet at Hank's house tonight," Archie said, and nodding at Joe and Sam, he added, "We can meet at your mother's house, Joe. I'll pick up Sam at eight forty-five."

Hank stared at the floor and said nothing.

"No," Joe said, realizing they had gone too far. "Sam stays with Hank. I'm going to my mother's house. I'll see y'all at nine."

JOE WAS FIXING A GRILLED CHEESE SANDWICH when the phone rang in his mother's study. He turned off the burner and went to answer the phone.

"Hello, Joe McGrath here."

"Hi, Joe. It's Susan Kelly."

"Susan, what a surprise. How are you?"

"Fine, thank you. . . . I have some information. I'm almost ashamed to share it with you."

"Why? Is it personal?" Joe asked.

"Well, sort of, I guess. I happened to overhear part of a telephone conversation Mr. Teague was having a few minutes ago. No, that's not true. I listened on purpose. I approached his office to give him a file.

He was bent over talking on the phone. I stepped to the side of the door and listened." She paused.

"Yes?"

"Mr. Teague said, 'I'm not shitting you, Robert.' And then he used a word I didn't understand: ark. A big boat, I guess. Anyway, he said, 'Damian's called an ark meeting tomorrow at ten a.m. at the junkyard. We'd meet sooner, but Damian's not available until then. It's important. Don't be late.' Not wanting to be caught listening, I went back to my desk. Does any of it make sense?"

"Yes. Think anyone suspects you were listening?"

"No, I don't think so."

"Good. I'm really busy right now. When things calm down, I'd like to have lunch or dinner with you. Interested?"

"Yes, I'd enjoy that."

"Thanks, Susan. Goodbye."

Joe put his feet on his mother's desk and leaned back. *I'll be goddamned. The junkyard, Adam's house. Seems we have an early morning appointment with ARC.*

CHAPTER 51

DAMIAN WALLACE

TUESDAY—MARCH 16, 1948

LIZABETH READ THE PAPER CAREFULLY, making corrections to the text and adding comments in the margins. She was using the late afternoon hours in her college office grading essays and tests, when she sensed something and looked up. Damian Wallace stood in the doorframe, studying her. She wasn't sure why, but it was unsettling.

A short man, no more than five feet six inches, in his forties, a noticeable middle age spread forming around his midsection. A full head of blond hair framed a face that seldom smiled, as if he were perpetually annoyed. His dress said college professor: brown shoes, tan wool slacks, an off-white shirt, and a tweed jacket with leather elbow patches. Sartorially, he topped off his dress by wearing brightly colored bow ties. Bright red today.

"Hello, Damian. Have you been standing there long?" Elizabeth asked.

"No," he said. "May I come in?"

"Of course. You know I have an open-door policy." She knew most faculty members kept their doors closed, including Damian.

Walking in, he closed the door. "Thank you. How's your semester going, Elizabeth?"

She studied him for a moment. Clearly, this wasn't a casual visit. "Fine. Full classes with bright and engaging young ladies. I trust you're having a similar experience."

"Things are going okay. It does get to be a bore at times. Some students aren't engaged. It seems young ladies prefer English lit to history." He tried to smile, but it appeared as if he had bitten a lemon. "Perhaps I should borrow the murder, mayhem, comedy, and sex in your Shakespeare plays to liven things up."

"Be my guest, but word of warning," she said, laughing easily. "It doesn't always work. I've had my share of disinterested students."

"Duly noted. How's your son doing? I hear he's been spending time in Montevallo looking into your husband's murder. That sounds futile since it happened so long ago."

"He's doing fine. Why the interest?"

"I'm concerned. I heard someone killed his young colleague. Aren't you worried that might happen to Joe or the darkie who's working with him?"

"Of course, I'm worried. Where did you hear about it?"

He laughed, although it sounded more like a hacking cough. "You know how things get around this small town and college. Everybody's talking. I have another question."

"Yes?"

"Are you asking around about something called A – R – C?"

"Why do you ask? Do you know what it means?"

"Clever. Answer a question with a question. No, I don't know. But several faculty members told me you asked them. Besides you, who wants to know?"

"None of your goddamn business, Damian."

"My, my, the language you use. I don't think the dean of your department would be impressed. Tell your son and whoever else has been asking about A – R – C to forget it," he said in a harsh, tight voice.

"Are you threatening us?"

"No. Quite the contrary, I'm giving you advice as a friend. I'm concerned for both of you. Who knows what could happen if you ignore it."

"Socratically speaking, Damian, since we are not friends, it follows your advice is incorrect and not applicable to Joe or me."

"As you will." Walking out, he turned. "Shall I leave the door open?"

She got up, slammed the door in his face, and took several deep breaths.

Feeling calmer, she placed the essays in a folder, left the unfinished ones for later, and went home, hoping Joe would be there.

JOE WAS SITTING IN THE LIVING ROOM reading the newspaper when he heard the front door open. "Mom, is that you?"

"Yes," she said, putting her briefcase on an empty chair. "How is Brendan's family? I feel so sorry for them."

He stood and hugged her. "As well as can be expected. His older brother, Colm, was a blessing. At the wake, he took control and alternatively had everyone in stitches and in tears with childhood stories. Are you okay?"

"I was until an hour ago," she said, sitting on the sofa and patting the cushion. "Come. Sit next to me. I need to tell you about a conversation I had with Damian Wallace. He's Geoffrey Wallace's son and like his father, teaches history at the college. You knew that, didn't you?"

"Yes. Archie told me that Geoffrey was to have been the hostile witness Dad wanted to call at the trial. Archie said he didn't think Damian was involved in this mess." Joe didn't mention what Susan had told him about Damian.

"Archie's wrong. I always considered Damian an odd duck," she said. "I know that sounds catty, but we have several male professors at the college like Damian. Anyway, he came into my office. Initially, the conversation was chatty stuff. School and classes." Elizabeth explained in detail the ensuing conversation, emphasizing the threats.

Joe massaged his forehead until she finished. "Unfortunately, it makes sense. Dad and Brendan's murders are likely connected. Now we have a link: the Wallaces."

"Geoffrey, Damian, Adam. Where does this end, Joe?"

"I don't know. But tonight, Sam, Archie, and I are going to make a call on the Pidd twins and try to fill in the missing links."

"How many more people do you think are involved?"

"No idea, but I'm sure there're more. And Mom, stop asking around about A – R – C. I don't want you taking any more risks, and I want Damian to think you're heeding his warning."

"Makes sense. What time are you going out tonight?"

"Nine."

"Promise me you'll be careful."

"Yes, ma'am."

"Good. I'll fix supper. I can't let you leave the house on an empty stomach."

"Thank you," Joe said. He paused and added, "Mom, be careful."

CHAPTER 52

PIDDVILE

TUESDAY—MARCH 16, 1948

J OE GOT TO HANK'S AT EIGHT FORTY-FIVE. A large truck was parked at the curb. Archie answered the door. "Hi, Archie. Your truck?" Joe asked, motioning toward the street.

"Yep. How do you like it? We can use it tonight."

"Pretty big, isn't it?"

"Sure 'nuff. This two-ton baby is the farm's workhorse, 1946 Chevy ten-wheeler. We haul all kinda stuff with it: crops, hay bales, supplies. If'n we take the sides off, it's a bobtail and can haul lumber and trees when we're clearin' land. Loggin' roads are rough and uneven, and this baby's got more clearance than a car. Three of us will be cozy in the cab.

"What if we have to haul the Pidds around?' Joe asked.

"We'll put the fuckers on the bed and tie 'em down."

"What fuckers you gonna tie on the bed of the truck?" Sam asked, as he and Hank came into the living room. Smiling, Sam added, "You best not be talkin' about my black ass."

Archie looked at Joe and said, "Well, I reckon we gotta abandon that plan. We were talking about the Pidds, Sam," he added, grinning.

"Glad to hear it," Sam said. "We ready to go?"

"First things first. Damian Wallace is a member of ARC and so is Adam. ARC's meeting at Adam's house tomorrow morning at ten," Joe said, describing in detail the conversation Susan overheard. "There's more," he added, explaining Damian's talk with his mother.

Archie let out a long, shrill whistle. "Sounds like we're gonna be busy boys."

"Yep," Joe said, satisfied pieces of the puzzle were falling into place. "Let's get to it with the Pidds. Then we'll plan what to do about the ARC meeting."

"Okay," Sam said. "But tonight, let's tie and lock up the Pidds somewhere safe, or they'll likely run off to one of the ARC boys and spill the beans."

"Agreed. Are we ready?" Joe asked.

"Yeah, once I put flashlights in Archie's truck," Hank said.

They went out to the truck. Hank climbed onto the bed with the flashlights, almost stumbling over a sledgehammer and a coil of rope. "Hey, Archie, what's with the rope and hammer?"

Archie smiled devilishly. "Thought we might need a little induce-ment to get the Pidds to cooperate."

"Fuckin' great. Can't wait. Everybody got their fire power?" Joe asked, pulling his jacket back showing his gun in the shoulder holster.

Sam gave them a look at his gun in a belt holster.

Archie pulled a four-barrel sawed-off shotgun from behind the truck's seat. "Never used it in anger, but it'll do big time damage."

"Okay, We're loaded," Joe said, eager to go. "Don't worry, Hank, we won't keep Sam out too long."

"I'll have eats and coffee waiting for you," Hank said, smiling. "Or maybe you'll bring back some white lightnin'." He paused, blinking. "Be careful."

"We will,' Joe said. He knew Hank was trying to act casual and supportive, but was hurting inside. Joe wanted to reply to him but decided it best not to. He jumped in the middle of the truck's cab and said, "Let's go."

Archie drove. The night was pleasant with a waning moon waft-ing among the clouds. They sat looking ahead stoically.

"I'm gonna use a back road around Columbiana. We'll hit the Pidd's house first," Archie said, repeating the plan they had agreed to.

"When we get there, park some distance from the house," Sam said. "Don't want to put them on notice with the truck's noise and headlights. You and Joe take a flashlight and approach the house on foot. I'll stay well behind you, covering your backs. I'll also be on the lookout for anyone comin' up the road."

"That'll work. Agree, Archie?" Joe asked.

"Yep," Archie replied. "They'll probably have dogs. Everybody here does. I got bags of leftover ham hocks and steak bones for them."

"Goddamn, you've thought of everything. You do this often?" Sam asked.

"Nope, but I got a good imagination."

East of Columbiana, Archie turned off the paved road onto a bumpy dirt road. "The house is 'bout half a mile up the road. I'll pull over before we get there."

Archie found a small clearing and parked the truck. He got a flashlight and a bag of bones. He handed the bag to Joe, put the shotgun in the crook of his left arm, and motioned Joe to follow.

They walked cautiously, taking each step carefully. Joe looked back and could barely see Sam in the faint moonlight. They soon saw the house with a single porch light on. It appeared no one was home. They passed a crudely written sign nailed to a tree trunk.

PiddVile
Pop 2

Joe couldn't help smiling at the misspelling. It made sense. The front yard looked like a salvage dump: an old truck and a car sat on blocks, and a variety of old appliances and threadbare furniture were scattered about. A dog started barking and ran toward them.

"Take a couple of bones out of the sack," Archie whispered. "When the dog gets close, hold the bones out so it gets a good sniff, then toss them as far as you can."

Joe did as Archie prescribed, and the dog ran after the bones. "Jesus Christ, I would have never thought of that."

"You've been away from Montevallo too long. Let's check the house and make sure it's empty."

"Stand to the side of the doorframe," Archie said. He pounded on the front door. "Dwight. Dwayne. It's Archie Hamilton."

No response. He tried again. No response. Using the flashlight, they looked inside the front windows. Nothing.

"Let's go visit a still," Archie said.

CHAPTER 53

MOONSHINE

TUESDAY—MARCH 16, 1948

BACK ON THE PAVED ROAD, Archie said, "It's on the left. I'll give you a heads up. It might be hard to spot. If we drive past state highway 28 sign on the right, we've gone too far. I'm told the still is one mile up the lumber road. I'll park before we get to it. We'll approach on foot."

"What if this source is putting you on? Are we headed up shit creek?" Sam asked.

"You got a better source?" Archie said, clearly annoyed. "If so, let's hear it."

"Calm down. We gotta stay focused," Joe said, trying to relieve the tension. "But Archie, I gotta ask a question too. Do you know if more than two guys work the still?"

"Sorry, Sam," Archie said. "My source is reliable, but it's always risky. The Pidds usually work it alone. I suspect the still's the crown jewel of 'the operation.' The Pidds probably feel like it's their baby."

"How do we deal with them?" Sam asked.

"Let me take the lead," Archie answered. "We'll play it by ear depending on what we encounter. . . . Okay, be alert. Getting close to the turn." Archie drove slower.

Joe soon called out, "I think it's comin' up."

Archie slowed to a crawl. "Yep, that's it. Here we go, pardners."

They passed a Private Property—No Trespassing sign. Archie drove at a snail's pace, dodging potholes and ruts. "This road's the shits," Archie grumbled. They came to a fence with a gate. The gate was wide open and Archie parked before he got to it.

Joe couldn't resist saying, "Well, it looks like the D-Dumbs lived up to their nickname if they are here. I'll take it as a good sign."

The men walked past the gate. On the left, Sam carried a flashlight and the sledgehammer; in the middle, Archie the shotgun and bone bag and a flashlight in his rear pocket; on the right, Joe the rope and a flashlight. The moon played hide-and-seek with the clouds. Sam and Joe used the flashlights only when the moonlight faded.

The road descended into a gully. Rounding a bend, a dim glow appeared through the trees. Turning off their flashlights, they heard water flowing.

Archie leaned over and whispered to Joe. "Probably a stream. Good. A still needs fresh water."

Joe gestured with his hands pushing downward, indicating to stay put. He studied the road and terrain leading toward the dim glow. The moon came from behind a cloud, and he could see the adjacent terrain better. There was adequate clearance on either side of the road for the men to spread out and approach the still in a flanking movement. Joe motioned to Sam to go left, mouthing the word "flank." Sam nodded. Joe moved right and motioned to Archie to use the middle of the road. Archie nodded. Joe swept his arms forward.

The road continued bending to the right. Joe estimated they had been fifty yards when the road straightened, and he saw an old, beat up, black Ford sedan. The men stopped and got their first look at the still. It was protected from the elements by a wooden shed with a sloping roof. The side facing them was open. Tarps used to close the opening had been rolled up, allowing access.

Joe was surprised. It looked more professional than the few illegal stills he had seen around Birmingham in his cop days. Those stills had been in the open and were cobbled together using discarded oil drums and corroded iron piping, a recipe for poisonous shine.

Several lamps were spaced around the area, and he heard a motor running in the shed. The lamps provided modest but ample light. The still materials were top quality: stainless steel containers and copper piping, which usually meant good quality shine. The setup had been done well and was obviously meant to last. Joe guessed the Pidds knew what they were doing, or whoever owned this operation would have never let them work it alone.

Joe had learned enough about illegal stills, the generic name for the entire process, to recognize the three major components that did different functions: the still, thump keg, and worm box. The names amused him. But, he knew only the meaning of worm box because the coiled pipe in it was shaped like a worm.

He put the still at six feet high and four feet wide. He couldn't see inside the still, but knew it should contain corn mash, fresh water, and yeast heated by a stone furnace, creating the fermentation and alcohol. When the alcohol turned to steam, it was forced through a copper pipe into the thump keg.

The thump keg, another heated barrel, was not as large as the still. He knew the keg was supposed to be filled with hot water, which re-evaporated the alcohol to filter out the residual mash, and then the alcohol steam flowed into the worm box.

Joe figured the motor he heard pumped the necessary cold water from the creek into the top of the worm box, as he could see water flowing out the bottom of the box. If everything worked correctly, the alcohol steam flowed down the coiled pipe surrounded by water, and condensed into clear liquid, and finally flowed through a filter out a spout into a bucket, resulting in shine.

Two men worked the still. Joe didn't recognize them, having never seen the Pidds. On Joe's left, one twin fed wood into the still's stone furnace. To the right, the other swapped buckets catching the clear liquid flowing out of the worm box and poured the new batch into Mason jars.

Joe saw two rifles leaning against either side of the shed. He gestured to Sam and Archie and held up his arms, as if holding a rifle, and pointed at the weapons. They nodded. Joe motioned them forward.

Archie moved quickly and called out, "Dwight. Dwayne. It's Archie Hamilton and two friends. Put your arms up and turn around real slow."

The two spun around, their eyes darting about, trying to size up the situation. The guy on the left moved toward the rifle.

"Stop, Dwayne, or I'll use this shotgun to make you look like corn mash," Archie said, leveling the gun at him. He stepped closer, as Joe and Sam encircled them on the right and left, handguns drawn. "Get on your knees and raise your hands over your heads," Archie shouted.

Dwight and Dwayne did as ordered. Joe and Sam got the rifles, removed the bullets, and laid the rifles on the ground well behind where they stood.

"Stand up," Archie said. "Keep your hands over your heads. Joe, frisk 'em. Make sure they're clean. Then check around for more weapons."

While patting them down, Joe noticed a scar under the right eye of the man on the left, giving him a fix on Dwayne. After looking in and around the shed, he said, "They're clean. Don't see any other guns."

Dwayne stared hard at Sam and said, "I knows the coon with ya, Mr. Archie. He's the one ya heped out o'er in Montevallo."

"You're goddamn right, Dwayne," Archie said. "And now he's gonna help me with your sorry asses."

Other than the scar, Joe didn't know how Archie could tell who was who. They looked like carbon copies of each other: scraggly, thin as rails, filthy clothing.

"Whatcha dong here, Mr. Archie? This here's private property. That white fella must be a revenooer," Dwayne said.

"I know this ain't your property. Whose is it? Chuck Holder's?"

Dwight and Dwayne stared at one another, as if beseeching the other to answer the question. They looked back at Archie, shaking their heads. It was so transparent; they might as well have uttered "Holder" in unison.

Raising his shotgun at Dwayne again, Archie said, "Last time. Is this Chuck Holder's property?"

CHAPTER 54

NAMES

TUESDAY—MARCH 16, 1948

Dwayne didn't answer. Archie raised the shotgun a bit higher. "I ain't waiting much longer." Joe, concerned Archie might pull the trigger, was about to step forward.

Glaring at Archie, Dwayne finally said, "Yeah. So what? He gonna be pissed when he know ya been up here."

"We'll see. The fella you think is a revenuer is somebody you gotta know. His name is Joe McGrath. Recognize the name?"

Dwayne squirmed. "I ain't never seed him before. But I knowed the name. He related to a lawyer man what git kilt during the trial, ain't he?"

"Bingo," Archie said. "If this was the county fair, Dwayne, we'd give you a kewpie doll." Gesturing at Joe, he added, "Meet lawyer Peter McGrath's son. And talk about pissed, Joe's pissed about his father's murder and now the hangin' of his buddy, Brendan O'Connor. Joe's got some questions."

"Nice to meet you, Dwayne," Joe said, spitting out each word sarcastically. "Let's start with a simple question. You killed your brother Darryl, and then let Jackie Simmons die in the electric chair for it, right?"

"Ya talkin' crazy. It was like Dwight and me and Poppa said. The darkie shot Darryl right in front of our eyes."

Joe cocked his gun's hammer and pointed it at Dwayne's face.

Sam walked over and said, "Hold on, Joe. Let me try and use a little of that stuff you call friendly persuasion on Mr. Dwayne."

Joe stepped back. Sam grabbed Dwayne by the throat with his right hand and lifted him two to three feet off the ground. His lower body twitched as if he had St. Vitus Dance. Sam held him for almost a minute before dropping him. Dwayne gasped for air.

Joe saw Dwight's face, a gawking mask of terror, probably figuring he was next.

Sam stepped back. "He's all yours, Joe."

"Thank you, Sam. Dwayne, did you kill your brother?"

Dwayne sat on his haunches, pale and trembling. He said nothing.

Joe motioned to Sam and pointed at Dwight. "I reckon it's your turn."

Dwight rocked back, groaning. "Yes sir, Dwayne shot Darryl. But y'all don't unnerstand. Poppa told us to say Jackie did it, or he gonna start usin' us like he use ta. Darryl and Poppa had us almost everday when we was kids." He looked up, his eyes pleading for help. "They beat us alla the time and used us, they used us, they . . ." His voice trailed off as he sobbed.

No one said anything. Joe felt sorry for the poor bastards. *Goddammit, why is everything so complicated?*

"Okay." Joe said, needing to move on. "Dwayne killed Darryl. Jackie went to the chair. Who killed my Poppa?"

"Yeah," Dwayne said, surprisingly relaxed. "It was like Dwight say. I kilt Darryl. Too bad Jackie goed to the chair for us. He were a nice colored. Beside our Poppa, other folks told us to keep saying he done it. I swear to ya, we didn't kill your Poppa."

Joe, pleased that Dwayne was talking, asked, "Who told you to keep saying Jackie shot Darryl?"

"The DA and Mistah Chuck, the man what owns this here property."

"And if you didn't kill my Poppa, who did?"

"I don't knows who kilt him."

"Who do you think mighta done it? How about your Poppa?"

"Could be lots of folks, I 'spects, including my Poppa. He were disrespected by your daddy. I did hear Mr. Chuck say one time something like that 'goddamn lawyer ain't long for this world.' All Dwight and I knows."

Joe stepped back, needing to collect his thoughts.

"Well, Dwayne and Dwight, while you're bein' so helpful, I got a couple of questions," Archie said, not wanting to let the Pidds relax. "Did you two throw the rock and note through Elizabeth McGrath's window a month ago?"

Without hesitation, Dwayne said, "Yes sir, we was told to," and he added, as if he knew the question was coming, "by Mr. Adam."

"Interesting. Y'all ever heard of ARC? A – R – C."

Looking clearly confused, Dwayne said, "No sir, ain't never heard nothin' like that 'fore." Dwight nodded in agreement.

"Just one more little thing. Did y'all kill Brendan O'Connor? And if not you, who did it?"

The twins stiffened. "We didn't kilt him. We don't know who done it," Dwayne said.

"Well, boys, I have a problem," Archie said, stepping closer to them and glaring. "You've been so helpful, and now you clam up on me. Lemme tell you the four ways you can die. You wanna be shot, held up by the neck by Sam, hung by a rope, or beat to death with this here sledgehammer? You got one of five choices: how you want to die or start talkin'. What'll it be?"

"Shit, tell him," Dwight pleaded.

"We didn't kilt him," Dwayne said, "It mighta been Mr. Adam or Mr. Damian. They been bossing us around a lot lately."

"How about Chuck Holder?"

"Coulda been. Don't really know."

"Were y'all at the river when Brendan was hung?"

"No sir. We did hep Mr. Adam git him in the car. Then Mr. Damian come and 'fore they drived off with him, they told us to git back home."

Joe's chin fell to his chest. He rubbed his forehead as if in pain. *It was Adam. And I introduced him to Brendan.* He looked up and inhaled deeply, hardly able to focus when he heard Archie say, "Well, shit, why didn't you tell us that in the first place? Answers a lotta questions."

Joe looked at Sam, who nodded and said softly, "It's okay."

His words helped Joe regain his equilibrium. He realized the Pidd twins were not as dumb as everyone made them out to be, and said,

"Sure does. Time to get back to town. We've got to talk about tomorrow. Where can we put these two to keep them quiet?"

"We'll take 'em to the farm," Archie said. "I got the perfect place. They'll be comfortable, well fed, and out of sight and out of mind. We need to slow the still down so it doesn't explode and create a fire. And we need to make it look like no one was here, including the Pidds."

"I can take care of the still," Sam said. He looked the setup over and said, "There's a generator in the back corner. It must provide the electrical power. Before I turn it off, secure Dwayne and Dwight and make sure you have the flashlights." He watched as Joe and Archie tied up the Pidds and got the flashlights.

When they were finished, Sam found several vents at the bottom of the still providing oxygen to the stone furnace. He closed them, which would slowly extinguish the burning process. He opened the tops of the still, thump keg, and worm box to release steam and pressure, and said, "Joe, fill the Mason jars with shine."

Sam turned off the generator and the lamps. The motor stopped operating. "Gimme some light, so I can unroll the front tarp and secure it."

Sam finished the job. "Done. There's one more thing. What'll we do with their car? We can't leave it here."

"I'll drive it back to Piddvile," Joe said. "You follow me and pick me up. Where're your car keys, Dwayne?"

He didn't say anything until Archie pointed the shotgun at him.

"In the ignition," Dwayne said.

"Good, I'll get the truck. Keep the boys company," Archie said, laughing.

While waiting for Archie, Sam asked the twins, "Why didn't you boys lock the gate?"

Dwayne turned to Dwight. "What tha fuck? Thought you were gonna do it."

Dwight shrugged.

"Shiiiiiit," Dwayne said, shaking his head in disgust.

When Archie arrived with the truck, he called out, "We'll put 'em in the back and gag 'em. Tie 'em to the side of the truck and to the tie-downs on the bed. Cover 'em with that piece of canvas. And we gotta make sure they can't peek out from under it."

"I'll sit in the back," Sam said, "and keep an eye on them."

"You don't have to do that, Sam. If we tie things good, they won't go anywhere," Joe said.

"Don't want to fuck this up at this point," Sam said "Besides, who'll look twice at a truck with two white guys in front and a colored guy in the bed? Business as usual, gentlemen."

"Well said, Sam," Archie said. "C'mon, let's tie 'em up." As he tied a rope around Dwayne's feet, he kicked at Archie. "You try that one more time, Dwayne, I'll kick you in the balls."

"Ready to go?" Archie asked.

"Lemme check," Sam said. "Dwight, Dwayne, if you can hear me, kick the bed of the truck." He heard two kicks, one from each side of the truck bed. "If I hear a chirp outta either of you, I'm gonna use my silencer, the sledgehammer. Understand?" He heard two more kicks. "We're ready, Archie."

Joe got the bone bag from the truck, started the Pidd's car, and called to Archie, "Follow me. I'm gonna stop on the other side of the gate and lock it, if there's a lock."

"Good idea," Archie yelled.

Joe stopped beyond the gate. It had an open four-dial combination padlock. He closed the gate, engaged the lock, spun the dials, and tugged. It was secure.

"Done," Joe said.

"All aboard," Archie yelled. "Next stop, Piddvile. Then Shoal Creek Farms."

Joe smiled, shaking his head. *Archie's enjoying the show.*

CHAPTER 55

A SHORT NIGHT

WEDNESDAY—MARCH 17, 1948

JOE PARKED THE CAR NEAR THE PIDD'S HOUSE. The dog lumbered up, barking like crazy. Sensing the dog was harmless, he tossed all the bones, figuring this may be his last easy meal for a while. Jumping into the Archie's truck, he said, "I've got their keys. Might add to the confusion about what happened to them."

"Maybe yes, maybe no," Archie said as he drove toward the main road.

JOE SNAPPED HIS HEAD UP from his chest and blinked his eyes when he heard Archie hollering out the window. "Doin' okay, Sam?"

"Yep, all's well," Sam shouted.

Archie had driven carefully, purposely avoiding any quick stops or starts or sharp turns, so as not to jostle Sam and the Pidds around.

A few miles from Montevallo, Archie said to Joe, "We're lookin' good. Not to fer to go." Joe was amused at his use of poor English even when it didn't matter.

Moments later, Archie said, "Oops, somebody comin' up on us awfully fast."

Joe looked back as a four-door sedan pulled alongside them. A white man leaned out the passenger's front window, waved a gun, and yelled, "Y'all gonna lynch the darkie in the back? We ken hep ya." He shot into the air. A white man in the back seat held up a bottle. "Waaaar Eagle."

When another shot was fired into the air, Joe pulled out his gun, and Archie reached behind the seat for his shotgun. Joe heard Sam yell for the Pidds to lay down. Then a third shot split one of the truck's side railings, and the sedan sped off.

"You okay, Sam?" Joe yelled.

"Yeah," Sam replied. "Lemme check the Pidds." Sam got two, loud foot stomps to his question. "They're all right. Keep on the lookout. Those cretins might be waiting for us."

"Right," Archie said. "I know a dirt road just ahead. It skirts town and comes out onto a road near the farm."

The remainder of the ride was uneventful, and Archie drove toward the main house whistling "Home, Sweet Home."

"Nice touch," Joe said. "Where're you gonna put the Pidds?"

Archie parked in front of the house and jumped out of the truck. "Be right back. Gotta get keys."

Joe looked at his watch: 12:42.

Sam, now standing in the back of the truck, asked, "What's he up to?"

"Damned if I know. He went to get keys."

Archie returned, jangling a ring of keys. "Sam, take the tarp off the boys and remove the gags. Here's a bottle of water. Give 'em a drink. I'll bet they're thirsty."

Joe got in the back and helped Sam. The Pidds seemed okay and appreciated the water.

"They still tied up good?" Archie asked.

"Yep," Sam replied.

"Get in the cab. We're going over to lock 'em up. You're gonna love the place," Archie said, laughing.

"Well, Mr. Mystery Man, where're we goin'?" Joe asked.

"City Hall," Archie said, pausing to enjoy their confused expressions.

"Sam, I don't know how much Joe told you about the farm, but we operate pretty much independent of the rest of Shelby County. Hell, the rest of most of the South for that matter. We try to live and let live. We also—"

"C'mon, Archie, get to the point. I told Sam about your socialist enclave," Joe said, smirking in mock derision.

"Oh, ye of little faith," Archie retorted, smirking back at Joe. "We have a City Hall, where there's a jail. Common issues and problems are resolved at monthly meetings of the entire community. But we do have the occasional miscreants in our midst. A trial is held with a jury drawn by lots, much as juror pools are selected everywhere."

Sam couldn't resist asking, "I suppose you're the presiding judge?"

"Doubting Sam," Archie said. "Prosecuting and defense lawyers, and a judge are assigned by the mayor. A new mayor is elected by the community every year, and the position has to be held by a colored person one year and a white person the next and so on. And it can be a man or a woman. I recuse myself from serving in any capacity in our City Hall."

Stopping in front of a nice, but unassuming, one-story wooden-framed building, Archie said, "Welcome to City Hall. Hank's company built it for us. Has a courtroom, office for the mayor and his assistant, and a communal meeting room. Jail's in the back corner. Get the Pidds."

Archie opened the building while Sam and Joe untied the Pidds and helped them off the truck. "How y'all feeling?" Joe asked.

Dwayne glared at him, saying nothing.

"Doin' okay," Dwight said. "Gag hurt, but thank ya fer the water."

Sam pigeonholed a thought. *Dwayne's the troublemaker. Dwight's more cooperative.*

"C'mon." Joe nudged Dwight toward City Hall. Sam followed, prodding Dwayne forward. They walked down a hallway that split the building into two: to the left the courtroom, mayor's office, and jail; to the right a large communal room, restrooms, and kitchen.

They pushed the Pidds to the jail, about twenty by twenty feet. A desk and phone faced the bars. There were two beds, one on each side of the cell, a sink against the back wall, and a small desk and chair. There was another small room within the cell.

"Welcome to the Shoal Creek Jail. This is gonna be your home until this mess settles down. You each got a bed. The sink's got two cups for water. You share the desk. Either of you write?" Archie asked.

Both Pidds looked at him like he was crazy.

"Hmmm, I guess not much, just nasty notes. The room in the corner has a toilet and shower. There's soap and towels. Hell, you even got a window. Don't waste your time trying to pry those bars open. Can't be done. You'll get breakfast in the mornin' and clean clothes. Shit, you boys gonna be on holiday. Get on in there."

Joe and Sam pushed them into the cell. Archie locked the cell door and asked, "Any questions?"

"Ya oughtta kilt us right now, Mr. Archie," Dwayne said, " 'cause if'n ya don't, Mr. Chuck or Mr. Damian gonna. I gotta tell ya, Mr. Damian a badass." Dwayne actually smiled and added, "Maybe we could works fer ya. We could built ya a still."

Archie laughed. "We'll talk it over. You boys sleep well. C'mon, Joe and Sam, we got work to do." He turned off the main light in the room, leaving on the single light bulb in the cell.

JOE AND SAM LEANED BACK on the sofa in Archie's study. They sighed, enjoying a moment of relaxation after the long, tense night. Archie came in from the kitchen with sandwiches and put them down on the coffee table. "Whatcha want to drink? Coffee's brewing. I got most anything you might want."

"Coffee and a beer," Joe said. He reached over and picked up two Mason jars he had brought in from the truck. "Or maybe, you want to toast Dwayne and Dwight with their shine?"

"Save it for Hank. I'll have coffee and a beer too. Thanks for the sandwiches," Sam said.

Archie got the drinks and sat in a comfortable chair. Looking at Joe, he said, "So, where are we?"

Joe took a swig of beer to wash down a sandwich bite and rubbed his eyes to fight off weariness.

"I mulled it over a lot as we drove back. When I first heard the ARC group was meeting, I was ready to interrupt their meeting and push hard for answers. As much as I'd like to get my hands on Adam and Damian, it's not a good idea right now. We've got no legal authority to bust in on the meeting. Adam could have us arrested for unlawful entry, trespassing, kidnapping, and illegal incarceration. Judges or cops might even be members of ARC. Shit, they'd lock us up for good."

"Joe's right," Sam said.

"Goddammit, I know he is," Archie said, clearly disappointed. "I'm enjoying this and wanna keep goin'. What's next?"

"Can we stakeout Adam's property to see who comes and goes to the meeting?" Joe asked.

"Yeah," Archie answered, nodding his head vigorously. "We'd have to get over there early to get set up."

"Good. Damian might think we're off the scent since he threatened my mother. But it won't be long before they wonder where the Pidds are. Knowing who most of the players are, we can decide how best to pick them off one at a time."

"I don't see an end game yet, Joe," Sam said. "Maybe we'll spook one of the ARC guys and the law gets involved. I doubt it. Seems to me, at some point we'll need help from the local cops and courts to close the door on this."

"You're right, Sam. Any ideas on who might help us, Archie?"

"Tough question. One guy comes to mind. Lemme think about it."

"Before you get too deep in thought, what time do we need to be on the stakeout?"

"No later than six o'clock," Archie said. "Things get busy on highway 17 soon after that. We'll have to leave by five thirty."

"I wanna go, but I shouldn't," Sam said. "If you're spotted, you'll have a better chance of talking your way out of the situation without me around. Putting a black man in front of those guys is like waving a red cape at a bull."

"Well, shit," Joe said, sighing. "But you're right." He looked at his watch. "It's almost two. We can nap for a couple of hours. I gotta call my Mom."

"And I need to call Hank. He expected us back at his place," Sam said.

"Use the phone in my office," Archie said, pointing at a nearby door. "You'll have to take turns. I'm tryin' to get a second line put in, but it moves slow out here and is damned expensive. Say, can y'all do your snoozing on the two sofas in the study?"

"Sure," Joe said.

Sam nodded.

"Good. Y'all make your calls. I'll set my alarm for four-thirty. Our cook, Gertrude, is in the kitchen by then. Folks rise early. I'll have her pack us a few sandwiches and drinks. And I'll tell Cal, who handles the jail, about our new residents and to get 'em breakfast and clean clothes. I'll introduce y'all to Cal and Gertrude and make sure they understand you have free rein on the farm. Sleep tight, detectives."

AFTER MAKING PHONE CALLS, Joe and Sam lay down on the sofas.

Five minutes later, unable to sleep, Sam propped his head in his hand and said to Joe, "Your Mom okay?"

"She was glad I called, but I know she's worried. How's Hank?"

"Answered the phone on the first ring. He was worried big time. I didn't tell him what we're doing this morning. Said we'd call later."

"Yeah, I didn't tell Mom either."

A few minutes later Sam said, "You know what I'm gonna do?"

"I have no fuckin' idea."

"I'm goin' over to the jail and have a friendly chat with Dwayne and Dwight. And I really mean friendly. Those peckerheads are ready to talk."

"Okay. Give 'em my regards. Good night, Sam."

CHAPTER 56

THE STAKEOUT

WEDNESDAY—MARCH 17, 1948

J OE STARED OUT THE WINDOW at a dull gray sky as first light formed in the east. He hoped it wouldn't rain, although Archie had said rain was predicted according to the *Farmer's Almanac*. Joe thought, *Hell, you might as well believe in voodoo dolls.*

They drove northwest of Montevallo through country covered with loblolly and shortleaf pine trees. With spring days away, the deciduous trees and brush had new growth as they struggled for their fair share of sunlight amongst the pines.

"You buy and trade vehicles on the side?" Joe asked, riding in a beat-up, light brown, two-door Ford sedan.

"Hey, not a bad idea," Archie said. "Didn't want to drive the big truck. Needed something that wouldn't attract attention. This is Cal's car. Besides its condition, it's smaller, and the color doesn't stand out."

"Hope we don't wreck it."

"Shit, Cal wouldn't care. Probably hopes we do. This is a 1942 model. I'd have to buy him a new car. Been to Adam's house?"

"Nope. You told me about it and the junkyard name."

"Yeah, I forgot."

"Did you bring your binoculars?" Joe asked.

"Yeah. Bausch and Lomb ten by forty-two. Bought 'em for huntin'. I think this expedition qualifies. They're in my satchel with the sandwiches and drinks, and the notebook and pen you asked for. We're almost to where Adam's property starts. You're the ex-cop. How do we do this stakeout?" Archie asked.

"Can't say until I see the layout," Joe replied. "Need a spot where we have a clear sightline to the entrance. It's gotta be easy to exit in the daylight. Is the real junkyard in use?"

"Not much. I think the old goat just wants to annoy Adam. Okay, here's the first part of the stone wall. I'll slow down unless a car's comin'."

Joe was impressed. The ten-foot high wall was built of stones of different shapes and darker colors, carefully woven in a tight, intricate pattern. They had driven about a quarter of a mile when Joe said, "Christ, how long is this thing?"

Archie laughed. "Over a mile along the highway. There's more you can't see. In a sec, you'll see the junkyard on the left, and then the entrance to Adam's."

Joe looked to the left and saw a dirt road adjacent to the south side of the junkyard, protected by a chain link fence. He looked back to see that the stone wall turned ninety degrees at the entrance to Adam's property and continued to the gate, an ornate design topped with Adam's initials, AMP. He also noted a pedestal in the center of the entrance ahead of the gate. He assumed it held a phone to call the house.

Joe turned back to the junkyard. It started roughly one hundred yards south of the entry and extended about fifty yards north. There was a noticeable rise in the terrain behind the yard.

"Drive past the junkyard. Is there a road on the north side?" Joe asked.

"I think there's one. Wanna check it?"

"Yeah."

"Yep, I see it," Archie said. He turned left onto a dirt road paralleling the chain link fence. Although early, the yard appeared unattended, but for the piles of junk gathering dust, dirt, and cobwebs. It extended about fifty yards up the dirt road, which dead-ended. The road appeared to serve no useful purpose.

When Archie stopped, Joe found an area where he thought the car could not be seen from the highway or junkyard.

"How about parking in here, Archie? It's a little tight."

"This'll work. Better than the dirt road to the south. I know the entry to the yard is off that road. I didn't see a gate on this road. Might get a few scratches in the brush, but Cal'll never know the difference," he said, laughing. "Direct me. I'll back it in."

They got the car where they wanted it and piled branches against the front end to hide it better.

Archie grabbed his pack and said, "Where to, detective?"

"The best spot is on the rise behind the junkyard pretty much opposite the entry to Adam's place . . . if it's high enough. Let's work our way behind the yard and up the rise."

They pushed through the brush and around the pine trees behind the fence, stopping often to see if there was activity in the yard. Nothing.

After about twenty yards, the rising terrain started inside the junkyard. Working their way up the slope, Joe knew the critical issue was the height. It was hard to estimate, but it had to be high enough to give them a clear sightline over the fence next to the highway where cars would turn onto Adam's road. At the top of the small ridge, they found a spot with a good sightline where they could lie down on their stomachs.

Archie pulled out the binoculars and set the focus. "Getting' a good view, Joe. I'm gonna hold it here 'til a car or truck comes by and check it out." He lay quietly, occasionally lowering the binoculars and blinking to relax his eyes. He had been watching for five minutes when a car approached from the south. "I'll be, it's Doc Smothers. Hell, I'd know him just by the red panel truck. I can read the slogan on the side: 'Doctor Willis Smothers—Your Shelby County Veterinarian.' People call him 'the animal chaser.' He's been our local vet as long as I can remember. Eighty-one years old. Good friend. Visits the farm a lot. Fact is, he's comin' out tomorrow. Always got sick animals."

"Let me take a look," Joe said. He made adjustments to the focus, and although the panel truck was long gone, a moment later he said, "This is great. Let's try another test. See if you can read a license plate number. Call it out. I'll write it down. Wish Alabama required front license plates. You'll have to wait for a southbound car. Then you should get a good look at the rear of cars turning onto Adam's road."

"Okay," Archie said. Another northbound car came by. "Didn't know that guy. You were right. Can't see the rear of the car well enough to see the plate." A few minutes later, a southbound car drove by. "Eureka! It's 58c543. Did you write it down?"

"Got it. I think we're in business," Joe said, checking his watch: 7:33. "Now we wait. Glad it's cloudy. Works to our advantage. A bright morning sun might have reflected off the binoculars or something else."

"Yep. Hope it doesn't rain. It'll be harder to see, even with the binocs. What the fuck, can't control everything. Want a sandwich?"

"Sure."

Archie got sandwiches and a thermos of coffee out of the satchel. As they ate, Joe asked, "Does the stone wall go around the entire six hundred acres?"

"Yep."

"Christ, must've cost a fortune. All on a small town lawyer's income?"

"So they say. But you haven't even seen the house, tennis courts, riding stable, and a huge fishing pond well stocked with bass. I hear tell the best clients of 'the operation' are invited here. Adam's also got acreage on the Coosa River over in east county. Built a hunting lodge there. It's rustic, not gated, but comfortable. I was there once 'bout ten years ago."

They relaxed as best they could, keeping their eyes on Adam's entrance and making small talk.

Joe approached Archie about the question that had been in his mind since he first saw his mother and Archie together. "Can I ask you something personal, Archie?"

"Sure," he said, looking surprised, then laughing, "as long as it's not about my love life, religion, health, or politics."

"It may be related to all of those. What's going on between you and Mom?"

"That noticeable?"

"Yep. You two lit up like Christmas trees when you came to the dinner party she had for Brendan."

"Are you upset?"

"No. Want to talk about it?"

"I could, but it's not my place. Elizabeth will have to tell you what she wants you to know."

"She's made discreet comments. I know she likes you."

Archie nodded, frowning. "It's almost nine o'clock. I think we should turn our attention to the ARC boys."

"My notebook and pen are to the ready," Joe said, knowing he had to let it go.

From then on, it was pure business. Archie watched every approaching vehicle. At nine fifteen, a Piggly Wiggly delivery truck turned onto Adam's road. It pulled out twenty minutes later. Joe recorded the truck's entry and exit time.

Five minutes later, a car came from the south, slowed, and turned right. "It's one of our boys. Damian Wallace. 58c329." Joe looked at his watch and recorded 9:20.

"Wow, Chuck and Anne Holder. 58c1267. I guess ARC's no longer exclusively male."

"I'll bet she's the only exception," Joe said.

Another car came with two occupants, "I'll be damned. Carlton Teague and Judge Jack Nowlan. He's the circuit court judge in Columbiana. Plate's 231 58. It's a county vehicle. Shit."

Cars came at an increasing rate. Archie missed a few when several cars were lined up to enter. The backup started clearing when someone opened the gate and checked cars in. By nine fifty, about twenty cars had entered. Archie had identified several doctors, a pharmacist, another college professor, a cop from Calera, and a lawyer from Alabaster.

At nine fifty-four, the red panel truck appeared from the north and turned left. Archie lowered the binoculars and blinked. "Jesus Christ, Doc Smothers is one of 'em. . . . Well, I'll bet that's all." When a car from the south sped into view with a red light rotating on top, Archie looked through the binoculars as it made an abrupt turn at Adam's. "It's Sheriff Cate. I don't believe it. District Attorney Sheldon Whitman's with him. They're in the fuckin' sheriff's car like they're on official business. Goddamn shameless."

"At least we know six guys in law enforcement and the judiciary not to approach for help," Joe said.

"There's probably more who couldn't make this hastily called meeting. It's ten o'clock. What now?"

"Let's wait a while longer for late arrivals, then get outta here."

"Yeah, wanna be long gone when the meetin' breaks up."

It started raining as they worked their way back to the car.

"You drive. I'm gonna lie down on the back seat," Archie said. "Too many people around here know me. Turn left at the highway. We'll go north, then over to 31, and back toward Montevallo on 25. Use the same dirt road I did last night to bypass the town."

Joe pulled out of the brush. The rain intensified. "Got lucky with the weather."

"Luck ain't got a fuckin' thing to do with it," Archie said, chuckling. "Careful planning, I'd say."

Joe grinned and nodded. He came to 17. It was clear both ways. He turned north. *There's got to be at least one weak-kneed weasel in ARC that'll talk.*

CHAPTER 57

SAM AND THE PIDDS

WEDNESDAY—MARCH 17, 1948

SAM LEANED ON A KITCHEN COUNTER in Archie's house, nursing a cup of coffee. He had walked around the farm and was still curious about this racial paradise in the middle of Alabama.

When Cal walked in, Sam asked, "Did the jailbirds appreciate breakfast and clean clothes?"

"Don't knows about the clothes," Cal said, accepting the cup of coffee Sam offered him. "They enjoyed breakfast. It was a big one, and they went right at it like pigs at a trough. How old are they? Can't tell white folks' age."

Sam laughed. "I'm with you. I figure 'bout forty-five."

"Whatever they are, they sho'nuff scrawny. Didn't they momma feed 'em?"

"They didn't have a momma for long. She up and left soon after they were born. Their poppa raised them, and it ain't a pretty story." He thought Cal looked pensive as if mulling something over.

"That's a shame. Boys need a momma. How come poor white families don't get along? Seem like they always fightin' with each other or kickin' the shit outta colored folks."

"Yep. You know, when folks brag about the Southern way of life, seems they forget those kinda things. . . . I want to talk to the Pidds. Can you let me in the jail?"

"Sho'. Arch told me you got the run of the farm."

"Does everybody call him Arch?"

"Yep. Jus' first names here. No highfalutin sirs or misters. Ready to go?"

"Yeah."

Cal poured hot coffee into a thermos and put it on a tray along with three cups, two apples, and two bags of potato chips. "We gotta take the boys a snack." He handed Sam an umbrella leaning next to the kitchen door. "Better take this. It's s'posed to rain.

As they walked toward the jail, Sam said, "Cal, if this ain't my business, you tell me. You and your family comfortable living here?"

"Why you asking?" He eyed Sam cautiously.

"Like you said, poor whites kick us around. So do a lot of other whites. Do you have those kinda problems on the farm?"

"Shit, Sam, the farm ain't perfect," Cal said, sounding surprised. "Whites blow up sometimes. So do colored folks. It's worked out by the community. The person what caused the problem, it's mostly men, gets punished. Could be a slap on the wrist alla way up to getting kicked off the farm."

CITY HALL WAS OPEN, and Sam saw several white and colored people in the mayor's office. When Cal opened the door to the jail, one of the Pidds was sitting on a bed; the other looked out the window. Both wore clean clothes, and their long hair was wet and dripping. The two turned to see who was coming in.

"Mornin', Dwayne. Mornin', Dwight," Sam said, unsure which was which. "Looks like y'all showered."

"Mornin', Sam. Sho' did. Feel good," the twin standing by the window said.

The twin sitting on the bed glared at Sam, who recognized the scar on Dwayne's cheek near his right eye.

"What's eating you, Dwayne?" Sam asked.

"Ya goddamned 'bout near kilt me."

"Yeah. But I didn't. We got a treat for y'all."

Cal put the tray on the desk. "Before I give you the treats, push the two breakfast trays under the food slot. Sam, stay behind the desk at all times, 'specially when they're handling the trays."

Dwayne pushed the trays under a slot on the floor.

"Y'all step back by the window," Cal said.

After they did, Cal poured coffee into the three cups. Placing one cup on the desk, he said, "This one's for you, Sam." He slid the tray into the cell.

"Thanks, Cal."

"I'll be off. There's a button under the right side of the desk drawer. It rings an alarm. Help will come runnin'. Keep the door open. When you leave, tell someone in the mayor's office to lock it." Looking back at the twins, Cal added, "I'll see you boys at lunchtime."

Dwayne had already sat down on the bed and was chewing on an apple, and mumbled, "Darkie, ya bettah stop callin' us boys."

"I can take it from here, Cal," Sam said. He sat and put his feet on the desk. He sipped his coffee, said nothing, and stared at the Pidds. As they ate, they cut nervous glances at Sam.

"Dwayne were jus' joshin'. He don't mean no harm," Dwight finally said.

"Like hell he was," Sam said. "Y'all gotta get a few things straight. Dwayne, the guy taking care you is named Cal. My name is Sam. The folks on the farm—white and colored—go by first names, including Archie. In fact, most folks call him Arch. You got that?"

"I reckon," Dwayne said.

Sam tried to keep calm, but Dwayne was testing his patience. "Reckon's not good enough. This farm's different. The coloreds and whites work together, live together, run this place together, and vote together on everythin'. You got two choices. Start actin' like everybody else. Or we're gonna be callin' you 'boys' as long as you're here."

"Yeah, in this here jail, Sam. When y'all gonna let us out?"

"Depends on how fast we find out who killed Brendan O'Connor. And on how well y'all cooperate. Let's start with cooperate. Tell me what happened the day you forced Brendan into your car."

"I done told ya what we knows," Dwayne said, glancing at his brother.

Dwight looked surprised and said, "Ya knows they's more."

Dwayne, shrugging his shoulders in disgust, said, "Okay, asshole. Ya tell him."

Dragging the chair in the cell up to the bars, Dwight sat and looked straight at Sam. "We grabbed Brendan off the street—"

"Whoa, back up. Start from the top."

Dwight wrinkled his brow, looking confused. "Mr. Adam told us to—"

"Do y'all have a phone, Dwight?"

"At our house?"

"Yes."

"Naw," Dwight said with a big grin, revealing an orthodontist's nightmare. "Ain't git 'nuf money fer one of 'em."

"Well, how did Adam get in touch with you?"

"Oh, I sees what from the top mean," Dwight said, looking pleased with himself.

Sam struggled to refrain from laughing; dealing with the Pidds was like trying to read a book after a bright light had gone decidedly dim. "Did Adam drive out to your house to talk to you?"

"Hell no. He ain't never been to our place. Rich guys don't give a shit. Mr. Adam jus' call Mr. Chuck. He sends a man out to fetch us. We git fetched and call him back. He say to get our butts over to Montevallo 'fore nine o'clock and be on the lookout for Brendan."

"Had you ever seen Brendan?"

"Ain't never laid an eye on him 'fore."

Christ, now I know how lawyers feel when questioning a hostile witness, Sam thought. "Okaaay. So how were you able to identify him?"

"Mr. Adam give us a good prescription. He was easy to pick out walkin' along Main Street. We knows most everybody in town."

"Did anybody see you pick him up?"

"No! We ain't dumb, Sam," Dwight said, clearly irritated. "We followed him past Julie's Café 'til he turn a corner to look at sumthin'. When nobody around, we stopped, shoved him down in the back seat, tied his hands, and gagged him."

"Did you punch him in the face or beat him?" Sam asked.

"Nope. Treated him like a jar of shine. We knowed we had to deliver him in good condition."

Sam chuckled at Dwight's use of a simile. "Where did you take Brendan?"

"We take him to the parkin' lot behind Mr. Adam's office buildin' like he say. Dwayne goed in to tell him we was there."

"What happened next?"

"Mr. Adam come out and look in the back seat. He were happy when he seed it was Brendan. He say we gotta wait fer Mr. Damian. Sho 'nuf, he come with two guys in his car."

Sam felt like he was pulling teeth. "Who were they?"

"Ain't never seed 'em 'fore," Dwight said, looking unsure of himself. "Well, maybe I seed one."

"When do you think you saw him?"

"Well now, musta been in the last year up at Mr. Chuck's warehouse in Pelham. He send me there a lot to deliver packages. Ya knows where it is?"

"I know Pelham, heading north toward Birmingham."

"Right. Anyways, he got a big warehouse up there with the biggest goddamn still you ever seed. It make the one we work look like a ma and pa operation. I goed in the office and give 'em the packages. A guy come in a door from the warehouse into the office. Mighta been same guy I seed with Mr. Damian."

"Could you show me the warehouse?" Sam asked.

"Yeah," Dwight said. "I even goed on weekends."

"Can you describe the men?"

"I ain't good at that sorta thin'. Dwayne?"

He shrugged his shoulders. "Me either."

"Well, I try," Dwight said. "They was white. I ain't good with age, but maybe they was forty. Wore overalls. Looked like working men. 'Bout it."

"What did Damian and the two men do?"

"He told the guys to put Brendan in his car. They done it like Mr. Damian say. He come over to me and Dwayne, and hand me a small notebook. He ask me if'n I was the one what wrote the note on the brick. You know 'bout that, right? The brick what we throwed in Joe's mama's house."

"Yeah. What next?"

"Well, now he say I want you to write what I tell ya. So I done it and he took the notebook. Mr. Damian get in his car with the two guys and Brendan, and they drived off."

"Wait a minute," Sam said, lowering his feet from the desk. He leaned forward and glared at Dwight. "Y'all told us last night that Adam and Damian sent you two home and then drove off with Brendan. What gives?"

CHAPTER 58

PIDD REVELATIONS

WEDNESDAY—MARCH 17, 1948

D WAYNE, STILL SITTING ON THE BED, SPOKE UP. "Shit, Sam. Ya guys was pointin' guns at us and tellin' us how we was gonna die. I jus' spit out what come to mind. It were like Dwight say. Mr. Damian and the two guys left with Brendan. Mr. Adam stayed at his office. We goed home."

"Okay. But why are you always riled up, Dwayne?"

"Fuck, if'n ya was white and poor, Sam, ya'd be riled 'cause most white folks, 'specially rich ones, be pushing ya around and callin' ya 'white trash' alla time."

"In case you're color blind, Dwayne, I'm a colored man. I get it all the time from whites. Let's see, the first time you saw me you said something like, 'Who the big darkie?' You got a problem with white folks. I gotta problem with white folks. I guess we ain't too much different."

"But I tries not to git riled up. I's tries to stay easy."

"Well, Mr. Easy, how'd you get the scar below your eye?" Sam asked, sensing an opening to a deeper truth. "Doesn't look like a shaving nick to me."

"Ain't none of ya goddamn bidness," Dwayne said, clearly unsettled.

"What's the matter? A guy get the best of you in a barroom brawl?"

Dwayne stared hard at Sam. "Hell no. I can takes care of myself."

"Did your Poppa cut you?"

Sam watched Dwayne's pugnacious stare fade to an open-mouthed look of despair. He leaned over and moaned, and said, barely audible, "How'd ya know that? Did Dwight tell ya?"

Sam didn't answer.

"We done told ya what Poppa done to us. How come ya ask me 'bout this?" Dwayne pleaded.

"Your Poppa done terrible things to you and Dwight. But you're letting demons control your life," Sam said, realizing he was treading on eggshells. "If you talk about it, maybe you'll feel better."

Dwayne looked up, blinking to clear tears. "Ain't too pretty . . . I were 'bout seventeen . . . Dwight stayed with a friend . . . me home alone with Poppa . . . he be drinkin' lotta shine . . . he come at me tryin' to pull my pants down . . . he wanted to do me . . ." Dwayne paused and wiped his eyes. "He pull down his pants and try to poke his big pecker up my ass . . . we started fightin' . . . I let him have a good one . . . knock him to the floor . . . he git up with a switchblade and swinged it at me . . . I's jump back, but he cut me . . ." Dwayne pointed at the scar on his cheek. "When he seed the blood, he stopped." Dwayne, breathing hard and sweating profusely, was shaking all over.

"You all right?" Sam asked.

"Yeah, I be okay," Dwayne said, wiping his brow and rubbing his eyes.

"Did your Poppa take you to a doctor?"

Dwayne, holding his head in his right hand, actually chuckled. "Shit, Sam. We ain't never goed to no doctor. Poppa tell me to close my eyes. He splash shine on the cut. Put a lotta Band-Aids on it and wrapped something' tight around my head. It git better after a while."

"But are you any better?"

"Whatcha mean?"

"Your Poppa fucked you and Dwight for years. He tried to kill you. Hell, he could have blinded you. That's what I mean."

"We git even with the old bastard when we—"

Sam interrupted Dwayne, thinking back to what Joe had told him about the Pidds and the trial. "At the trial years ago, your Poppa made y'all say you didn't kill Jackie Simmons. Isn't that right?" He realized there was more to this story but didn't want to move too fast.

"Yeah, I done told ya what I knows."

"I know you did. Now I see you and Dwight right here. I was jus' wondering, what happened to your Poppa?"

"He were kilt in a accident."

"Musta been tough on you two."

"Yeah," Dwayne said, looking confused. "It were."

"How and when did your Poppa die?"

"What ya wanna know for?"

"I'm trying to understand things, Dwayne. No harm in that, is there?"

"No, I reckon not. He were kilt in a truck accident two years after the trial."

Sam glared at Dwayne. "Did you and Dwight have anythin' to do with your Poppa's accident?"

Dwayne stood and walked to the back of the cell, and stared out the window, shielding his eyes with his hand from the bright sunlight.

Sam waited patiently.

Dwight, still sitting in the chair facing Sam, fidgeted as he looked at his brother, waiting to see what he would do.

"You wanna talk about it, Dwight?" Sam asked.

"Dwayne, we oughtta tell him," Dwight said. He waited, and when his brother said nothing, he continued. "Shit, can't do no harm now. After the trial, Poppa keep tryin' to do us. But we's fought him off. He say he gonna kill us alla time. He were drivin' us crazy, Sam. One night after he passed out from the shine, we took the floor boards outta his Model T truck. Opened the transmission and loosen up the brake band and put everythin' back like it were. Make it look like a failure. Next mornin', he goed down the hill, try to slow down, but goed over the edge of the road and rolled down the gully. Car stopped on top of him."

"Did y'all mean to kill him?"

Dwayne spun around and shouted, "Yes," and then said in a quieter voice, "No." He sat on the bed, holding his head. "We jus' wanted to scare the shit outta him. We loved him. Anyways, we sho' tried. He jus' don't let up. We tried to—"

Sam cupped his chin in his right hand and gently rocked back and forth, looking thoughtfully at the twins: Dwayne still hunched over, holding his head, and Dwight staring at him, a blank expression on his face. Having heard them confess to the murder of their father,

Sam knew he could now be judged complicit. And yet, even with that and as obnoxious as they were, Sam was conflicted about his feelings. He pitied them, but after hearing their father's story, he felt compassion and understanding for them too.

Sam stood. "I gotta get goin'. Y'all talk about what I said. Don't forget Archie said he might talk to you later about workin' out here. Sure as hell isn't my call, but if you lived and worked here, everybody would treat you with respect. But you would have to return the favor. I'll come see y'all again."

As Sam walked out the jail door, he glanced back and saw Dwayne, his head cocked to the side with a quizzical expression on his face, staring at him.

CHAPTER 59

THE MEDALLION

WEDNESDAY—MARCH 17, 1948

J OE HAD BYPASSED MONTEVALLO and was nearing the farm. He looked into the back seat. "Archie, we just passed town. Want me to stop so you can get in the front seat?"

"No. Well, I reckon the stakeout went okay. I missed identifying a few folks, but I got most of 'em."

Joe nodded. "Think anyone in ARC will talk straight to us? I mean without us getting tough. Maybe someone weak-kneed or a member who joined for the business and social benefits."

"They're all in it for the latter," Archie said. "It's risky to judge folks beyond what they let you see on the surface. To answer your question, I'd say Doc Smothers, the vet. Couldn't believe it when he turned into Adam's place. I've known Willis since I was a kid. He always teases me about our lifestyle on the farm. But he's never said or done anything that made me think he was involved in 'the operation.' "

"If we talk to him tomorrow, how do we approach him?"

"Slowly and carefully. If he catches the drift of what we're interested in and doesn't want to talk, we're done with any side door entry into ARC."

Joe turned onto the farm's entry road. "Maybe dit's best you talk to him alone."

"Yeah. I was jus' thinking that. If you and Sam are in on it, I doubt he'll say much. He'll be here about ten. I'll invite him to stay for lunch.

He seldom says no. You and Sam go back to town later today. I'll handle it."

As Joe and Archie got out of the car, Sam walked up from the jail. "The two super sleuths. How'd it go?"

"Okay. Did you talk to the Pidds?" Joe asked.

"Sure did. They said a few interesting things."

"C'mon in the house," Archie said. "We have a lot to talk about. I'll ask Gertrude to fix lunch."

JOE AND ARCHIE TOLD SAM about the stakeout. He was explaining his meeting with Dwayne and Dwight when Gertrude walked into Archie's study with a tray of food.

"Hey, y'all. Arch told me you boys had a short night and a long mornin' and be mighty hungry," she said, a diminutive black woman as thin as a rail. Joe couldn't tell if she was fifty or seventy, but she had a smile that brightened your day. "I made y'all my best egg salad sandwiches and coleslaw and sweet iced tea."

"Thank you, Gertrude. I know we'll enjoy it," Archie said. "Dig in, fellows."

Between bites, Sam finished telling them about Dwayne and Dwight.

"Christ, they killed their father too," Joe said. "Even if they didn't intend to, it's either second degree or manslaughter. What do we do with these two? Let them go or turn them in?"

"Who? The authorities you and Arch saw going to the ARC meeting at Adam's?" Sam asked. "The Pidds would be released in a flash, and then ARC'd be on our tails. Arch, did you mean it when you told the Pidds you would talk to them later about working on the farm?"

"Yeah. But they gotta change a lot. Sounds like you made progress with them. Hell, they could help maintain our vehicles."

"Yeah, your brakes for sure," Sam said, laughing. "I'm gonna talk to them again. Of course, it's your call."

"Keep talkin'. I'm all ears," Archie said.

"One other thing," Sam said. "We know it was Damian and two other men who took Brendan. Let's use Dwight to try and find the guy he thought he recognized. Two of us will take Dwight to Pelham, let him show us the warehouse, wait and watch until the guy comes out, follow him, and at the right moment, grab him and bring him here for a friendly chat."

"Yeah," Archie said. "Why not? You two and Dwight go tomorrow while I deal with Doc Smothers. The guy might cooperate if we say we're gonna turn him in for the murder of Brendan. He might open up and push it back on Damian and the other guy."

"Slow down," Joe said, his voice rising. "You're right, Archie. We're in big time, but we can't keep kidnapping people and holding them as prisoners until we're good and ready to let them go. We could end up behind bars, not the killers we're looking for."

"Okay. I agree," Sam said. "But what do you propose we do?"

Joe massaged his chin in thought and said, "We gotta move on Adam and Damian. Everything points at them."

"And Chuck Holder," Archie said.

"Right," Joe agreed. "We also need help from someone in law enforcement we can trust. Archie?"

"Tough call. If I gotta pick now, I'd say Raymond Chapman. Too bad we can't get help from outside Shelby County."

"Damn, I got it," Joe said. "Remember when you told me about Stanford Ramsey and Chuck Holder? Do you have any idea what it was about?"

"Not really. Since Stanford said the deal went sour in the twenties, it may have had something to do with prohibition. Was Stanford involved in bootlegging back then in Birmingham?"

"Don't know, but he coulda been. He loves money. But what's important is that he has a beef with Chuck. Stanford never gives up until he gets even. Here's his chance."

"Consider this," Sam said, looking worried. "What if instead of Chuck, he decides to get even with you and me over Mahogany Hall and the warehouse fire insurance thing?"

"Yes, always a possibility," Joe said. "But I think Stanford's put Mahogany Hall behind him. We covered our tracks well in the fire insurance job. He's politically well connected in Montgomery. If I can sell him on getting even with Chuck, maybe he'll put me in touch with the right people in the Alabama Attorney General's office and the Alcohol Beverage Control Board. Hold the right red meat in front of those folks, and maybe they'll want to play."

"Big maybes," Archie said. "Over the years the state has made feeble passes at shutting down 'the operation.' But well-placed bribes and people in the right places have thwarted any attempts. The state's gonna want to work with local law enforcement. We know we can't trust Sheriff Cate, Judge Nowlan, or the DA. If the state asks, give them Chapman's name."

"Okay. Here's where Stanford comes in," Joe said. "He has a motive to help us if he wants to. And he knows the ropes in Montgomery as well as anyone. And Sam's right, he has a motive to get even with us too. Hard to weigh the risk."

"I'm game to give it a try," Archie said. "Sam?"

"Okay. Joe's plan is risky but less than what I suggested. If you call Mr. Ramsey, give him my regards."

"Huh?" Archie asked.

"Sam worked with me on the prostitute murder case," Joe said. "When this settles down, we'll fill you in."

"Yep, it's quite a tale, Arch," Sam said. "Colored boy and white boy work together to solve big murder mystery."

"Sam loves to be dramatic. But I can top him," Joe said. He pulled the medallion out of his pocket and held it up. "I saw this half buried in the dirt the morning we found Brendan's body. I put it in my pocket. It must be Damian's unless Adam or another ARC member joined them when they hung Brendan." He handed the medallion to Archie. "Notice on the front it's embossed A – R – C, and on the back, the Greek letter beta is stamped on it. We know what ARC stands for. What do you suppose the beta character means?"

Archie studied the medallion. "Wow, this is something. When we met at your mother's house, I said ARC had been described to me as a secret fraternal society. Since most ARC members were in college fraternities, they might use Greek letters to identify the members. If the medallion is Damian's, he's the Beta."

Archie passed the medallion to Sam, who looked it over and said, " I think Archie's right. My Dad and a lot of his buddies were members of Birmingham's only colored Masonic Lodge. They used a lot of symbols to denote different stuff."

"Okay, I'll call Stanford. Archie talks to Doc Smothers," Joe said. "Well, Sam, I guess you get the day off."

"Nope," Sam said. "I'm gonna talk to the twins tomorrow. I'm making progress, especially with Dwight."

"Fine," Archie said. "But we have to work around Doc Smothers. He'll arrive at ten and probably leave at two. You and Joe can come back after two. Probably best you leave here now."

"Arch, my car's at Hank's," Joe said. "We'll get out of your hair for a while. Can someone drive us there?"

"Yeah. I'll ask Cal to do it. His car's still out front. Call me if anything changes."

CHAPTER 60

STANFORD RAMSEY

WEDNESDAY—MARCH 17, 1948

J OE SAT IN THE BACK SEAT OF THE CAR, hardly listening as Cal and Sam discussed the day's events. Tuning them out, he gazed out the window at the spring farm fields as he thought about how to approach Stanford Ramsey. Joe valued Archie's judgment, but he was worried about Raymond Chapman. *Sure, the sheriff, judge, DA, and another cop were at the ARC meeting, but we don't know who else in law enforcement, including Raymond, wasn't there.* Joe realized he had little choice, as time was running out. Too many people knew of their activities, and if the Pidds slipped away, Joe and Sam might as well get out of town. "Not gonna happen," Joe mumbled.

"Whaddaya say?" Cal asked.

"Just thinkin' out loud," Joe answered, as Cal pulled up to Hank's house.

"Thanks for the ride," Sam said.

"Y'all welcome. Any time."

"We tried to be careful with your car," Joe said, "but it probably got a few scratches when we parked in the bushes."

Cal laughed. "Shit, y'all coulda put a hundred scratches on my car. Ain't nobody gonna be able to tell the difference."

"That's good. I'm goin' to my mother's house. I'll call y'all later."

ELIZABETH WASN'T HOME WHEN JOE GOT THERE AT ONE O'CLOCK. Looking through his note pad, he found Stanford Ramsey's home phone number. He dialed the operator.

"Stanford, it's Joe McGrath."

"At last," Stanford said, congenially. "I've been expecting your call."

"Well, here I am. Sorry it's taken so long to call," Joe said, deciding to play whatever the game was.

"How's Birmingham's newest private detective doing? I hear you're still working with Sam Rucker."

"I'm doing okay. Sam has his own firm in the Ankle. We work together on investigations. In case you've forgotten, colored and white folks are frequently involved in the same problems."

"So they are. After you and Sam had resolved the Abernathy affair, you moved to greener pastures."

Joe rolled his eyes at Stanford's description of murder as an affair but kept his voice steady and factual. "I'm in Montevallo working on my father's murder. I told you about it last November."

"Aha, I remember. Your father was murdered over twenty years ago. I questioned whether you could find the murderer after so long a time. Had any luck?"

"Yes. But I need your help."

"My goodness, Joe, why should I be inclined to help you? I don't recall that I owe you any favors."

"True. The situation in Montevallo has become worse and more personal. You never met my young sidekick at the police department, Officer Brendan O'Connor, who helped Sam and me crack the Abernathy case. He joined me at the detective agency. Last week, he was abducted off a downtown street in Montevallo, and," Joe said, struggling to keep his voice calm, "we found him hanging from a tree. Our work is now more urgent and dangerous."

"That's terrible. I'm sorry. . . . But I still fail to see how I can help you."

"A local farmer and rancher, Archie Hamilton, is also workin' with us. He said you had bought a few horses from him over the years. Do you remember him?"

"Sure. Who can forget Archie and his socialist sanctuary? I like him, but I find his brand of altruism a sham to maintain a content and reliable labor force. But it's about time I bought a few more horses from him. I'll have to get Adam Paige to handle legal issues and appraisals. He's a good horseman."

Joe had to admit he was interested in Stanford's view of Archie's farm, and his mention of Adam, but he let it be. "I wish it was as simple as horses. How about some help with Chuck Holder and what people down here call 'the operation'?"

There was silence for several seconds. "What do you know about Chuck Holder?"

Joe caught the decided change in Stanford's voice, a tonal shift from congeniality to harshness. "A couple of things. We suspect he's involved in Brendan's murder. Secondly, Archie told me Chuck stiffed you in a business deal about twenty years ago."

"Hmmm, Chuck's not only a cheat, he might be a murderer. But I can't arrest him."

"No. And neither can I. I have no legal authority to do so. We can't trust law enforcement in Shelby County. We know the sheriff, circuit court judge, DA, and at least one other cop are close to Chuck and work together."

"I'll bet there's even more. I would be tickled pink to see it shut down. What do you want me to do?"

"We'd like to get help from the state. The Alabama Attorney General's office and the Alcohol Beverage Control Board. The state has made feeble efforts to stop 'the operation' but politics and bribes always overcome their efforts."

"So I've heard."

Joe paused and knew it was time to stop beating around the bush. "Stanford, you're well connected in Montgomery. Do you know anyone at the state level we could trust and work with on this?"

"Possibly. Let me think about it. I'll make a few discreet calls. If I have anything concrete, I'll call you back later today. How do I reach you?"

Joe gave him his mother's number. "Thanks. I appreciate your help."

"You're welcome," Stanford said, snickering. "How do you know I won't call Chuck or someone else and leave you hanging out to dry?"

"I don't. But I do need to take care of some overdue laundry. . . . Time is of the essence. I have to trust you Stanford."

"I'm touched."

The phone line went dead. Joe didn't know if Stanford was joking, serious, or being sarcastic.

JUST AS ELIZABETH OPENED THE FRONT DOOR, the phone rang. She had seen Joe's car in the driveway and called out, "Joe, I'm home early. Short day at the college."

"Hi, Mom. I'm in the study. I think this call's for me. I'll be out in a few minutes."

"Hello. Joe McGrath here."

"Stanford Ramsey. I've got a few minutes. Important meeting at five o'clock. Got two names for you, the straightest arrows I know in Montgomery. Henry Baxley, Assistant Attorney General. And don't laugh, James Bourbon on the ABC Board. I gave you a rousing endorsement. They're close to Governor Folsom, whom I don't personally care for. He's popular statewide, even with the Negroes. He was swept into office a year ago January running on a populist platform and has been pushing a reform agenda. Baxley and Bourbon knew of your work in Birmingham and are interested in what you told me. They're meeting in Baxley's office at nine o'clock tomorrow morning to discuss it. They'd like you to be there. If you can't make it, call right now. The number's CApital 7371. Let me know what happens."

"Thanks. I'll be there. I may—" Joe heard a click.

He called Archie and explained Stanford's help. He asked if Baxley and Bourbon could stay at the farm if they agreed to get involved, explaining it was the best way to hide them from ARC and others while they planned the next steps. Archie said yes and reminded Joe not to come to the farm tomorrow before two o'clock.

Joe then called Sam and brought him up to date. He told Sam he'd pick him up around one-thirty.

AS JOE HELPED ELIZABETH CLEAR THE DINING ROOM TABLE, she said, "I've been worried sick about you. And Sam and Archie too. Is this anywhere near over?"

"Mom, I wish I knew the ending. But I think the next couple of days will tell the tale. Remember, if anybody threatens you, call me immediately. If you can't reach me, call Raymond Chapman's office."

"It's that bad?"

"It could be. Cornered murderers are unpredictable and capable of anything. I'm going to bed. Not much sleep last night. I'm driving to Montgomery tomorrow for a nine o'clock meeting. I'll be gone before you're up. I'll be back later in the day."

"Always on the go. Be careful. Good night, sweet prince," she said, smiling as she kissed him on the cheek.

Joe lay in bed, unable to turn off his churning mind. Like a chess game, not only was the next move difficult, the myriad number of subsequent moves and outcomes seemed daunting. He played the various moves as best he could but gained little solace from the mental exercise. The end game that most concerned him was the one involving his mother, the Queen, and the threat the two Black Knights, Adam and Damian, posed to her.

CHAPTER 61

MONTGOMERY

THURSDAY—MARCH 18, 1948

Joe spent his drive to Montgomery thinking about what to tell Baxley and Bourbon. While he wanted their focus on Brendan's murder, he figured they might be more interested in 'the operation' since it affected revenues from state-controlled liquor stores. While he wanted to bring up his father's murder, he realized it would be a mistake at this point. The Pidds were important witnesses in Brendan's murder and 'the operation.' Too much information about his father's murder would inevitably bring up the Pidd's past actions and jeopardize the whole deal.

He arrived at the Assistant Attorney General's office at eight forty-five. The receptionist showed him into his office.

"Joe, nice to meet you," Henry Baxley said, extending his hand. "Glad you're early. James Bourbon should be here momentarily."

Joe put Baxley at about his age and height. Well dressed in a light gray three-piece suit with a blue tie. Nice looking dark-haired man but for his weak chin, which was at odds with his ramrod posture. Joe couldn't get a clear read on him. Shaking hands, he said, "Good morning, Mr. Baxley."

"Henry's fine outside the courtroom. Let me introduce Mrs. Stenson, a court reporter par excellence. With your law enforcement background, I'm sure you understand we need a record of our discussion in case things should go to more formal legal proceedings."

"Of course," Joe said. "Good morning, Mrs. Stenson."

She nodded politely. "Good morning."

Joe smiled at her. She was a small, nondescript woman with a squeaky voice, perfect for a court reporter.

"Ah, James, welcome," Henry said. "Meet Joe McGrath."

The two shook hands.

James was the antithesis of Henry. Short. Overweight. Black suit poorly fitted. Pudgy face with a big smile. Immediately friendly and garrulous. Joe figured he was a guy he could work with.

"Gentlemen, we'll sit around my conference table facing Mrs. Stenson," Henry said. "Speak clearly to make her job easier. Mrs. Stenson, interrupt us if you miss something or need a break. Let's proceed."

He made a few introductory remarks for the record, and then said, "Joe, we're interested in what was conveyed to us about the situation in Shelby County. As you may know, over the years attempts were made to shut down the illegal alcohol activities in the county to no avail. We needn't review that sordid history. I talked to Governor Folsom last night. He supports our involvement, subject to our discussion this morning. James and I want to hear what has transpired since you started your work in Shelby County. You tell your story. Then we'll ask questions."

"Early this year I started spending time in Montevallo trying to find information that might lead to the murderer of my father twenty-five years ago. His murderer was never found. It's been a long time. I've had little luck. But I became aware of 'the operation.' And then Brendan was killed," Joe said. He proceeded to explain in detail the events that had occurred since he first came to Montevallo. He was precise, careful to include the dates, times, and names relative to each event, but left out his meeting with Jason Partlow.

Joe felt Henry's hard stare, as he held his hands in the steeple position, his fingertips nearly touching his mouth, and said, "Interesting. Actually, fascinating."

Joe, concerned that this was likely to be more confrontational than he had expected, said, "What's not fascinating is Brendan O'Connor's death and its manner."

"Sorry. Didn't mean to sound facetious. Last night, one of my men researched our files concerning Brendan's death. We learned more from you this morning than we found. Is your father's murder in any way related to Brendan's death?"

"I have no proof of that."

"I hope the authorities in Shelby County are having more luck with the case."

"Not as far as I know. Nothing's been announced or reported. Besides, I don't trust most of them."

Henry cupped a hand around his chin as if to hide it. "So you told us. We'll come back to the 'trust' issue later. If I understand the complete sequence of events, I would classify Adam Paige and Damian Wallace and the two unnamed guys as murder suspects. At this point, Chuck Holder is a likely accomplice. Anne Holder is a maybe based on your observations. Do you agree?"

"Yes. But don't forget the Pidd twins," Joe said.

"Aha, the Pidd twins. How could I forget? Their fingerprints are all over much of what you've told us. Of course, they're accomplices. Do you believe what they told you?"

Joe didn't want to move this fast, but Henry was forcing him. "Yes. Why don't you come to Archie's farm and interview them yourselves?"

"We may. Another subject. The trial transcripts. Where are they?"

"Oh, I forgot to tell you," Joe said, slapping his head and then smiling. "Sorry, couldn't resist. They're in the safe in my Birmingham office. Put them there a month ago when things started to heat up. We can get them whenever you want to look at them."

"Good. We're even," Henry said, returning the smile. "Will Susan Kelly talk to me? I need to corroborate what you told us."

"Probably. Should I ask her?"

"Not yet. Have you got notes from the stakeout you and Archie Hamilton did?"

"Not with me. I can get them for you at any time."

"Good. Do you have the ARC medallion?"

"Yes." Joe pulled it out and held it up so both men could read the front and back as he explained it to them. Then he put it back in his pocket.

"I'd like to have it."

"No, not today. I'll give it to you when it's clear we're going to cooperate and move ahead together on this."

Henry's hand went back to his chin. "Hmmm."

"For Christ sake, Henry," James said, "why don't you stop acting like a prosecutin' attorney. I thought this was gonna be a discussion. You're treatin' Joe like a hostile witness. I wanna ask him 'bout 'the operation.' I can't tell you how much those Shelby County boys have cost the state over the years, but they been doin' it so long, it must be substantial. Shit, they probably think they can get away with it forever. Can I ask a few questions?"

Joe thought Henry looked chagrined when he said, "Sure. You go ahead, James. Just doing my job."

"Thank you," James said, not hiding his frustration. "Joe, you told us 'bout the list of names you got from the stakeout, but do you know how large ARC or 'the operation' groups are?"

"No to both. But we know ARC is larger than my list. Besides a few of its members being involved in Brendan's murder, it seems their attention is on 'the operation,' which is certainly much larger. It's their bread and butter. ARC manages it, but a number of others are involved. Workers for the stills, truck drivers for distribution, office personnel, and so on. A lot of these people probably depend on it for their livelihood."

"Where do you suggest we start with ARC?" James asked.

"We need to find a few members who will talk to crack it wide open. In fact, today Archie Hamilton is going to have a talk with Willis Smothers, the vet. Whether or not Archie has any success with him, you could have a go at him."

"Okay," James said, nodding. "Does 'the operation' have a central office?"

Joe was surprised. "Good question. I don't know, but they must. We can show you the still the Pidds were working. Didn't look for records, but didn't appear to be any. Dwight Pidd told Sam Rucker he'll show us where the warehouse and big still are in Pelham. He goes to the office often to deliver packages. It's likely there are some records there."

"Yeah, makes sense," James said, rubbing his cheek as if in thought. "Henry, I wanna hit those stills and talk to them ARC guys. Where are you on this thing?"

"Still thinking."

"While you think, consider this," Joe said. "As soon as ARC gets any hint that the state is involved, they're going to close 'the operation' down and destroy records. You need to have search warrants, so you can hit the homes and offices of Adam Paige, Chuck Holder, Damian Wallace, and the stills as soon as you start."

"Tall order, Joe," Henry responded. "Especially for a guy who could be charged with trespassing, kidnapping, and withholding evidence if things don't work out in his favor."

Joe felt his temples starting to throb, but he controlled himself. "I didn't come to Montevallo looking for ARC or 'the operation.' I had never heard of either of them. Then one of my best friends was hung to death by men my mother and I know well. Sure, I worked around the edges and over the boundaries. But after what I've told you, how can you fault me for what I've done?"

"Just want you to know the possible legal outcomes," Henry said, holding up his hand as if signaling peace. Glancing at James, he added, "Of course, we want to go after ARC and 'the operation.' And I hope it leads to the men who murdered Brendan. Question: How best to proceed?"

When Henry offered no answer and James remained silent, Joe said, "Here's my suggestion. You and James drive to Archie Hamilton's farm early tomorrow morning. Dress casually and don't use a marked car. If you have an antenna, store it in the trunk. It'll attract unwanted attention. Archie has plenty of spare rooms, and you can stay overnight there. You can interview the Pidds. Hopefully, we can get Willis Smothers to come to the farm and you can interview him. I don't think we should reach beyond those three. We have control over them but not others. Too risky."

"Okay," Henry said, "What's next?"

Joe was pleased Henry was softening up and asking his advice. "Time is of the essence. We can't control the situation. Too many leak possibilities. If you're satisfied with what you hear tomorrow, you need to have someone in Montgomery ready with a judge to issue search warrants. Best scenario: the warrants get issued tomorrow afternoon. Your guys bring them to Montevallo. And we go to work Saturday serving the warrants and doing the searches."

"If I agree, I need two things," Henry said, his hand moving back to his chin. "One, I'll have to get a few more guys to come up here early Saturday morning to help us. Second, I can't go forward so quickly without the cooperation of at least one Shelby County law enforcement office. I know you don't trust most of them, but is there anyone we can work with?"

"Montevallo Police Chief Raymond Chapman is the best bet. Archie knows him well and doesn't think he's involved with ARC or 'the operation.' I'll try to arrange to have Raymond come out to the farm and talk to you tomorrow afternoon. And I agree, you'll need more manpower. Archie, Sam, and I can help. You may want to deputize us."

"Hmmm. Don't need the colored boy. Normally work with the sheriff, but I understand your concern about him. My office will research state and federal law. James, what do you think?"

"I'm ready to go. Joe's right, you'd be amazed how quickly illegal liquor operations can shut down if they get wind trouble's brewin','" James said, laughing at his own joke.

"Okay, Joe, if Governor Folsom agrees, we'll be at Archie's farm early tomorrow. I'll talk to the governor later today and call you. Where's the farm and how do we get in touch with you?"

"Good. Thank you," Joe said. He gave them directions to Archie's farm and contact phone numbers. He looked at his watch: 10:15. "I need to get back to Montevallo and get things arranged for tomorrow. We'll be waiting. Probably start with the Pidds."

Driving back to Montevallo, Joe wished he had more control over the events likely to occur. Yet, he saw no other way forward. Sure, he and Archie and Sam could take it on as vigilantes and hope for the best. But there were more pitfalls in that approach than the ones Henry had mentioned. "What the hell," he said, "the die is cast."

CHAPTER 62

DOC SMOTHERS

THURSDAY—MARCH 18, 1948

"Good to see you, Doc Smothers," Gertrude said. "I done cooked up my fried chicken for you. You doin' okay?"

"My goodness. Thank you, Gertrude," the vet said. "You know how much I love it. I'm not doin' too bad for an eighty-one-year-old. How are you?"

"I be doin' jus' fine. This here other platter has turnip greens and black-eyed peas. I be right back with biscuits."

"Archie, you're a lucky man to have such a good cook. It's gonna be a light supper for me tonight."

"Yep, she's a good woman. How'd it go with the animals?"

Gertrude quietly put a plate of biscuits on the table.

"I gave the calves and foals shots they were due. You gotta have your handlers go easy with the big stallion's ankle. I'll check him in two weeks. Everythin' else looked okay."

The two men ate lunch over small talk, and then Gertrude served lemon meringue pie and coffee.

"Willis, I was in town early yesterday mornin' and saw your red truck heading toward highway 17. Figured it must be you. Did you have business up north?" Archie asked.

"Yep. I had a few clients around Alabaster. On the way back, I stopped at Adam Paige's house."

"Checkin' up on Adam's horses?"

"Nope. Not this time. Jus' another damn meetin'."

"The vet and the lawyer," Archie said, laughing. "What's the matter? Did you get sued for improper conduct with an animal?"

"Why, you dirty old man," Willis said, putting on pompous airs. "It was a right proper meetin' of gentlemen to talk about how things are goin'. I always thought you should be a member."

"Sounds like the Chamber of Commerce. I never joined. I don't mix well."

"Yeah, I know," Willis said. "It's not the Chamber, but most of the time it's kinda like that. Social and business talk."

"I guess I never heard of the group. What's it called?"

Willis squirmed in his chair, obviously uncomfortable. "It's a secret fraternal organization. Hell, I've said too much, Archie. Don't you go and tell anybody what I said. You hear?"

"I'm not talkin' to anyone." Archie smiled, hoping to calm Willis down. "But I think I may have heard about your group. Years ago, old man Harris came to see me. He was the president of the bank. Remember?"

Willis nodded, still looking unsure of himself.

"He asked me if I wanted to join a secret social fraternity made up of local prominent men. I thanked him, but said that sort of thing wasn't my cup of tea. Besides, I hate meetings. He told me the group was called ark, which confused me. I didn't know if he was talkin' about a boat or what."

Willis cracked a grin. "I can tell you it wasn't a boat. . . . I never knew Harris talked to you 'bout us."

"I guess he did it on his own," Archie said, grinning back at Willis.

"You made the right decision. You wouldn't have fit in. I mean . . . we've talked about this many times. You live side-by-side with Negroes as if they were jus' like you," Willis said, shaking his head. "You and your daddy have always walked against the grain. Goddamn it, Archie, most folks don't like it."

"I've told you many times how I feel. The only difference between Gertrude and me is our color. Okay, I admit, she's a better cook."

"We got our Southern traditions. You ignore 'em. Even make fun of 'em."

"I don't make fun of slavery, which has never completely gone away. I don't make fun of denyin' people a good education. Or jobs. Or housing. Or—"

Willis interrupted. "You gotta admit there's a difference in the races."

"I was gonna say I don't make fun of lynchings."

"Christ, that's different. I've always opposed lynchings. Governor 'Big' Jim Folsom does too."

"Listen to us," Archie laughed, hoping to lighten things up, "we sound like two old broken records. Even though we see things differently, we're still friends. I wanna keep it that way."

"I got no beef with you, Archie. I like Negroes. They work for me, and I do work for Negro farmers. I'm not a racist."

Archie shook his head vigorously. "Shit, Willis. We're all racist, jus' different stripes. Some don't show it. Some wear it on their sleeves. And some don't even know they are. But what really bothers me are the ones who cause harm and even death to people."

"Our fraternal society is not like the Klan. We don't go around burning crosses or buildings or killing people," Willis said, emphatically.

"Okay. Do you remember young Joe McGrath? He's Peter and Elizabeth's son?"

"Sure," Willis said, raising his eyebrows. "He's been around town lately asking about Peter's murder. That's been so long ago, maybe it's time to let it be."

"There's no statute of limitation on murder or grief. Wouldn't you want to know who did it if your father or son had been murdered?"

"Absolutely. I don't condone murder. Archie, where the hell are you going with this? Do you think I had something to do with Peter's murder?"

"Of course not. Did you hear about Brendan O'Connor? He worked for Joe. He was found hanging from a tree next to Shoal Creek."

"Sure did. Terrible. Hard to imagine who might've done it. Haven't heard they have any suspects," Willis said. A look of recognition engulfed his face. "You know who did it, don't you?"

"Maybe." Archie realized he had to make a tough judgment. "We gotta trust each other here. I don't want what I'm about to tell you to go right back to your secret group. If all 'the operation' did was . . . don't look so surprised, Willis. Most everybody knows somethin' about 'the operation.' I was gonna say if all 'the operation' did was liquor, I might let it go. But I will go after the men who murdered Brendan. Do we stop or go on?"

Willis rubbed his forehead nervously. "I made an oath with this group not to reveal names or activities, and to report any outsider who asked questions about us. You want me to violate my oath?"

"Did 'the operation' pay you a split from the sales?

"Hell no. What do you think I am? I'm in the group for the social and business contacts."

"Did you mean it when you said you don't condone murder?"

"Yes."

"Don't you think the question of murder is outside the bounds of any oath you took?"

Willis took a deep breath, and as he scratched his cheek, he looked more relaxed. "You're right. Okay, let's go on. You have my word. I won't say anything."

"This is tough stuff. I found it hard to believe. Damian Wallace and two unknown workin' type men took Brendan in a car out to the river. Unless someone else joined them, they hung him. Adam is also likely involved." Archie paused to observe Willis's reaction.

He shook his head, apparently distressed. "Jesus Christ, how could they do such a thing and why? You think Damian and Adam are members of . . . oh, what the fuck, it's called ARC, A – R – C. You've been baiting me all along, haven't you?"

"If I had asked you up front about ARC and Damian and Adam, you would've clammed up on me. Right?"

"Probably. How'd you know all this?"

"Two days ago, Damian went to Elizabeth's college office and said he had heard that she and Joe were asking around about something called ARC. He denied knowing what it meant, and added he brought it up only because he wanted to protect them. Then he basically threatened Elizabeth, when he said she and Joe better stop askin' around."

"Maybe Damian was sincere and trying to help them out."

"Doesn't work, Willis. The same day we learned from another source, who will remain unnamed, that Damian had called a meeting of ARC at the junkyard at ten o'clock yesterday. Everybody knows the junkyard is Adam's estate. We figured Damian and Adam were both members of ARC and were upset with Joe's investigative work about his father's murder."

"Did you know I was a member of ARC before I mentioned it today?"

Archie realized he had to lie or reveal their stakeout. "No. But I got it when you told me you stopped at Adam's for a meeting after your vet work in Alabaster. The timin' was right."

Willis shook his head, clearly upset. "I still can't believe they would do such a thing. Why?"

"Hard to say. Brendan's murder, and here I know I'm reachin', might be related to Peter's murder."

Willis removed his glasses, placed them on the table, lowered his head, and rubbed his eyes, as if seeking relief from a bad dream. "What do you want to know?"

"At your meetin' yesterday, did you hear anything related to what I've told you?"

"Indirectly, but pretty much things you already know. Adam mentioned Joe, and said he was back in town with the colored guy, Sam Rucker. Damian said he told Elizabeth to tell Joe to stop asking around about ARC. He did seem upset when he added that she was uncooperative. Anne Holder asked how we were going to control Joe and Sam. Adam said they were workin' on it. No talk about Brendan. Most of the talk, and there was a lot of it, was about 'the operation.' " Willis paused. "When I was leavin', I noticed Adam, Damian, Chuck, and Anne huddled in the corner having a serious conversation."

"Is Anne a member of the group?"

"No. But she comes to meetings with Chuck occasionally," Willis said. He smiled weakly. "Some say she runs the Holder part of 'the operation.' I've said enough. What are you gonna do?"

"Honestly, I don't know. I'll talk to Joe, and we'll decide our next step."

"Move carefully. I don't think any of them are killers, but they aren't bashful about protectin' their interest. They're my friends and good customers."

"I know. Don't forget, I'm your friend and good customer too . . . and always will be. Thanks for the advice and for trustin' me. I won't discuss our conversation with anyone but Joe."

"If you've deceived me, Archie, I won't take kindly to it. I better take my leave. Thanks for lunch. Tell Gertrude I enjoyed the fried chicken."

CHAPTER 63

DECISION TIME

THURSDAY—MARCH 18, 1948

J OE GOT BACK TO MONTEVALLO just before noon and went to his mother's to call Stanford Ramsey. He was the kind of guy who wanted to be kept in the loop and could cause trouble if excluded.

"What have you got?" Stanford asked.

His abruptness and question put Joe on edge, and he decided to tell him as little as possible. "I met with Henry Baxley and James Bourbon this morning. They're considering things and will let me know what they decide."

"When?"

"They weren't specific. They need to talk to the governor."

"Any problems?"

"No. Baxley asked tough questions, and at times I was unsure if he'd work with us. Bourbon was easy to work with."

"Not surprising. Bourbon plays easy but gets tough when he has to. Although Baxley was doing his job, his background explains his demeanor. He comes from a dirt-poor family in Rainsville on Sand Mountain. Worked his way through college. Graduated from University of Alabama Law School with highest honors. Bright kid, but he's always looking back over his shoulder, afraid his past will catch up and devour him."

"Thanks, very descriptive," Joe said, thinking of how Baxley had reacted to the Pidds as if he wanted them to go away. "But how do you know?"

"My job is to know. Call me as soon as you hear from Baxley. That's it for now."

Joe held the dead phone, shaking his head. Vintage Stanford.

SAM AND JOE ARRIVED AT ARCHIE'S FARM shortly after two. The three went into the study to debrief the day's events.

Joe gave a blow-by-blow account of his meeting with Baxley and Bourbon. He focused on the two men's personalities, including what Stanford said about Baxley's background, adding, "Stanford pushed me hard for details. I didn't give him specifics."

"You worried about him?" Archie asked.

"I'm always worried about Stanford. One moment he's helpful, then he puts a knife in your back. We won't know until this is over which version we've got."

"We have to hope Baxley doesn't turn his back on the Pidds because of his prejudices about poor white people," Sam said. "Ain't it strange how people who better themselves often look down on their past. I don't mean just white folks. Colored folks do it too."

"Weird world, Sam," Archie said. "Anything else, Joe?"

"Yeah. We need to involve Chief Raymond Chapman to satisfy Baxley. I'll call and ask him to come out here tomorrow afternoon. If Baxley gets cold feet, I'll call it off with Raymond."

"Good. Before we decide how to handle the Pidds and Doc Smothers with Baxley and Bourbon, I'll tell you 'bout my talk with Doc. It went pretty well, but I know he's having a hard time acceptin' that members of ARC could be murderers."

Joe stood and paced the room, full of nervous energy. "Do you think Doc Smothers will keep his mouth shut?"

"Said he would," Archie answered. "I've known him a long time and trust him, but like Stanford and Adam, the waters are muddy now." He then described his conversation with Doc.

"Okay," Joe said, pausing briefly to stare out the window, "let's deal with Doc first. Arch, how do we get Doc to come out tomorrow to meet with Baxley and Bourbon?"

"I'll have to level with him. If he spooks, we'll have to be ready to move early Saturday morning or the cat might be out of the bag."

"I got a suggestion," Sam said. "If Doc balks, tell him that since he's a member of ARC, he's likely to be arrested. Might put the fear of God in him."

"Not a bad idea," Joe said. "Both the Pidds and Doc need to recognize they are subject to arrest. The Pidds are involved in still operations, but more seriously, they're accomplices in Brendan's murder. Baxley got it immediately. Their best bet is to open up to Baxley and hope he goes easy on them."

"Sit down and try to relax, Joe," Sam said, smiling. "Take an edge off. It's gonna get tense enough later. You're right about the Pidds. I doubt they really understand their situation. Arch, let's talk to them. If you dangle an opportunity to work on the farm in front of them, maybe they'll cooperate even more. Sure would help with Baxley."

Archie looked skeptical. "Okay, but they have to come around a lot, especially Dwayne. You wanna join us, Joe?"

Ignoring Sam's suggestion to relax, Joe said, "No, let's don't overwhelm them. Arch, a couple of things before you go. Can we bring the Pidds up to your study when Baxley and Bourbon interview them? Better setting than the jail. When are you gonna call Doc Smothers?"

"Yeah, we'll use the study. I'll call Doc now. What time should I ask him to come?"

"How 'bout eleven o'clock?"

"Sounds good. Let's go, Sam."

JOE USED THE PHONE in Archie's office to call Chapman.

"Police Chief Raymond Chapman speakin'."

"Hi, Raymond. It's Joe McGrath."

"Hey, Joe. I shoulda gotten back to you sooner. Fact is, we don't have any credible leads on Brendan's murder. It's strange, but it seems everyone in town has clammed up the last couple of days. Not even idle gossip. Don't get it. Don't worry, we're still workin' the case."

"Good. But not why I called," Joe said, realizing he had a good opening. "I need your help. Can you come to Archie's farm for a meeting tomorrow afternoon at two o'clock?"

"Yeah, I s'pose. What's up?"

"Might have some leads concerning the murder."

"I see," Raymond said, sounding a bit miffed. "So the ex-homicide detective's been working the case?"

"I've never stopped. Can you make it?"

"Yeah. I'll be there."

"Thanks." Joe hung up, feeling things might work out after all.

He finally relaxed, and lay down on a sofa in the study and fell asleep.

"JOE, WAKE UP," GERTRUDE SAID, gently shaking his shoulder, "you got a phone call from Montgomery. Use the phone in Archie's office."

Startled, he looked up, got his bearings, and said, "Uh, thanks, Gertrude."

After she left, he went to the office. "Joe McGrath here."

"Henry Baxley. I talked to the governor. We'll be at Archie's farm no later than eight in the morning. I'm bringing three men and will have several on standby in Montgomery to get search warrants if we need them. You all set?"

"Yes. Police Chief Chapman will be here at two."

"Good. See you tomorrow. Goodbye."

Joe checked his watch: 5:25. He realized he had slept almost two hours, when he heard several voices.

ARCHIE WALKED INTO THE STUDY followed by Dwayne and Dwight with Sam in the rear. Joe could hardly believe what he saw. The twins were well dressed in neatly pressed khaki slacks, and dark brown shirts and shoes. Most striking, they were clean-shaven, and their long, scraggily hair had been cut neatly, making them look ten years younger. Joe smiled as their eyes darted about the room, looking at Archie's house.

Dwayne's eyes finally focused on Joe. "Hello, Mr. Joe . . . uh, I's mean Joe. Archie say only first names out here. Ya okay?"

"I'm doing well, Dwayne. Nice haircut."

Dwayne looked pleased, touching the nape of his neck. "Archie git the farm's barber to cut it. And Cal done bring us these here duds."

"Y'all doin' okay?" Joe asked.

"I reckon we be fine." Dwayne paused and looked around the study again. "I ain't never seed such a house. It's . . . It's . . . It's—"

Sam, realizing Dwayne couldn't find a word to express his feelings, said, "Marvelous."

Dwayne grinned, "Yeah. It's marvelous."

"Everybody sit down," Archie said, showing the twins where to sit. "We had a good discussion this afternoon. I think we know where we stand, and we're ready for Baxley and Bourbon."

"Dwight, you've been quiet," Joe said. "You doing all right?"

"Yes," Dwight answered, but his look of despair said otherwise. "I knows y'all don't think much of us. Hell, I don't blame ya. But I wants ya to know we's didn't go out to kilt Brendan. Jus' git him in the car like Adam say."

"I know," Joe said. "But do y'all understand that according to the law, you are accomplices to his murder and could be prosecuted for it?"

"We knows," Dwayne said. "We gonna coperate with Mr. Baxley and hep out. But I gotta tell ya, we gonna try to hep usself out too."

"Good," Joe said. "All you can expect any man to do." Turning to Archie and Sam, he added, "I talked to Raymond. He'll be here at two."

"Right, makin' progress," Archie said. "Let's go in the dinin' room. Gertrude's fixed a good supper. I invited Cal to join us."

It was one of the more interesting supper parties Archie ever had. When Gertrude came in to serve the first course, she said, "Dwayne and Dwight, Archie said you were special guests tonight. I hope y'all enjoy these few simple dishes I've prepared." The supper, which was more a dinner, consisted of a gumbo-style soup, a simple salad of fresh lettuce and tomatoes followed by a succulent roast beef with roasted red potatoes and vegetables, and iced tea.

The table conversation included sports, politics, and laments about women. The Pidds held their own in the ensuing exchanges, especially when Alabama football and Birmingham Barons baseball came up. The twins tried to follow the etiquette conventions of the others, but at times they were so overwhelmed with the quality and quantity of food that they shoveled it in as if there was no tomorrow, and maybe they were right. Dessert was a rum-spiced bread pudding and coffee.

Halfway through the meal, the phone rang. Archie ignored it until it stopped. Then Gertrude came in and tapped him on the shoulder. "Doc Smothers is on the phone for you."

"Excuse me, he's returning my call. Be right back."

"WHAT'S THE STARTING LINEUP for an Auburn football team?" Joe asked, repeating the opening line of his joke. When no one responded, he answered, "Seven pigs a-snortin' as linemen, three mules a-runnin' as backs, and one confused jackass quarterback who can't do shit."

Archie returned to a room full of laughter, and four men shaking their heads, feigning disgust. Wanting to get back to business, he said, "Doc Smothers will be here at eleven."

"Any problems?" Sam asked.

"He was reluctant. But I convinced him it would be in his best interest. The table's set for tomorrow."

After supper, they all went into Archie's study. He served everyone a brandy.

"Well, gents," Archie said, "we got an early start tomorrow. I say we call it a night. Dwight and Dwayne, you're gonna bunk upstairs. It's a nice room with a bathroom. Cal will show you where it is."

"C'mon, fellas," Cal said.

Dwight and Dwayne said good night and dutifully followed Cal.

Joe looked at Archie askance. "Are you gonna put a guard on them?"

"Nope. Their choice. If they sneak out, so be it. But they know if they do, we'll find them, and they'll pay the consequences. I think they're okay. Dwayne's the wildcard."

"Big gamble," Joe said.

"No bigger than yours with Stanford Ramsey," Sam said.

CHAPTER 64

THE INTERVIEWS

FRIDAY—MARCH 19, 1948

J OE SAT AT THE ROUND BREAKFAST TABLE, sipping coffee, staring distractedly out the window at a sunny day and ignoring the conversation of the others. He had been pleased to see that the Pidds had not bolted last night and knew he should have called Stanford by now. He decided to put it off until later when he knew more about what was likely to happen. Looking back to the men at the table, he listened to what Archie was saying.

"Dwight and Dwayne, we got two important gentlemen comin' here to talk to you. Alabama Assistant Attorney General Henry Baxley and James Bourbon. He controls the state's liquor. Call them Mr. Baxley and Mr. Bourbon. They'll use my study for the interview. Y'all tell 'em the truth like we talked about yesterday. Any questions?"

"No," Dwight said, emphatically.

"You okay, Dwayne?" Archie asked.

"Yeah," Dwayne said. He paused, looking unsure. "Tell the truth."

"Good," Archie said. "Y'all gonna be with them alone. This is your chance to impress Mr. Baxley. C'mon, let's help Gertrude and clear the table. They'll be here soon."

HENRY AND JAMES ARRIVED AT THE FARM SOON AFTER EIGHT. They had three Alabama Highway Patrolmen with them who were assigned to the Attorney General's office as special investigators: Larry Marriott, Doug Pettus, and Owen Smith. The men met in Archie's living room to discuss the day's planned interviews. At first, Henry objected to Sam's presence in the meeting, but acquiesced when Joe insisted he be present. The discussions went reasonably well. Henry made it clear he would make the final decision on whether or not to proceed with a more intensive investigation.

When conversation ebbed in the living room, Archie said, "Henry, you use my study for your interviews. Dwight, you and Dwayne take Mr. Baxley and Mr. Bourbon to the study. Y'all can talk in private."

Joe couldn't sit still, but he took a deep breath and rubbed his forehead. He realized Archie was putting the success of the remainder of the day in the twins' hands. Sam had told him earlier that they were ready. Joe hoped he was right.

Joe studied the three highway patrolmen while Sam and Archie talked to them. They were nearly a matched set: thirty something, tall, athletically built, closely cropped dirty blond hair, square jawed, and when they stood, ramrod postures. Joe wondered if their physical characteristics were prerequisites to being in the department, which he knew was run like a military organization. They dressed casually and were armed. He heard Pettus say they had a couple of shotguns in the car. The most significant difference between the three was Marriott's large, jug-shaped ears. Joe chuckled to himself, knowing it would be a mistake to mention the ears.

He got antsy again and checked the time: 9:57. Fifteen minutes later, the four men walked in from the study. Heads popped up in the living room, waiting to hear how it went.

"We had a good talk with Dwayne and Dwight," Henry said. He smiled. "We're on first names now. They remind me of the people I grew up with in Rainsville. Hard working but always near or over the edge of the law."

Joe thought, *this sounds good*, realizing Henry was not reacting to the Pidds as Stanford implied he might.

"They corroborated your story, Joe. I'm sure you coached them well. I'm prepared to proceed unless we hear something contradictory from Smothers or Chapman. As you suggested, Dwight says he can show us to the warehouse in Pelham. He said it's open on

Saturdays at eight, and office staff work half a day. James is rarin' to go. . . . Doc Smothers is coming at eleven, right?"

"Yes," Archie said. "Want coffee and a sweet roll?"

"Sounds good," James said, an eager gleam in his eye.

ARCHIE INTRODUCED WILLIS SMOTHERS to Henry and James. When Willis realized their positions, he said, "What's going on, Archie? Why are these men here?"

"For some routine questions. Just talk to them, Willis."

"And if I don't want to?"

Joe was about to speak, when Henry said, "Willis, as Archie said, I'm the Assistant Attorney General of the State of Alabama. I'm conducting an investigation authorized by Governor Folsom. We can do this the easy way and talk, or with a quick phone call, I can get a court order requiring you to cooperate. What'll it be?"

"Let's talk," he said, glaring at Archie.

While waiting for the interview to conclude, the mood in the living room was decidedly somber with the exception of Dwight and Dwayne. They kidded around and tried to make jokes with the others, not understanding the problem Willis presented. Joe realized his moment of hope earlier might be short lived.

After only thirty minutes, the three men came into the living room looking none to happy.

"Willis refused to cooperate," Henry said. "When he understood we were interested in both Brendan O'Connor's murder and the illegal liquor activities in the county, he said—"

Willis interrupted Henry and said, "You lied to me, Archie. You said you were interested in only the murder. All these guys want to talk about is 'the operation.' How could you treat me like this?"

"I didn't lie to you, Willis. We wouldn't be here if Damian and Adam hadn't killed Brendan. But since they probably did, it brings 'the operation' square in middle of this mess. And now Henry and James are investigating both issues. And I wasn't lying when I told you it was in your best interest to come out here and talk, and I still believe it."

Willis looked tired and beaten. "I'll take my leave, gentlemen.'" He turned and took a step toward the front door.

"Sit down, Willis," Henry yelled.

He hesitated and then turned around, looking at Henry as if he didn't understand him.

"I said sit down," Henry repeated.

Willis did as he was told.

"Doug," Henry said.

He leapt up and stood at attention. Joe thought he might salute. He didn't. "Sir," Doug shouted.

"Until I tell you otherwise, you are responsible for Doctor Smothers. You will remain with him at all times. Absolutely no telephone calls," Henry said. Turning to Archie, he asked, "Is there a bathroom in the house with no doors or windows one could crawl out of?"

"Yes, the one in the kitchen."

"Good. Doug, the doctor can use that bathroom while you stand outside the door. He can have food and drink as he needs, and can walk the house and grounds accompanied by you. Don't let him out of your sight. Got it?"

"Yes, sir." Doug sat by Willis.

"Am I under arrest?" Willis asked, wearily.

"No. But I will hold you incommunicado until I'm sure it's safe to release you. I can't risk it. You might tip off 'the operation.' We'll make you as comfortable as possible."

"I need to call my office. My receptionist knows I'm here."

Archie noticed Henry's frown and said, "I'll call his office. I know the receptionist well. I'll tell her we've got some sick animals with serious problems, and Willis continues to work on them. I'll say he asked me to call and tell her he'll be here into the late evening, and she should close the office at one o'clock as usual on Friday."

"Makes sense," Henry said. "Thanks, Archie."

CHAPTER 65

RAYMOND CHAPMAN

FRIDAY—MARCH 19, 1948

W HEN ARCHIE ANNOUNCED that Gertrude had set out a buffet-style lunch on the dining room table, Joe caught Sam's eye and winked. They both shook their heads as if all they ever did here was eat.

Joe soon realized it was a stroke of genius by Archie and Gertrude. It gave the group, including Willis, a chance to enjoy a good lunch and socialize. Three smaller tables had been set up for the men after they filled their plates. The seating arrangements the men chose fascinated Joe.

Archie, Larry, and Dwayne sat together. Joe sat at a table with Henry, Owen, and Dwight, and noticed that Henry had studiously avoided any interaction with Sam. This worried him, but nothing was to be done about it at this time.

Willis and his new companion, Doug, sat with James and Sam. After a while, Joe heard the four men laughing frequently. From what little he could hear, James was regaling them with stories about still raids that had gone awry.

Over coffee and coconut cream pie at the dining room table, Henry said, "Joe, join us when we interview Chief Chapman. You can explain the situation to him and judge his reaction since we've never met the man. If he's not on board, we have a bigger problem than the doctor presents."

"Okay," Joe said, "I suggest we take a break until he arrives. Relax. Read a book. Archie's got a great library in the study. I'm gonna take a walk. See you when Raymond arrives."

"Chief Chapman, thanks for coming to talk to us. Can I call you Raymond?" Henry asked.

"Of course."

"We want to discuss with you why we're here."

"Joe said y'all had information on Brendan O'Connor's murder."

"Yes, but there's more. I'll let Joe explain."

"Raymond, the murder and the local illegal liquor business called 'the operation' may be related. The liquor business appears to be managed by a secret group called ARC." Joe told him what he had told Henry and James. He closed by saying, "That's what we know."

"Well, you and Archie and Sam have certainly been busy," Raymond said, adding angrily, "Why didn't you come to me with this?"

"We didn't know if we could trust you. Sure as hell couldn't trust anybody else in local law enforcement. I wish—"

Henry cut in. "Raymond, did you know of 'the operation' and the illegal liquor activity in the county?"

"Of course. Everybody knows about it. I bet even you knew about it. But none of it went on in my jurisdiction." Raymond smiled. "Well, I suppose people in the city bought and drank illegal liquor. But it's been going on for years. Why didn't the state or feds stop it?"

Henry, ignoring the question, asked, "What do you know about ARC, A – R – C?"

"Not much. Heard it mentioned a few times but paid it no mind. Thought is was kinda like a secret Elks Club. Why are you questioning me like this? You think I'm guilty of something, and if so, what?"

James spoke up before Henry could speak. "Raymond, Henry's got a habit of treatin' everybody like they're up to somethin'. Shit, you shoulda heard him goin' at Joe yesterday. He don't mean no harm. Jus' doin' his job. We don't think you're guilty of anythin'. But we need the support and help of someone in local law enforcement."

"I would have come to you," Joe said. "But the more we learned about the involvement of guys like Cate and Whitman in 'the operation,' we didn't know if we could trust you. Archie says you can be trusted. I don't know you that well."

Raymond looked at the three men and settled a stern gaze on Joe. "You're right, you don't know me well. Lemme tell you a story. When I came to work for your Uncle Andrew in '33, he pulled me aside one day. He told me about the bootlegging and stills in the county, said they were controlled by important people and not much could be done about it. I've never forgotten what he said next: 'Raymond, they'll offer you money, a lot of it. Don't take it. Always be a good and honest cop.'" He paused and added, "And I always have."

Joe nodded twice to thank Raymond, and said, "Henry, Uncle Andrew was my father's brother and was police chief when Dad was killed. He died in 1935."

"I see," Henry said. "Raymond, where are you on this? Do you want to help us or not?"

"The state's made a few passes at 'the operation,' but no action. Are you serious?" Raymond asked.

"You bet we are. Governor Folsom has approved what we're doing. Are you in?"

"Yes."

"Can you keep your mouth shut?"

"Yes," Raymond said. He smiled. "But I reckon you're gonna have to hope I'm answering you truthfully."

Henry smiled. "I'll take that chance. I'm gonna call Montgomery and get search warrants issued as soon as we're finished here. We need more help. Can any of your officers be trusted to help us?"

"You bet. Start with Officer Jeff Davis. Good, honest kid. Joe, Archie, and that colored man Sam know him. We're a small force. I got three more we can use if you need them."

Joe looked down but said nothing. At least Raymond hadn't called Sam a boy.

"Good," Henry said. "Don't tell Davis or any of the others what's going on, but bring them with you tomorrow morning at six thirty. Anything else?"

No one answered.

"Raymond, you probably need to make sure your officers are on duty for tomorrow morning," Henry said. "I'll call Montgomery."

CHAPTER 66

HENRY BLOWS A FUSE

FRIDAY—MARCH 19, 1948

J OE WALKED INTO THE STUDY AND NOTICED he was the last to arrive. Unusual for him.

"Glad you could make it, Joe." Henry smiled weakly.

"Wouldn't have missed it." Joe thought his smile was more a smirk.

Henry stood and placed his hand on his hips. "The search warrants will be here in a couple of hours. Six men are coming. A lawyer, Tim Benchley, who'll have the warrants. And five more highway patrolmen—Bruce Carrow, Stan Burton, Bud Strickland, Steve Dawson, and Wilbur Jones. They're driving two unmarked cars with radios. We'll have warrants to search the homes and offices of Adam Paige, Damian Wallace, and Chuck Holder, as well as the still on Holder's property and the Pelham warehouse. If we find any information pointing to others of interest, it will provide us enough probable cause to search those locations. Arrests will be made where appropriate. Questions?"

"How we gonna split up for the searches tomorrow?" Joe asked.

"We'll meet here at seven in the morning to discuss that and other details about the plan. With Raymond's help and all of you, I think we have enough resources to meet our initial needs."

Sam said, "I'd like to make a suggestion—"

"I didn't ask you a question, boy," Henry said.

The room went silent. Sam leaned over and slowly stood, accentuating his height and build. "Mr. Baxley, in case you haven't noticed, I am not a boy. I stand before you as a proud colored man."

"I don't care what you stand before me as. If I had you in my hometown on Sand Mountain, we'd take good care of you. Sit down."

Sam remained standing. "Sir, I've heard of the sundown towns on Sand Mountain. Rest assured, I'll not be visiting there soon."

"Oh, damn it, Henry. Sit down. Let Sam speak," James said.

Henry glared at everyone, especially James, and sat.

Sam appeared unflustered, and said calmly, "There are enough potential sources of leaks in this operation that it could sink quicker than the Titanic. Mr. Baxley, I suggest we hit the warehouse in Pelham first. As Dwight told you, the office opens at eight on Saturdays. It's the likely location of records and personnel directly related to 'the operation.' It's also the farthest one from here. If we try and time all hits at once, a small mistiming might give someone the opportunity to call the warehouse and warn them. I also suggest we allow adequate time for the warehouse search to be completed before launching the other hits. I suspect the information there will better direct the entire plan." Sam sat.

Henry stood and said, mustering as much sarcasm as he could, "Well, how many of you would like to listen to and work with this eloquent, smart-ass colored," pausing, he spit the next word out, "guy?"

Archie, James, Joe, and the Pidds stood.

Joe looked around the room, and said, "Gentlemen, I assure you that you want Sam Rucker on your side in a fight."

In short order, all the men were standing, although a couple of the highway patrolmen hesitated for a moment.

Henry started to exit the room, when Archie said, "Time for supper. Raymond's going to join us. Let's go to the dining room."

JOE FOLLOWED THE OTHERS TOWARD THE DINING ROOM and noticed James had managed to take Sam and Henry by their arms. He escorted them to the table, where the three men sat side-by-side, Sam in the middle.

Joe sat on the opposite side of the table facing James. Try as he might, he couldn't keep his eyes off the three men and tried to listen to their conversation. He noticed the others at the table were talking quietly, their attention also turned to the same men.

He caught snatches of James's jokes. At first only Sam laughed, but one of the jokes finally brought forth hearty laughter from all three. Joe admired James's ability to break the ice in tense situations. The entire table had relaxed and voices rose in lively cross-table conversations. *I was right about James,* Joe thought. *Not only can we work with him, he's a peacemaker and a leader.*

Gertrude served another excellent supper with the help of two white women, both about forty, rather plain looking, and dressed in black dresses with white collars. Joe noticed they caught Henry's attention, and yet Joe thought he looked at them thoughtfully rather than in anger or surprise. He hoped this evening would calm Henry down so they could work together as a rational, focused team.

After supper, it was brandy and cigars in the study. Sam and Henry continued to seem comfortable with one another. The six men from Montgomery arrived and were introduced. Men drifted off to their bedrooms over the remainder of the evening, leaving only Archie and Joe in the study.

"Big day tomorrow," Archie said. "I'm off to bed."

"I'm right behind you after I call Stanford. He's expecting it. Good night."

Joe went into Archie's office and picked up the phone to place the call.

He paused and looked at his watch: 10:25. He put the receiver back in its cradle. *Goddammit, I'm not gonna call him tonight. Too late. I'll do it tomorrow, hopefully after everything's all over.*

CHAPTER 67

THE BLITZKRIEG

SATURDAY—MARCH 20, 1948

JOE AWOKE ON SATURDAY as the day's first glimmer of light filtered through the window blinds. In a hurry, he didn't shower or shave. Before putting on his jacket, he strapped on his holster and gun. He went to the dining room. Gertrude was putting a large platter of scrambled eggs on the sideboard next to plates of bacon and toast, a bowl of grits, and an urn of coffee. Dwayne and Dwight were at the table, eating large servings.

"Good mornin', Joe," Gertrude said, smiling brightly. "Got a good breakfast here for y'all. Sounds like you gonna be busy today."

"Mornin', Gertrude. Yep. Busy day comin'. Thanks for the breakfast. Mornin', Dwayne. Mornin', Dwight."

Dwayne shoveled a huge amount of grits into his mouth, barely nodding.

"Mornin', Joe," Dwight said. "Looks like stormy weather. Did ya see 'em dark clouds comin' at us from the southwest? Our Poppa always said they was a bad omen."

Joe peered out the window. It did look ominous, but he wasn't worried about bad omens, only that windy, wet weather might hamper their operation. "I don't think your Poppa's right. Hell, today's the first day of spring. Gotta be a good sign. Let's just say they cancel each other out."

Joe finished and went to the study to wait for the seven o'clock meeting. Raymond had arrived with Jeff Davis and his other three officers—Wally, Jerome, and Mack—at six thirty to meet with Henry, who explained to the four officers what they were doing and why. Raymond then introduced his men to the others as they drifted into the study.

"OKAY, MEN, HERE'S THE PLAN AND THE ASSIGNMENTS," Henry said, authoritatively, trying to sound less strident than yesterday. "Doug Pettus and Willis will stay here. You two can relax, play cards, enjoy Gertrude's food. We're going to work in four five-men teams, and I'm gonna keep Raymond and his officers assigned to teams in Montevallo to avoid any jurisdictional questions. To start, I'm going with Sam's idea. We'll hit the Pelham warehouse at eight thirty. I reviewed the plans last night with Raymond. He said to allow thirty minutes to get to Pelham, so the team will leave at seven fifty to have some wiggle room. James is the Team One leader, joined by Owen, Tim, Steve, and Dwight."

James tapped Henry on the shoulder and whispered in his ear. Henry grabbed his chin and smiled. "And Sam. James wants some muscle. Tim will help James look over the documents they find. Steve, I'm moving you to Team Three."

Henry handed James the warehouse search warrant and explained to everyone the procedure for serving it and conducting the search. He added, "The warrants limit our search only to apparatus and paperwork possibly related to illegal liquor activity. If we find anything, we'll have probable cause to expand the search throughout the premises. It's a judgment call. The other three teams will depart the farm no sooner than nine-thirty and only after Team One calls and gives the green light. Teams Two and Three will cover Montevallo. Team Two will hit Adam's home and office. Larry is the team leader supported by Joe, Wally, Jeff, and Bud. Team Three is responsible for Damian's home and office. Raymond is the team leader supported by Jerome, Archie, Steve, and Mack. Team Four handles Holder's house, office, and the still on his property in that order. I'm the team leader supported by Stan, Bruce, Wilbur, and Dwayne."

Henry paused and looked around the room. Everyone appeared to be listening intently. "Be sure you have weapons. We brought enough shotguns to have one in each car. Remember, we don't go in with guns drawn and blazing. They are to be used only in self-defense. This is not a search and destroy mission, but a search for incriminating evidence. With Raymond's car, we have four cars with radios. Each team leader will drive one car. Owen will drive a truck Archie said we could use. It's covered and can be secured, so Team One has a large vehicle to bring back documents and any people they arrest. If you need help because you're able to arrest more people than you can handle, call Raymond or his office. He'll have officers ready to assist on a moment's notice. We'll use frequency 155.010. Raymond says the range limit of the radio is about twenty miles, so we may not always be able to stay in touch with each other. Pass messages around if need be. Questions?" Henry smiled and added, "Sam?"

"None. It sounds like an excellent plan, Mr. Baxley."

"TURN RIGHT," DWIGHT SAID. "It's jus' down the street on the left."

James checked the rear view mirror and Owen was in sight. "Got it," he said, slowing down so he could check the layout as a light rain started. It was a quiet, scruffy looking area. The warehouse was the biggest building, with a few smaller ones scattered about. "We're five minutes early. This looks perfect. I'm gonna pull in that dirt lot on the right side. I'll park in those trees where we can observe the warehouse."

While they waited, a woman arrived, knocked on the warehouse door, and entered after being identified.

"I seed that women afore," Dwight said. "She work in the office."

"The door's locked," James said. "I don't want to knock and announce the search warrant. One of them might make a phone call before we get in. It's not standard procedure, but we'll have to force our way in and hope for the best. Dammit, Dwight, why didn't you tell me that?"

Dwight, a hangdog look on his face, brightened up, and said, "I gots an idea. Them folks knows me. I'll jus' knock and say it's me, and tell 'em I got packages from Mr. Chuck. Betcha they open the door."

"Great idea." James looked at his watch. "Let's go."

James and Owen drove slowly into the warehouse parking lot, making as little noise as possible. Before they got out of the car, James said, "Okay Dwight, you're on. If they open the door, Owen and I will be on either side of you and will push it wide open and rush in."

It worked. James led them through the front door of the warehouse at exactly eight thirty. He displayed the search warrant and announced it, as he held up his ID. He told the two men and the woman in the office to stand in a corner away from their desks and phones.

When the door to the interior of the warehouse wouldn't open, Sam kicked it open with one well-planted foot. The three men tending the still were quickly rounded up and put in the corner with the office personnel.

"Sam," Dwight said, pointing at one of the men who tended the still. "That's the guy. He was with Mr. Damian."

James and Tim were searching the desks for information. Sam interrupted them and told them what Dwight said. James whispered in Owen's ear.

"What's your name?" Owen asked the man whom Dwight had fingered.

"None of yer fuckin' business," the guy said.

"It'll be my business when I put my boot in your ribs."

Sam walked over and added, "My boot'll work your other side. Don't want you to feel unbalanced."

"Roscoe, ya fuckers."

"Well, Roscoe, you're under arrest for operating an illegal still and as a suspect in the murder of Brendan O'Connor," Owen said, pulling out handcuffs. "Put your arms behind that support column."

Roscoe did nothing until Sam grabbed him by the neck and shoved him against the column. Owen handcuffed him.

"There's a safe over here," James called out, looking at the others crouched in the corner. "What's the combination?"

No one spoke. Sam walked over and loomed over them with a scowl on his face. The woman said, "I know it. I'll open it."

She did and all the papers were added to what James and Tim had found. James told Owen to handcuff the other five people and then to search the area of the still for documents. He told Sam to keep an eye on the six.

James and Tim sat at a desk and started reading through each piece of paper. It was time consuming, and Owen added more documents to the pile.

After about thirty minutes, James took off his glasses and rubbed his eyes. "We got more stuff to look at, but we've seen enough to put half of Shelby County behind bars."

He used one of the office's phones and called the farm. "It's James. Go at nine thirty."

Forty minutes later, after the document review was complete, James said, "Owen, we're done. Use the car radio and try to get Raymond or Larry. Tell 'em we'll load the truck and car with the documents and the six people we've arrested, and then head back."

Ten minutes later, Owen came back from the car, dripping wet. "Fuck, it's raining harder. I finally got a connection. Raymond told me to tell y'all somethin' funny is going on. Damian wasn't home. He called Larry and he said Adam wasn't home either. They want us back in Montevallo pronto."

CHAPTER 68

DESPERATE MEASURES

SATURDAY—MARCH 20, 1948

RAYMOND STOPPED, and Joe slid into the back seat of the police car. Jerome was sitting in front. "Raymond, I'm concerned about my Mom. Let's stop by her house first."

"On our way," Raymond said.

"Have you talked to Henry?"

"Yep. Chuck didn't skip. Didn't find anything useful in his house but found some interesting stuff in his office. They arrested Chuck and are on the way to the still, then back here. Henry said Anne Holder was a shrew, constantly yelling and berating them. Didn't find anything implicating her in 'the operation,' so they couldn't arrest her. You find anything at Adam's house?"

"Nothing," Joe said. "No Adam. No incriminating papers, although he's too smart to leave any lying around. His wife finally told tell me he left the house in a hurry just before nine. Somebody tipped him off. Larry, Jeff, Bud, and Wally are at his office now."

"Pretty much the same at Damian's house. Except his wife wouldn't say anything. Steve, Archie, and Mack are at his office. Want me to park in the front of your mother's house?"

"Yes. I have a key."

As they entered the house, Joe called out for his mother. No answer. The living room, study, and dining room appeared fine. Joe was surprised to see the door to the kitchen closed. His mother never closed it.

He opened the door slowly, one hand on his gun. A chair had been knocked over. Back door was ajar, apparently a forced entry. Two muddy scuff marks on the floor.

"Christ, do you think Adam and Damian kidnapped your mother?" Raymond asked.

Joe had been looking out the back door. His mother's car was parked in its usual place. There were fresh tire tracks on the muddy alleyway. A sense of dread overwhelmed him. "Goddammit, I knew something like this might happen. The Black Knights," he said as if talking to himself and added, "Yes, who else could it be, unless they sent their goons to do it? C'mon, let's get over to your office."

JOE RUSHED INTO THE POLICE OFFICE LOBBY ahead of Raymond and Jerome, and called out to Sam and James who were talking to the desk officer. "Sam. James. We've got a big problem."

"Yeah," Sam said, "we heard Adam and Damian flew the coop."

"Worse. Someone kidnapped my mother. Forced entry into her house through the back door. Signs of a possible struggle in the kitchen. Her car's still there. Has to be Adam and Damian or their henchmen."

"Well, it's not one of the guys who helped Damian with Brendan," Sam said. "The guy Dwight fingered is in a cell."

"How the hell do they think they can get away with somethin' so blatant?" James asked, looking utterly surprised.

"Dammit, I don't want to debate their fuckin' state of mind," Joe answered. "I want to find my Mom. Ideas?"

Before anyone replied, the desk officer's phone rang. He answered and said to Raymond, "Chief, someone wants to talk to you. Won't give his name. Want to take it in your office?"

"No. I'll take it here," Raymond said. He took the phone, scratching his head with his free hand. "Chief Chapman speaking."

Joe watched as his expression quickly faded from his stern cop mode to a furrowed brow and look of concern.

"Who is this?" Raymond asked, putting the phone back in its cradle. Turning to Joe, he added, "He hung up. Didn't recognize the voice. It was muddled like he was speaking through a tin can. I'll try to repeat what he said verbatim, 'Raymond, tell Joe McGrath, the colored bastard, and the state's guys to be out of town by sundown or Elizabeth McGrath's a dead woman.' That was it."

Joe felt frozen in a bad dream. Not thinking clearly, he blurted out, "Where's Archie?"

"Over at Damian's office," Raymond replied.

"I'll go to Damian's office and help with the search," James said. "Archie can come back here. Tim, you go to Adam's and help them."

Raymond called to the officer standing nearby. "Jerome, take these guys to Adam Paige and Damian Wallace's offices. Bring Archie Hamilton back here pronto."

"Goddamn," Archie said. "I don't believe it. Elizabeth. This is crazy. Maybe they want to stick it in your eye, Joe, and are willin' to go down and take her with them."

Joe massaged his temples and pushed his head back, looking upwards. "We gotta find her. Any idea where they might've taken her?"

Archie paced around. "Best bet. Adam's hunting lodge, unless they've left the county."

"Is there a phone at the lodge?"

"I think so. Don't know the number."

"It doesn't matter. You can't call the lodge," Sam said. "If they answer, they know we're on to them. If they don't answer, they might leave or kill Elizabeth. We gotta go out there. This bad weather will work to our advantage."

"Right," Joe said, nodding vigorously. "Archie and Sam, let's get organized and get moving. Raymond, can Jeff join us? We need a police officer to make the arrests. You need to stay here to keep things on track."

"Sure, I'll send Jerome to get him," Raymond said. "But in this case, you could make citizen's arrests."

"I'll call Hank and ask him to join us," Archie said. "He helped Adam build the lodge and knows it better than me. I was there only once."

"Raymond, you got a conference room with a blackboard we can use?" Joe asked.

"Yep." He pointed to a door.

JOE HAD THE CAR'S HEADLIGHTS ON, and the window wipers were having a hard time combating the heavy rain. The wind built in intensity and the clouds behind them looked even darker. Sam sat beside him. Hank was in the back seat. Joe checked the rear view mirror to ensure the car with Jeff and Archie was behind them. It was. They had decided to drive two cars in hopes they would be returning with Elizabeth, and with Adam and Damian in handcuffs.

"Hank, how much longer before we're there?" Joe asked.

"About fifteen minutes. Christ, this weather's the shits."

"Yep. It'll give us cover to approach the lodge. Go over the layout again. You did a great job explaining it in the conference room. But a refresher doesn't hurt."

"Well, it's one story. A big living and dining room spans the entire width of the lodge, almost a hundred feet. The back includes the kitchen, four bedrooms, and two bathrooms. A big deck encircles the lodge. There's a front door, and doors on both sides of the big room, and one in the back off the kitchen. Big fireplace on the right front facing the living room. Dining area's on the left side."

"The deck is about eight feet off the ground. Right?" Joe asked.

"Right. The lodge has a large basement, but it's mostly to protect the upper floor when the Coosa River floods. If this rain keeps up, it might."

"The height works to our advantage," Joe continued. "Tell us when to park the car before we can see the lodge. We'll sneak up to the base of the deck. I'll go up on the deck and peek in a window. Damn dark for midafternoon. The lights should be on. Makes it harder for them to see out the windows. I'll try to get a fix on things and come up with a plan to move in."

As the rain and wind intensified and lightning flashed behind them, Joe worried there might be a tornado, wreaking havoc with their plans. The sky darkened.

The rain was now blowing almost horizontal. Joe slowed down and focused on driving.

"You're gonna turn right soon just after a barn," Hank said. In a few moments, he added, "Here it comes. Lodge is a quarter of a mile up the road."

Joe turned onto a muddy dirt road, pleased to see that the area was well wooded, as he edged to the right and stopped. He waved to Jeff to pull up on his left. Rolling the window down, he said to Archie and Jeff, "Headlights off now. Hank'll tell us where to park, and we'll go on foot from there." After explaining the rest of the plan, he drove forward as slow as possible.

"Joe, park here," Hank said. "The lodge is about a hundred yards."

Joe left the keys in the car and told Jeff to do the same. He then led them forward in the driving rain, and they were soon soaked. Raymond had given them slickers, but they didn't use them since the rain would've bounced off of them noisily. They all wore dark clothing. They'd left the shotguns behind, and wrapped their handguns in protective cloth, but that proved futile in the deluge.

When the lodge came into view, Joe saw it was well lit inside. He motioned the men to spread out. They moved forward, crouched low, and huddled under the deck. A Buick sedan was parked nearby.

Joe whispered in Archie's ear to overcome the howling wind. "I'm going up. Keep everybody quiet."

Joe felt like a snake as he slithered up the steps of the deck. He paused near the top and peered out. He saw no one at the windows to the right and left. He crawled across the deck to the left window, careful with each move to test the wooden planks for looseness. Standing up on the right side of the window, he peeked, ever so carefully, around the window frame.

Adam and Damian were sitting at the dining room table eating sandwiches and drinking beers. Damian's back was to him, but Adam was facing him and had a gun beside him on the table. No other weapons were apparent.

Ducking down, Joe crawled to the window to the right of the fireplace. Peeking in, he had a view that gave him both hope and chilled him. Elizabeth, still wearing her nightgown and slippers, was tied to a chair: her arms to the armrests and her legs to the front legs of the chair. She appeared okay, and he saw the door behind her on the right side of the lodge was closest to her. He took a quick look at the deck area on the right side and saw two wooden chairs.

The wind subsided briefly, and he could see Adam looking at Elizabeth as he shouted something. Joe thought she replied, and then he saw Adam laughing, as if he were mocking her.

Joe wanted to pull out his gun, jump through the window, and go in blazing.

CHAPTER 69

TOUCH OF REDEMPTION

SATURDAY—MARCH 20, 1948

J OE RESISTED HIS IMPULSE to go it alone and slid back down the steps. Under the deck, he knelt, motioned the men to cluster around him, and whispered. He explained the situation to them, and asked Hank, "Are there steps up to the deck on the right and left?"

"Yeah."

"Good. Listen carefully. Only time to say this once. Hank, go around the deck to the stairs on the right. Creep up to the window on the left. Wait a good half-minute to give the rest of us time to get in place. Then throw the deck chair next to the window through it, jump in, and help my mom. Sam and Jeff, you go around the deck to the stairs on the left, creep up and get ready to kick in the door. Sam takes Adam. Jeff takes Damian. Archie and I will go up the front stairs and kick in the door. Arch helps with Adam and Damian. I'll see to Mom. Walk carefully on the steps and the deck. Test each footstep to make sure a board isn't loose. Our cue to kick in the doors is when Hank breaks through the window. We wanna get these guys, but first priority is to save my mom, so do whatever's necessary. Check your guns. They'll probably fire, unless they're too wet. Ready?"

The men looked at him solemnly and nodded.

"Let's go," Joe said.

SAM WAITED, JEFF BY HIS SIDE, LISTENING FOR BREAKING GLASS. Nothing but the rain and wind. Then two sharp bangs. It was time. He stepped back and gave the door a savage kick and a second kick.

As the door flew open, Sam saw Adam shoot his gun at Archie but miss, and then turn toward Elizabeth and fire. Sam jumped forward, grabbed Adam's right arm, and yanked it up pointing toward the ceiling as he fired again. Sam saw Damian coming toward him. While holding Adam's arm, Sam deftly balanced on his left leg and with his right kicked Damian in the groin. He fell to the floor clutching his crotch.

Sam pulled Adam's right arm backwards even more, causing him to scream in pain, drop his gun, and fall.

"Jeff! Gimme handcuffs. Cuff Damian."

"You black motherfucker, you almost broke my arm," Adam yelled as Sam cuffed him.

Sam left him on the floor and said, laconically, "I shoulda shot you."

He looked across the room. Archie was on his knees over Hank who lay on the floor. Joe was untying Elizabeth.

"Jeff, take this," Sam said, handing him Adam's gun. "I'm going to help Joe and Archie. Watch these guys. You're the cop, but I wouldn't hesitate to shoot if they try anything."

"Will do," Jeff said. "Damian's not gonna be any trouble."

Sam walked to Elizabeth. She seemed okay. He stooped down and saw Hank's bloody shoulder. Archie was tending it.

"He took the bullet in the shoulder that I'm sure was intended for Elizabeth," Archie said. "He jumped in front of her just as Adam fired."

Joe massaged Elizabeth's ankles and wrists, and asked, "How's Hank, Archie?"

"Not sure. Gotta get him to a hospital," Archie said.

"Let me take a look," Sam said. He tore Hank's shirt off and examined him. Sam took off his soaked jacket and his shirt, which he tore into strips. "I'm gonna bandage him as best I can. Hope it'll stop or at least slow the bleeding. Archie, look for a first aid kit in the kitchen or bathroom."

Archie found a kit and handed it to Sam.

"Thanks. Good. Iodine. Hydrogen peroxide and bandages. Now, please get a car so we can take Hank to the closest hospital that'll take coloreds."

"Columbiana's will. I'll be right back."

As Sam worked on Hank, he could hear Elizabeth and Joe talking.

"You feeling better, Mom?"

"God, I was worried no one would know where we were."

"Archie figured it out. Thank him."

"I will. . . . I can't believe this has happened. If Hank dies . . . "

Sam thought she was crying.

"I remember you and Hank and Adam as boys. Such good friends, playful and understanding. You won't believe what Adam said. He said they should have hung you and Sam instead of Brendan. Damian added they probably should have shot both of you like their daddies did Peter."

"They said that?" Joe asked.

"Yes."

"I'm about finished with Hank," Sam said. "His pulse is pretty good. Joe, why don't you help Elizabeth walk around a bit? Archie went to get a car. Elizabeth should go with Archie and Hank. You, Jeff, and I can take Adam and Damian to the Montevallo jail."

Joe nodded as he helped his mother up.

When Archie returned, Hank was carried to the car, and Sam and Joe helped Elizabeth into the car. Sam then found additional blankets, wrapped them in a slicker he found in the lodge, and laid one over both Hank and Elizabeth. Archie drove off.

Once back in the lodge, Sam said, "Jeff, please go get the other car. We'll load the cretins and take 'em to Montevallo."

"Okay," Jeff said. He placed the gun on the table.

Sam lifted Adam and Damian under their armpits and put them in dining room chairs. Damian was hunched over, moaning in pain. Adam glared at Sam, still complaining about his arm.

Joe walked over to Adam, lifted his head up, and tore his shirt open. A medallion hung from his neck. Joe yanked it off and looked at it. "So you're the ARC Alpha."

He turned to Damian. "And you're the Beta." He pulled Damian's shirt open. No medallion but several scars below his throat. Joe fished out of his pocket the medallion that he had carried around for ten days, and held it in front of him. "This belongs to you."

Damian looked like a cornered animal. "Where the fuck did you get that?"

"By the oak tree where you murdered Brendan."

Sam watched Joe pick up the gun on the table and check the chambers. *What the hell's he doing?* But Sam couldn't find words to stop him when Joe pointed it at Adam. He'd never seen Joe with such a malevolent expression of hatred.

"Who tipped you off?" Joe asked.

Adam looked up, still in pain, but said nothing.

Joe cocked the gun's hammer.

"Stanford Ramsey, you dumb ass," Adam blurted.

Sam thought it wasn't possible, but Joe's visage looked even more evil.

"You shits don't deserve to live," Joe said. "This is for what you did to Brendan and what your fathers did to my father. You're first Adam. If it weren't for Hank, you would have killed my mother. Don't worry, Damian, you're next."

Sam took a step to Joe's side and gently touched his forearm. "Joe, You'll find no redemption for your hatred if you pull the trigger."

Joe kept staring at Adam, but he slowly lowered his arm. He uncocked the gun and handed it to Sam.

Joe turned and walked away. Sam saw Jeff standing by the front door, his mouth agape, and figured he had witnessed the entire scene.

CHAPTER 70

JOE'S REMORSE

MONDAY—MAY 3, 1948

J OE AND SAM HAD RETURNED TO BIRMINGHAM A WEEK after the
rescue and the other arrests had quieted down. He also had to
make sure his mother was doing all right, which she was, especially
with daily visits from Archie.

Still rattled to have learned that Stanford Ramsey had tipped off
Adam, Joe called him a few days later.

"Well, high time I heard from you," Stanford said. "Your escapades
in Shelby County have been big news all over the state."

"You almost got my mother killed, you motherfucker."

"You got what you wanted. I got what I wanted, Chuck Holder.
Adam kidnapping your mother was an unintended consequence, a
stupid one. Don't keep me in the dark next time."

The line was quiet. *How could I have been so stupid to trust him?*

The brief conversation had exacerbated the melancholy that had
haunted Joe since Brendan's death. Dark thoughts cluttered his mind,
impeding any understanding. Not the least of which was why in his
zeal to find his father's murderers, he had pushed on after his young
sidekick was killed with the final thrust that almost led to the death
of his mother and Hank.

Unable to focus on business, Joe had asked Sam to run the office
for a few weeks while he worked with his psychiatrist, hopefully to
bury the demons. Sam readily agreed, and Joe called Dr. Wayne

Theroux's office. Joe had first seen him last year, when Theroux slowly led him to the source of his irrational jealously in his relationships with women: feelings that had started to well up in him when he was fifteen and his mother started seeing other men after his father's murder.

Dr. Theroux put his notebook down and peered over the top of his glasses. "Joe, it's been four weeks, two and three times a week. It's time you go back to your normal activities, and we go to once a week. How do you feel about that?"

"I'll give it a try." Joe said. "But I'm still having trouble understanding why my mother dealt with this so much better than me."

Theroux was a man he had come to like and admire. Medium height, paunchy around the middle, about fifty years old, rumpled graying hair, a salt and pepper beard, and blotchy skin that gave the appearance of someone who drank too much. He wore a tweed wool suit and a bow tie, and always had a pipe in hand.

"Your mother's obviously a strong woman," Dr. Theroux said, cleaning his pipe and tamping in fresh tobacco. "I'm pleased to hear she and Archie are going to get married. A good sign. She's moving on."

Joe went to his office the next day for the first time in almost a month. Sam and Sally and the others greeted him warmly. However, he sensed they were treating him like fragile glass. He understood. They were probably right. Sam asked Joe to join him in the conference room.

"Things are going well, partner. Dave and John have been carrying the load. We have a few more clients. Nothing big. But it'll help pay the bills. Sure you're ready? Don't need to rush it."

"Yep. I'm not crazy, Sam. Needed to straighten a few things out. I'm okay. I've followed events in the newspaper but fill me in on the latest."

"The biggest news is that Robert Beauchamp is going to defend Adam. You know who he is, right?"

"Sure. Best criminal defense attorney in Alabama if not the South. Is he defending Damian and the others?"

"Don't know. The trials have started. Watch the papers. . . . Say, I got the invitation to Elizabeth and Archie's wedding in June. Great news."

Joe smiled. "Yes. Mom's delighted. Me too."

"Are you surprised?"

"Nope. Mom told me recently that Archie had proposed years ago. She said she loved him but wasn't ready to make a commitment. I think the recent events changed everything. She's retiring at the end of this semester, and will sell the house and move to Archie's."

"All sounds good."

Joe put his hand on Sam's shoulder. "Thank you. You've been my rock. After what's happened the last few months, I couldn't have made it without you."

CHAPTER 71

THE WEDDING

SATURDAY—JUNE 19, 1948

J OE LEANED AGAINST AN OAK TREE, watching the wedding reception play out under a beautiful late evening summer sky. There
was less than an hour of sunlight left, so oil lanterns had been placed
among the tables on the lawn where guests sat eating and drinking.
A small band providing dance music was playing Glenn Miller's "In
the Mood." Earlier he had walked his mother down the aisle for her
wedding to Archie Hamilton. His son, Arthur, had been his best man.
Joe's daughter, Jane, was a flower girl as was Archie's granddaughter, his grandson the ring bearer. Elizabeth's sister from Boston was
Matron of Honor.

Archie and Elizabeth had wanted a small wedding, but the guest
list grew to almost two hundred people. Hank and his wife, Mattie
Ruth, had been accorded honored guest status, and he read a biblical
passage during the ceremony. His shoulder had healed but the use of
his left arm was limited.

Joe's fiancé, Diane, was at his side, when he had announced their
engagement after the toasts to the bride and groom. There were cheers
when he said they would marry early next year. Sam and Yolanda
were present along with her two loyal servants, Pearl and Frederick.
Joe and Sam's Birmingham office was there: Sally Bowers, Dave
Williams, and John Stavos. Jeff and Raymond were present. Jeff's
retelling of the rescue over the ensuing months and years became a

county legend, including his description of the 'field goal," Sam's balletic kick into Damian's groin. Archie's employees were present, which now included the Pidd twins. After they testified for the prosecution and with the help of Henry Baxley, they were given suspended five-year sentences subject to their employment on Archie's farm.

Joe enjoyed being back to work, and the wedding ceremony was a moment of joy and celebration. Yet, as he leaned against the tree, he felt the dark cloud forming and realized he might never get over his father and Brendan's murders. Looking up, he saw Sam approaching.

"A wonderful day, Joe. You doing all right?" he said, knowing the answer by the look on Joe's face.

"Off and on. Off right now."

"Go back to on. Damian's been sentenced to death. I'm sure you heard that his execution has been postponed pending an appeal to the Alabama Supreme Court."

"Right," Joe said, sarcastically, "while Adam all but walks free."

"Twenty-five years in prison is not free. He turned state's evidence, as did Roscoe and his buddy. They hung Damian out to dry and ran for cover. I'm sure Beauchamp orchestrated it. And the blood samples the coroner found under Brendan's fingernails matched Damian's."

"Yep. But they can't even get many convictions concerning ARC folks and 'the operation.' "

"Not quite," Sam said. "Chuck Holder got twenty years for bootlegging and operating stills. A few people received suspended sentences along with substantial fines. A number of others have been fined. The Attorney General's staff is still working on the names found in the papers in the warehouse and in Holder's office. Folks are on pins and needles wondering if they'll be tagged. But yes, your good friend Anne Holder got off scot-free. So did Doc Willis. He's a good man who got caught in the middle. You know all this, right?"

Joe finally smiled. "Yeah, but there's something I have to learn. 'What's gone and what's past help should be past grief.' "

"You're right. Your old buddy, Shakespeare, isn't it?"

Joe even laughed and said, "Yep. Paulina in *The Winter's Tale*, Act III, Scene 2."

"Your mother would be proud. I wish I could say I knew the quote. But to hell with it. Going back to work Monday?" Sam asked.

"You bet we are."

Acknowledgments

Apologizing in advance to anyone I've overlooked, writers and friends who read and commented on all or parts of the manuscript include David Beckman, Armando Garcia-Dávila, Karen Hart, Scott Kersnar, John Koetzner, Kevin Konicek, Steve Laruccia, Liz Martin, and Linda McCabe.

Suzan Reed, who has designed the covers for three of my books, is an extraordinary graphic designer. Her imagination continues to amaze me with this noir-style cover for *Touch of Redemption*.

Barbara Stone Laruccia edited my manuscript with a keen eye for my grammar and punctuation mistakes. In addition, Armando Garcia-Dávila, Karen Hart, and Linda McCabe provided much needed editorial and plot advice.

Any errors remaining in the book are mine, and mine alone.

Liz Martin, my lovely wife and an English major, rolls her eyes at my use of Southern slang and colloquialisms but continues to be my constant companion and staunchest supporter of my work.

About the Author

Waights Taylor Jr., born and raised in Birmingham, Alabama, lives in Santa Rosa, California. His professional career included twenty-four years in the aviation industry and then twenty-two years in management consulting. When his professional career was coming to an end, he turned to writing.

31876609R00180

Made in the USA
San Bernardino, CA
22 March 2016